John Searle

Nick Fotion

PRINCETON UNIVERSITY PRESS
PRINCETON AND OXFORD

Published in 2000 in North America, Central America,
South America,the Caribbean, and the Philippines by
Princeton University Press, 41 William St., Princeton,
New Jersey 08540. All rights reserved.

First published in 2000 by Acumen
Acumen Publishing Limited
17 Fairfax Road
Teddington
TW11 9DJ, UK

ISBN: 0-691-05711-7 (hardcover)
ISBN: 0-691-05712-5 (paperback)

Library of Congress Card Number: 00-107340

Designed and typeset in Century Schoolbook
by Kate Williams, Abergavenny.
Printed and bound by Biddles Ltd., Guildford and King's Lynn.

www.pup.princeton.edu
10   9   8   7   6   5   4   3   2   1

John Searle

Philosophy Now

Series Editor: John Shand

This is a fresh and vital series of new introductions to today's most read, discussed and important philosophers. Combining rigorous analysis with authoritative exposition, each book gives clear and comprehensive access to the ideas of those philosophers who have made a truly fundamental and original contribution to the subject. Together the volumes comprise a remarkable gallery of the thinkers who have been at the forefront of philosophical ideas.

Published

Thomas Kuhn
Alexander Bird

John Searle
Nick Fotion

Charles Taylor
Ruth Abbey

Contents

Introduction

John Searle was raised in the tradition of analytic philosophy, but he transcends that tradition. One reason is that he writes on a variety of topics even though his tradition encourages its supporters to focus narrowly on certain aspects of one or two topics. In his long career, Searle has written extensively on such subjects as philosophy of language, philosophy of mind, the nature and structure of social institutions, context (what he calls Network and Background), ontology, science and causality.

But beyond that, he has brought all these topics together – he has synthesized them so as to form a single "big picture" philosophic stance. As will become evident later in this work, his stance is in large part reactive. It reacts against the strong and broad based contemporary tradition of postmodernism that is intent on, indeed seems to delight in, deconstructing just about everything in view – especially our sense of what is real. Searle's stance reacts also against the dominant view in psychology and philosophy of mind that severely deflates consciousness to the point of ignoring it completely or not taking it seriously when explaining mental phenomena. Interestingly, in his defence of reality, consciousness, and his sense that a big picture philosophic stance makes sense, Searle incorporates many of the views that he reacts against. He mixes his views with those of those with whom he disagrees. Yes, he says, we know things only from a certain point of view (aspectually), and yet we still can meaningfully think of ourselves as being in contact with the real world. Yes, he also says, science can explain consciousness in terms of what non-consciously goes on inside our head. Yet he adds that that need not undermine the importance of consciousness. And, yes, analytic philosophy's fondness for detail has a point, but that need not deter us from also engaging in big picture or "synthetic" analytic philosophy. Searle's seemingly unholy mix of conflicting views makes him liable to attack from all sides. At the same time, the mixture makes his own views intriguing and original. The mixture also makes John Searle one of a kind; and one with whom anyone interested in what is happening on the contemporary philosophic scene must come to terms sooner or later.

Another reason Searle transcends analytic philosophy is that what he says about language interests not only philosophers, but also linguists; what he says about the mind interests not only philosophers but also psychologists; what he says about the social world interests not only philosophers but also social scientists; and what he says about cause and scientific explanation interests not only philosophers but also scientists. His writings then, are of interest to the many rather than the few.

Still another reason has to do with the way he writes. In the jargon of the American West where he was raised, Searle is a straight shooter. What he says, he says clearly and straightforwardly. Although he does not completely eschew jargon, he uses it sparingly. His attitude is that if he cannot express himself directly and clearly, this is a sign that he does not know what he is talking about. However, sometimes Searle is apparently too straightforward. When dealing with those who disagree with him, his attacks are often frontal and even confrontational. As a result, Searle's readers, especially those who are not sympathetic with him, are more likely to attend more to his confrontational style rather than to the content of what he is saying. I cannot recall how many times I have heard the charge from both philosophers and non-philosophers alike that Searle directs many insults at his opponents but only a few arguments at them. For that matter, the charge is often made that he presents few if any arguments even on behalf of his own views – especially when the topic is the nature of the mind. To be sure, his opponents seem to Searle to be the ones bereft of argument. They are said to be prone to name calling and *ad hominem* appeals. The resulting back-and-forth scuffling kicks up lots of dust which, not surprisingly, serves to draw attention to Searle, the alleged cause of it all.

One goal, then, in writing about Searle, and to a lesser extent about his opponents, is to settle the dust. Once this is done, the reader will presumably be in a better position to see just how cogent Searle's stance is on various individual philosophic issues. A second goal is to show how Searle's views on the various topics he writes about connect to form a synthesis. He himself shows how he does it in his 1998 book *Mind, Language and Society: Philosophy in a Real World*. In fact, he does it for the benefit of the professional philosopher, but most especially for the informed general reader. He seems to think that part of his task as a philosopher is to make his ideas accessible to a wider audience, a task that he evidently enjoys. Still, it is sometimes useful to get the good news not only from the horse's mouth but also from someone who stands at a slight distance from the horse and who can therefore hear what the horse is saying more objectively.

Searle's 1998 book is divided into three parts corresponding to the three major subjects of his overall philosophic stance. The first subject he takes up is the mind. It is here where the dust of controversy is the thickest and may be why he features the mind at the beginning of this book and, in fact, why he spends more time on this subject than any other. But a more likely reason is that we can then appreciate better what he wants to say about the other two subjects. That is, once we understand how the mind works, we are in a better position to deal with social reality since that reality is a construction of the mind. In turn, once we understand social reality, we can understand how language, his third major subject of his writings, works. Searle insists that the three are tied together closely. Reality is one rather than many. Even so, since both social reality and language are products of our mental powers, it makes sense for Searle to explain his overall philosophic position by starting his tour of reality with the mind before taking us to see the rest.

The present work starts the tour at a different point. It starts with his philosophy of language, then to the mind and from there to social reality. This is the path that Searle actually took in his career. He initially made his reputation with his writings on language and it was only after he had already established himself as a outstanding philosopher in this field that he moved to address questions on the philosophy of mind. Although his concern with issues surrounding our understanding of mental phenomena are still with him, he broadened his interests in the 1990s in order to write about social reality, more particularly how that reality comes to be created.

However, the main reason for starting with Searle's work on language is not to trace the history of his intellectual development but to gain an understanding of what he says about language, making it easier to explain how and why his ideas evolved to those concerned with the mind, and from there to social reality. So Chapters 1–4 (Part 1) of this study explore Searle's thoughts on language. In these chapters we see him focusing his attention on speech acts, a concept that he learned about from his mentor John Austin. Speech acts are for Searle the minimal units of language communication or, better yet, the minimal units of actual language use. We don't use language by just referring or just predicating, i.e. we don't normally go about the world uttering expressions such as "That painting" and "red" or "is red." Rather we say "That painting is red" while talking, let us say, to a friend who as yet has not been in the gallery where the painting in question is hanging. Thus, referring and predicating play their roles within speech acts. It is not as if we refer and predicate and then, by doing so, build up to uttering speech acts.

Focusing on speech acts, Searle's self-appointed task is to come to understand them better. He wants to know the details of how they work or, putting it differently, how they are to be analyzed. As just noted, this account forces him to attend to referring (done within the speech act) and predicating. But even as the simple example of the red painting shows, knowing how a speech act works involves taking into account the context concerning the speaker and the situation in the gallery. However, many speech acts are contextually richer. For example, when a commander tells a soldier to bring him the report, understanding the speech act presupposes knowing about rank and military traditions. Similarly when the priest marries the young couple, the context of the church and its traditions come into play. So we see that speech act analysis already shows the way to Searle's future interest in understanding social reality and quickly takes us beyond a view of language as simply a string of words organized in this and then in that way. This means that we cannot completely understand language and its workings by simply looking at language itself. If we look only at language, commands, promises, congratulations, declarations of war and the like will make no sense. Speech acts are embedded in a context.

But there is more to a speech act than referring, predicating and a context. A speech act is a kind of *act*. As such, Searle (and Austin before him) realized that speech acts cannot be understood without taking intentions into account. When we communicate with one another we do so intentionally. This is how speech acts differ from emotional reactions expressed in part in linguistic form. If I utter a series of unprintable expressions as, in total darkness, I futilely fumble to fit my key into the door lock, I am not using language intentionally. What I say counts as an event or an uncontrolled reaction, not an act. But if I say, in a calm, clear and deliberate voice, "There is a stranger at the door", "Please close the door", "You're hired" or "Congratulations", I speak intentionally. As such, each of these utterances is a speech act.

Intentions and other mental concepts are involved in speech acts in other ways. I not only speak intentionally when I say "I promise to be in my office tomorrow" but also, within the promise, I express the *intention* that I will be in my office. Other speech acts express different mental states. When I describe today's weather in Atlanta as sunny I express a *belief* that the sun is shining. When I request that you hand me that sandwich I express the *hope* that you will do so. Similarly when I congratulate you for winning your tennis match I express *happiness* in your success. So speech act theory is infused with mental concepts. Just as we cannot fully understand what a speech act is without taking the social and physical context into account, so we cannot understand this theory without taking a variety of mental concepts into account.

There is still more. Speech act theory must not just give an account of intentions, beliefs, wishes and similar concepts, but also of Intentionality (capitalized on purpose). Whereas intentions have to do with what we intend to do or are doing, Intentionality is concerned with the "aboutness" feature found in language. One way we come across aboutness is in the beliefs we hold when we describe the world. In saying that the moon is out, I express a belief and this belief is about the status or the condition of the moon. Another way aboutness manifests itself within language is more direct. When I say that the moon is out tonight I am talking about the object we call the moon.

Thus, after writing extensively about speech acts in the first part of his career Searle could have moved to expand his understanding of these acts by focusing attention on social reality (an important part of the context of these acts) or he could have focused on the mind. He actually chose the latter first, probably because interest in philosophy of mind and in the study of psychology was on the increase in the 1970s and 1980s. In those days, cognitive psychology and the more specific theory that claimed we can better understand the workings of the mind by making an analogy to a computer were the rage. Searle realized almost immediately that many researchers and thinkers who were caught up in this rage were saying things about the mind and mental phenomena that were at variance with what he wanted to say. Coming as he was out of his work on speech acts, concepts such as beliefs, intentions, desires, and Intentionality made sense and seemed important to him. But to those who wanted to develop new concepts that carried the authority of the "cognitivist" discoveries in psychology, neuropsychology and related sciences, Searle's everyday concepts seemed obsolescent to say the least.

It is understandable, then, that Searle would move to write a book titled *Intentionality* (1983), and beyond that to write other books and articles in philosophy of mind soon after finishing the major things he wanted to say about language. In the present study, these writings on the mind are addressed in Chapters 5–8 (Part 2). Chapter 5 is on the topic of Intentionality. His discussion here sets the framework for his main portrait of the mind and also addresses the issue of how Intentionality found both in language and the mind relate to one another. Chapter 6 deals with his notion of Background (or context) since it becomes clear quickly that just as language use is embedded in a context, so is the mind. Chapters 7 and 8 deal directly with the mind. They are concerned with his major work on the mind, *The Rediscovery of the Mind* (1992a). They are also concerned with the dust raising controversies between Searle and his "enemies" who, as already noted, come at him from all directions.

While continuing to do battle in the arena of philosophy of mind, Searle moved to address issues pertaining to social reality. His major work here is *Construction of Social Reality* (1995a). This book and other related writings on this topic are discussed in Chapters 9 and 10 (Part III, which also includes Chapters 11–13). In this discussion the connections back to speech act theory and to his theory of the mind are evident. Indeed, most of social reality seems to be constructed from older concepts, especially from his work in philosophy of language. At this point, one can appreciate why it makes sense to discuss Searle's theory of language in the first four chapters and then philosophy of mind in the next four before turning to social reality.

Chapters 11 and 12 are clean-up chapters. In the main they are concerned with Searle's ontology but also with what he has to say about epistemology. Searle has discussed these topics throughout his career although as yet he has not devoted full length works to them. It is interesting to note that his realist stance in ontology fits hand in glove with many of his early works. A speech act telling us that the car over there is blue is about that car, that real blue car over there. It is not about some impression, set of sense data, etc. of the car. Language's Intentional powers point to reality. But the mind's Intentional powers do the same. When I see the car I really see the car; and when I see a student come into my office I do so because a real tuition paying student has come in.

The last chapter in this work pulls together all that preceded it and, to some extent, draws certain conclusions about Searle's overall philosophic stance. In the end, the hope is that readers will have come to appreciate John Searle as a philosopher they must know about if they are to have any sense of what is going on in philosophy today.

Two final introductory comments are in order. First, I do not attempt in this work to canvass all the topics that Searle has written about. For instance, I say nothing in the text about his paper "Deriving 'Ought' from 'Is'"(Searle 1969: Ch. 8). I avoid the topic since, even though this paper is well known, and widely reprinted, it represents an isolated foray by Searle into the realm of ethics and value theory. As such it is hard to put it into the larger canvass of his "synthetic analytic" stance. I also say nothing of another early Searlian foray – this one into the realm of campus politics. As a young faculty member at the University of California at Berkeley, he sided with the student movement in those far off days when many students in the United States decided that the society in which they were living needed radical surgery. Clearly in a book of this size one cannot cover every topic and do justice to each.

Secondly, in this study I keep commentary by others on Searle's position to a minimum. There is a growing collection of items (already numbering many hundreds) listed in *The Philosopher's Index* on John Searle. Most of these articles, discussion notes and reviews attempt to use Searle for target practice. To try to take even a representative sample of these works into account and then construct what Searle's reply to them would be would needlessly complicate the presentation. As a result, the reader would lose sight both of Searle's stance on particular issues and his overall philosophic stance. So I refer and comment on the views of others only if it serves the purpose of helping to explain Searle's position.

When convenient, I insert reports of these commentaries into the body of the text. At other times if the commentary by others seems intrusive, but still worth reporting, my reports are found in endnotes. Above all, I try to keep the explanatory line as straight and as clean as possible. To do so is to be very Searlian.

Part I

Philosophy of language

Chapter 1

Searle's speech act theory

Background

John Searle's first major work, *Speech Acts*, appeared in 1969. By then, the tradition of language analysis within which it was framed had matured. Indeed, it was already in the second stage of development.

The first stage was strongly influenced by the many accomplishments of science. By the end of the nineteenth century, the revolutionary notion of "natural selection" developed by Charles Darwin in his *The Origins of the Species* in 1859 and *The Descent of Man* in 1871 had taken hold. Soon after, in 1905, Albert Einstein presented his special theory of relativity to the world, followed by his general theory in 1916. About the same time, electrons and other subatomic particles were discovered, and Max Planck and Niels Bohr developed their versions of the atomic and quantum theories. Science was on the move. If the changes in science that Copernicus, Brahe, Kepler, Galileo, Newton, Harvey and others had brought about in earlier centuries were revolutionary, the more recent changes toward the end of the nineteenth century and the beginning of the twentieth were equally revolutionary.

The newer revolution differed from the older one in many ways. Science now was more mature. It had a history of success in many areas both on the theoretical as well as the practical level of engineering and medicine. Instruments of observation and measurement were more sophisticated than in the past. The newer science also had a broader base since psychology and the other social sciences had joined the family. Before the turn of the century,

Wilhelm Wundt (1912) and others in Germany had taken the study of psychology out of the philosopher's hands and placed it into those of the laboratory oriented psychologist.

However, it wasn't long before Wundt's form of laboratory research, which stressed introspection, was replaced by behaviourism. Now, John Watson (1919), the champion of behaviourism, could say that psychology is a proper science. Watson argued that the subject matter of psychology is external (human and animal) behaviour and that such a subject matter can be studied objectively. If, instead, psychology were defined as the study of inner mental phenomena or characterized in terms of what could only be known through (subjective) introspection, he thought that it was doomed never to be a science the way physics and chemistry are sciences.

Freud was also making his contributions to psychology at this time with his psychoanalytic theory. Although his work derived more from the medical setting rather than from the laboratory, and although it did not seem to be so objective as the work done by the behaviourists, it was, none the less, widely accepted as being both scientific and revolutionary. It was scientific insofar as what he discovered was based on clinical observations. But it was also revolutionary in that what he discovered suggested strongly that the mind possesses unconscious thoughts and forces, the importance of which had been grossly underestimated by almost everyone up to that time.

While all this was going on in psychology, Max Weber was doing what he could to turn sociology, if not into a laboratory science, at least into an empirical study. Understandably, in the glow of all these developments in the physical and the social sciences, there was optimism that all the individual sciences could be unified under the banner of science, and that scientific progress was inevitable. As part of this new revolution, there were even significant developments in fields of study related to but not strictly speaking part of science: viz., in logic and mathematics Bertrand Russell and Alfred North Whitehead were among the many contributors. In addition to making direct contributions to these fields by presenting us with new systems of logic and mathematics, many of contributors to these fields (though not necessarily Russell and Whitehead) came to the view that claims made within these fields had a special status. They were viewed as nothing but language claims and, as such, not about any *thing*. What claims made within logic and mathematics tell us is how certain linguistic expressions relate to other linguistic expressions. Thus they were said to be quite different from those claims or assertions made within the sciences. The sciences use language to make "vertical" assertions about what is out there in the world. In contrast, logic and language were said to make "horizontal" assertions. So if one says "If x, then y" this is just another way of saying "If not y, then not x", or if one says "Not not x" this is just another way of saying "x". Also if one says "I have four apples" this is the same as, or equivalent to, saying "I have two apples plus two more", or even "I have three apples plus one more". These claims containing "if–then", "and" and "plus" were taken as telling us something about the meaning of these expressions.

In so far, then, as the studies of logic, mathematics and even the meaning of terms are studies of language, and in so far as it was evident that these studies help us to think more clearly about whatever problems face us, it seemed plausible to pay more attention to language than had been done in the past. That is, if logic and mathematics are the instruments by which we think, it was thought that must be important to look carefully at these instruments in order to understand better how they work, and how they can help us to improve our thinking. It didn't take much imagination to extend this outlook to language in general. What was also needed, it was said, was a better understanding of the meaning of all sorts of concepts that we use when we engage in serious thinking about any subject matter. An aspect of this outlook was that if we failed to engage in this analysis of language, we would probably fall into error when doing philosophy, theoretical work in the sciences and, in fact, when doing any sort of serious thinking.

Quite naturally many of those who took this "linguistic turn" (Rorty 1970) early in the twentieth century, directed their attention first and foremost to the language of science. After all, they had a strong admiration for science and, in fact, many of them were even making contributions to one or other of the sciences. Further, the startling successes of the various sciences suggested that the use of language within the sciences was different from, and probably superior to, the use of language found in the street. Street, or ordinary, language, was viewed as full of ambiguity, vagueness, inconsistency and was said as well to be replete with unscientific and anti-scientific concepts. As an instrument of thinking, ordinary talk was worse than unhelpful. It actually muddled our thinking. One of the many ways it did this was by encouraging us to reify concepts. Because expressions such as "the average man", "the mind", and "red" often appear as nouns in ordinary language sentences, it was said that we are tempted to suppose (wrongly) that the average man really exists someplace (surely someplace near the centre of our country), that there is such an entity as the mind or soul (that separates from the body at death), and that there is an entity such as redness out there some place (perhaps in the world of Ideas).

In contrast, when employed by the great scientists, scientific language adheres more closely to logical principles, uses mathematics properly, defines its terms more carefully, and closely ties our use of these terms to observation. Because it does all these things, scientific language approaches being an ideal language. Not surprisingly, when we use it rather than ordinary language, it was thought that we would be less prone to fall into error.

Quite naturally as well, if the focus of analysis at this time was on scientific uses of language, heavy emphasis was inevitably placed on understanding what scientists do when they describe some event or process. Science uses language mainly to issue descriptive claims about the past, present and the future. These claims can be specific in the form of a temperature reading, a report about the height of a plant or one concerning the number of people in a room. Or they can be general in the form of some law of science such as that gases expand when heated or that learning is facilitated the more it is rewarded. Scientific claims can be theoretical in nature as well. Indeed, much of the progress in the sciences of the nineteenth and twentieth centuries was measured by the proliferation of theories – the theory of evolution, relativity theory, atomic theory, quantum theory, psychoanalytic theory and so on. But no matter what kind of claims were being made within science, since they were based directly or indirectly on observation, they were thus assessable as either true or false. As such, they earned the status of synthetic (informative) claims.

But, as viewed at the time, there were also analytic claims to consider. These were also said to be assessable on a true–false dimension. However, their status on this dimension is determined not by observation but simply by an analysis of the terms in these claims, that is, by an internal (i.e. "horizontal") analysis of the sentences themselves. Logical and mathematical claims were, of course, included under this analytic heading. But so were other claims. If my uncle really is my uncle, I know (analytically, that is, by the meaning of "uncle") that he cannot be the mother of my cousins. Similarly, I know that nothing can be a square triangle, not by observation, but by analyzing the meaning of "triangle" and "square". And, finally, I know (analytically) that if something is red it has to be coloured.

In the hands of those who formed what was called the Vienna Circle (e.g. Rudolph Carnap, Herbert Feigl, Otto Neurath, Moritz Schlick. Friedrich Waisman), and some of their allies (e.g. A. J. Ayer, C. W. Morris) in the 1920s and 1930s many of these thoughts led to further thoughts – ones that sounded more radical. For these philosophers, who later came to be called Logical Positivists (or even Logical Empiricists), only certain claims counted as meaningful. They were willing to count the synthetic claims of science (and those of everyday observation) as meaningful since being able to make such claims is what contributed to science's success. They could also count as meaningful the analytic claims of logic and mathematics since these, after all, formed the basis for how we think. But, for the Positivists, it seemed that if we made any other kinds of claim we would be talking nonsense. Listen to Ayer as he (in)famously tells us about his version of the Positivist principle of verification – the principle that was supposed to tell us which sentences are to count as meaningful, and which not.

> The criterion which we use to test the genuineness of apparent statements of fact is the criterion of verifiability. We say that a sentence is factually significant to any given person, if, and only if, he knows how to verify the proposition which it purports to express – that is, he knows what observations would lead him, under certain conditions, to accept the proposition as being true, or reject it as being false. If, on the other hand, the putative proposition is of such a character that the assumption of its truth, or falsehood, is consistent with any assumption whatsoever concerning the nature of his future experience, then, as far as he is concerned, it is, if not a tautology, a mere pseudo-proposition. The sentence expressing it may be emotionally significant to him; but it is not literally significant. (Ayer 1952: 35).

Thus, to Ayer's way of thinking, claims made in art criticism, ethics, philosophy, and religion are meaningless. They are neither true nor false. This is to say that they are not rationally assessable in any fashion. They are allegedly more akin to screams of pleasure and displeasure than anything else. Those who make these meaningless claims think otherwise of course, but for Ayer all this shows is that they are not thinking clearly.

The second stage of the analytic movement was in clear reaction to such extreme claims. The criticism of the Positivists and their allies came from many directions. Even during the Positivist heyday there were some who thought that scientific language (and research) was not the exclusive possessor of meaningfulness. Early in the twentieth century, G. E. Moore and a bit later Gilbert Ryle thought that our street language made more sense than the Positivists would allow and, as a result, it too was worthy of study. After all, it *was* the language most of us use when we think about various matters in our lives. In addition, it didn't seem to them that it was quite so flawed as the Positivists thought. So, giving barely a nod in the direction of the impressive developments in science, logic and mathematics, these philosophers came to the conclusion that much of the philosophy done in the past could be purged of many of its errors if more attention were to be paid to ordinary language. For them, ordinary linguistic (or conceptual) mistakes led to bad philosophy. Others joined this line of thinking after World War II including Paul Grice, R. M. Hare, H. L. A. Hart and Peter Strawson.

But, more than any others, it was Ludwig Wittgenstein, after he had broken with the Logical Positivists, and John Austin who saved ordinary language from the Positivist dustbin that they reserved for meaningless claims. Both argued that ordinary language can do more than enable us to make descriptive claims. Wittgenstein made this point by saying in his *Philosophical Investigations* (1953) that we can play what seemed like an indefinite number of "language games" within ordinary language. He said that engaging in scientific activity is not a single language game, but is itself a host of different games (i.e. linguistic activities). But, in addition, he said there are non-science games we can play with language. We can give directions, make promises and so on. Austin said much the same in *How to do Things with Words* (1975) in a more systematic way. In that book he argues that utterances such as "I promise to meet you at the park" are not assessable as either true or false. Yet he says that they are perfectly meaningful since they are assessable as well formed or ill-formed in other ways. He then tells his readers how to make these assessments. For example, a necessary condition for making a well formed promise is that the one making it possess the ability to carry it out. Another necessary condition is that what is promised takes place in the future. It would be an ill-formed promise if I promised today to do something for you yesterday. Commands such as "I command you to do as I say" are also meaningful, but they too are not assessable as true or false. Austin again goes on to tell us how they can be assessed. Thus a necessary condition for making a command is that the one issuing it must have some sort of authority over the one commanded. If the private "commanded" the general, we would either laugh or be seriously concerned about private's career opportunities in the forces.

Austin goes on to argue that other allegedly meaningless utterances have meaning. He discusses "Hello", "You are excommunicated", "I pronounce you man and wife", "Please help me" and scores more. Of course, for Austin, the favoured claims of the Positivists are also meaningful. He calls them constatives initially, and contrasts them with the variety of utterances to which he is fixing our attention. He calls all these other utterances, performatives. Performatives get their name because it seems to Austin that these uses of language are "doings" or linguistic performances. In making a promise Sam, the speaker, puts on a linguistic performance and, if the situation is right, suddenly finds himself bound to doing something in the future for someone – usually the one to whom the promise was made.

Late in the book Austin puts all his cards on the table. He says that constatives (true and false claims) are performatives as well, since uttering a true or false claim such as "(I say) the grass is green" is as much a doing as is "I promise to mow the lawn". So, in the end, all uses of language are performatives. But, since it is clearer than before that there are different kinds of performatives, he feels obliged to identify what kinds there are in order to tell us how they are alike and unlike one another. It is as if, once he realized how subtle, diverse and powerful the language to which we are married is, what it needs is understanding, not divorce.

Enter John Searle

It is in this setting, then, that we begin to see what Searle is up to in *Speech Acts*. By 1969 the terminology but not the subject matter had changed. Instead of talking about performatives (in language use), the expression "speech acts" had come into fashion. Austin had discovered speech acts and told us many interesting things about them. He had done the exploratory work. Searle, Austin's student, set himself the task of carrying on his mentor's work by presenting a more complete and systematic account of speech acts.

Before examining Searle's account of these acts it is helpful to make two preliminary comments. The first deals with subject matter. Searle makes it clear up front that the main focus of *Speech Acts* is the philosophy of *language*, not linguistic *philosophy* (1969: 3–4). The latter is a method for dealing with philosophic problems. If we engage in language analysis in order to understand better the mind/body problem, the relationship between science and ethics, the nature of reality (ontology) and how we come to know anything (epistemology), we are doing linguistic philosophy. The study of philosophy of language might eventually help us to do (linguistic) philosophy so it is certainly important to engage in such a study. Nonetheless, our attention in the study of philosophy of language is on language itself. Linguists also study language, but much of their work is concerned with this or that particular language. In contrast, Searle's concern is to show us how language works across national and ethnic borders. He wants to show us how language – any language – works.

The second comment has to do with Searle's style of doing philosophy, and in particular with doing linguistic analysis. Searle is not obsessed with borders when it comes to making distinctions unlike some philosophers who say, for example, that unless we can find the bright line to help us sort all utterances into either the analytic or synthetic bin, we do not really understand that distinction. Or they say that unless we can find a different bright line to help us distinguish between making a promise and not making one, we do not understand what a promise is. These border obsessed philosophers sometimes go on to argue that the lack of a bright line undermines distinctions such as that between analytic and synthetic utterances and concepts such as promising.

Searle will have none of that. For him, not to know whether "Green objects are extended" is synthetic or analytic is to grant that we already know a lot about this distinction. We wouldn't be able to make the call that it is a borderline claim unless we could distinguish it from other claims far from the border. We all know "My uncle has siblings" is analytic, while "My uncle has two brothers and one sister" is synthetic even if we had never used or heard these utterances used before. Our sense of how to use our native language tells us what is clearly analytic, synthetic and what is not clearly one or the other. Searle's style, then, is to look for clear-cut or paradigm cases first, and then worry later about the borderline cases. That means that in giving an account of assertions as a kind of speech act, he does not focus right away on fictional assertions, where it might be difficult to say whether and in what sense they are true or false. Rather, he focuses on ordinary assertions such as "(I say) that is a large tree" and "(I say) John is deeply in love with Mary". It also means that he is perfectly willing to grant that certain non-paradigmatic uses fall right on top of some not-so-bright line having to do with whatever distinction we are trying to make. As a result, for example, we may not be able to decide whether an alleged promise is really a promise.

Fixing his attention, then, on everyday uses of everyday language, Searle begins his analysis of speech acts by more or less dividing his work load into two parts. I will separate the two parts more than he does for purposes of simplifying the exposition. Part one I will call the analysis of the structure of speech acts; part two, the analysis of the process of communicating by issuing speech acts – structure and process for short.

The structure of a typical speech act is pictured below.

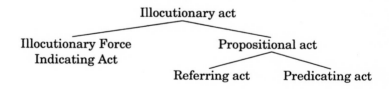

The following sentences, taken from *Speech Acts*, help explain what all this means. Searle says:

> Imagine a speaker and a hearer and suppose that in the appropriate circumstances the speaker utters one of the following sentences:
> 1. Sam smokes habitually.
> 2. Does Sam smoke habitually?
> 3. Sam, smoke habitually! [This one might be deviant, that is, one that a normal English speaker might not utter.]
> 4. Would that Sam smoked habitually.
>
> (1969: 22)

When a speaker utters any of these sentences the referring act is the same. Sam is the person being referred to. The predicating act is the same as well in all the sentences: viz., smoking habitually. The referring act and the predicating act taken together make up what Searle calls the propositional act. The propositional act tells us what we are talking about. It is the content or subject matter of the speech act (i.e. the propositional content). But it definitely doesn't say anything by itself in the normal sense of saying anything. Uttering just the propositional act is like uttering (or writing) "Sam's habit of smoking". If a speaker uttered that much, and no more, the hearers would likely be puzzled. They would be tempted to say something like "Yes, you are talking about Sam's habit of smoking; that is your subject matter. But what do you want to tell us about it?" To "tell us about it" the speaker needs to complete the sentence by somehow issuing an illocutionary force indicating act.[1] The term "illocution" is John Austin's from his *How to do Things with Words* (Austin 1975: 98). The prefix "il" is taken to mean "in", and "locution" as "speech". So "illocution" means "in speaking" or "in saying" something. In 1 above the indicating act is brought about by word order. That order tells the hearers that the speaker is making an assertion about Sam's smoking. In 2 the word order and the question mark signal that a question is being asked. In actually saying something in both 1 and 2, the speaker has now dealt with his hearers' puzzlement. They know he is asserting, asking a question, issuing a request (3) or expressing a wish (4). When the illocutionary force indicating act is added to the propositional act, Austin and Searle say that the speaker has issued a full speech act which they dub an illocutionary act (an act of actually saying something).

Communication

Unfortunately, understanding how speech acts work to bring about communication requires something more than just knowing about the structure in the sense of the linguistic representation of speech acts. One part of the something more has to do with intent and, in so doing, has to do with seeing communication as a process. There is no intent in screaming "Ow!" or "G.. damn it!" as one steps solidly on nail while walking barefooted. The latter scream is, of course, in English as is, perhaps, the former. Presumably Russians scream in other ways when they step on nails. Still, these emotive "uses" of language are not acts because they lack intent. Or, as it might be put, we don't scream on purpose. Screams are emitted, not issued purposefully, so they are better thought of as events, not acts. In contrast, speech acts require intent or purpose. When Sam says to Henry "It's raining now" he issues a speech act with the intention of letting Henry know about the weather conditions outside. His intent is not necessarily formed as the result of prior deliberation. More than likely it is non-conscious in that it seems to be simply built into the action of saying "It's raining now". It is much the same when we hit a ball with a bat in baseball. The swing is intentional even though the decision to swing is not necessarily made in advance, but a split second before the ball hits the bat.

So Sam's intention is to send a message to Henry about the rain. But in communicating with Henry, Sam has another intention, again probably a non-conscious one. This one is to get Henry to recognize that the message sent to him is sent intentionally. The second intention, then, is to get Henry to recognize the first intention. Presumably the second intention is to help make it clear to Henry that Sam is responsible for the speech act issued. If, then, a question arises about the truth, correctness, appropriateness, etc. of the speech act, the hearer can point to the speaker as the one responsible for its issuance.

Assume, then, that Henry is clear about the message and about Sam's intentions. So far so good. But there is another intention lurking in the seemingly innocent speech act issuance of "It's raining now". Searle argues that Sam intends Henry to receive his message via the rules of language exhibited in "It's raining now". Unless the message to Henry is delivered via the rules which Henry understands, and Henry recognizes that the message is intended to be delivered by the rules, we do not have communication. What we have, even if Henry comes to think that Sam is telling him "It is raining now", is an accident. It is as if Sam were talking in English to Henry who only understands German but still, magically, Henry comes to the right conclusion about what Sam has said.

The analysis, then, of a simple speech act is not so simple. This should not be surprising. The analysis of the simple act of throwing the ball is not so simple either. That analysis might tell us how the thrower flexes his back, how he steps to the side and pushes off of his back foot, how he bends his knees slightly, how he pulls his throwing arm back over his head all the while keeping his other arm in position to maintain balance, how he turns his shoulder as he throws, how he keeps his head up and so on. The whole act (equivalent to an illocutionary act) of throwing might be done seemingly as one simple, almost thoughtless, motion, and yet be extremely complicated under the analyst's eye.

It is the same with speech acts except, as we will see shortly, matters are far more complicated than with throwing a ball. But before discussing these complications, two very important points related to what has already been said need to be addressed. The first deals with the first intention discussed above, having to do with delivering a message to a hearer.

Consider a second speech act that Sam issues to Henry. Sam says "Shut the door". Henry gets the message via the rules of English and fully understands Sam's intentions. So Sam has achieved what Searle calls illocutionary effect. Communication has taken place via his illocutionary act issuance. But Sam wants something more. He wants that door shut, and shut now. However, Henry has recently become non-compliant. He says in response "Go to hell!" What Sam has failed to achieve by his speech act is the perlocutionary effect (via his perlocutionary act of trying to get Henry to shut the door). The terminology is Austin's (1975: 101–32),[2] but Searle stays with it. The perlocutionary effect (and the corresponding perlocutionary act) is not literally part of the speech act as is attested by our example. The perlocutionary effect is a causal response to an already fully delivered linguistic act, and so it is not strictly speaking a part of that act. It is what results from speaking (uttering a full illocutionary act).

The two are often confused because part of the speaker's intent in issuing a speech act is to bring about the perlocutionary effect. Also, confusion comes about because success in achieving illocutionary effect (success in communicating via a speech act) is very often followed by success in achieving the perlocutionary effect (the desired causal result of many speech acts). Searle thinks that confusing the two effects can lead to bad philosophy. Hare (1952: 13–14) gives an example of this confusion of which Searle would approve. He says that Charles Stevenson's (1945) persuasive theory of ethics is concerned with perlocutionary effect. It characterizes ethical discourse as an instrument used to get (cause) people to do as we wish. Stevenson seems to be telling us that ethical discourse is an instrument of manipulation and propaganda.

But, for Hare, ethical discourse is no such instrument. Rather, if we focus on that discourse's illocutionary (strictly linguistic) features, as he does, we see that it prescribes (advises, directs) people about their behaviour and backs its prescriptions with reasons. Far from being an instrument used mainly to goad or prod people into action (i.e. the Stevenson thesis), moral discourse (speech acts) leaves the decision making in the hands of those to whom we issue prescriptions. Good work in philosophy of language on Hare's part thus gives us a significantly different answer to the what-is-ethics question and shows the value of doing philosophy of language well.

The second point concerns the rules of language. For Searle *"speaking a language* is engaging in a rule-governed form of behavior" (1969: 41). The rules of a language act as bridges in giving meaning to sentences so as to enable speakers to send messages and have them understood by hearers. These rules are, however, not merely regulative in nature. Regulative rules help modify behaviour we already engage in. These rules have to do with how, when, how much and what we eat, when and how we exercise, how long and how hard we work, how fast and how we drive our cars and so on. Linguistic rules eventually develop so that they regulate our linguistic behaviour. But initially they do so with constitutive rules.

These rules create new behaviour forms. Searle makes analogies to games to help us understand his sense of what constitutive rules are. Knowing what it means to win a set in tennis makes sense only in terms of one of the invented rules of that game. It is not as if the game had a long history and then along came the rule makers to tell us how to regulate the game by modifying it in this way or that. Rather before the concepts of match, set, ace, net, court, racket, (tennis) ball were "invented" there was no game of tennis as we know it today. In a similar way, language rules generate "institutions" such as promising, contracting, commanding, declaring war, etc. where seemingly there was nothing before. There is more to say about these constitutive rules and the institutional facts they generate. However, it is best to wait for that discussion (in this work, see Chapters 9 and 10 especially) since Searle's most extensive treatment of these matters takes place later in his career.

The following is a summary of the discussion thus far. Searle's account of speech (illocutionary) acts is very general. He tells us that the linguistic structure of these acts includes the sub-actions of referring and predicating (to form propositional acts that possess propositional content) and the act indicating how we are illocuting (telling others what we are doing with the language we are using). Put together properly, these sub-actions form complete speech acts. These complete or full-bodied acts, he adds, are the minimal units of language communication. That is what makes them interesting for the study of philosophy of language. Here is how Searle talks to us about these same thoughts.

> The reason for concentrating on the study of speech acts is simply this: all linguistic communication involves linguistic acts. The unit of linguistic communication is not, as has generally been supposed, the symbol, word or sentence, or even the token of the symbol, word or sentence, but rather the production or issuance of the symbol or word or sentence in the performance of the speech act. To take the token as a message is to take it as a produced or issued token. More precisely, the production or issuance of a sentence token under certain conditions is a speech act, and speech acts . . . are the basic or minimal units of linguistic communication. (1969: 16)

Searle is not suggesting here that it is easy to identify the precise nature of these minimal units. Often we say one thing but mean something else. That is, a gap often develops between what he calls sentence meaning and speaker meaning. The gap can be so great that we can even mean the opposite of what we say, as with irony. "Yes", the professor says to Cool Eddy, "I can see you are working hard from all the sweat on your brow". At other times we say one thing and mean what we say, but mean something else as well as in "There is a cobra just off of your right foot" (but meaning also something like "You had better slowly move your foot away from where it is"). But in addition to many other kinds of uses where we say one thing but mean something else, there are uses where we say one thing but mean something more. If the lady says "No", is she saying "It isn't raining", "Don't touch me" or what?

We will see in Chapters 2–4 what Searle's various strategies are for how hearers decipher what speakers say to them. But speakers can also help their hearers. This is possible because of what Searle calls the Principle of Expressibility. In essence the principle tells us "Spell it out". If the lady says "No", and her boyfriend doesn't "get it", she can spell it out by saying "I don't want you to touch me"; and if Cool Eddy doesn't understand his professor's irony, he can say to him "Look Cool Eddy you're a good for nothing lazy bum". In other words, "whatever can be meant can be said" (Searle 1969: 19).

The Principle of Expressibility is important for Searle since it makes it possible for him to begin his analysis of language by attending to actual uses (sentences), and from there move to speech acts. What the principle says is that we can analyze speech acts by restating what is said so that it now coincides with what is meant. In effect, then, sentence meaning and speaker meaning become identical. With coincidence we are closer to getting an explicit "portrait" of whatever speech acts we wish to analyze.

For Searle, once we come to understand the speech acts sent in our direction either because of the help we get from the speaker or because we know how to decipher what others say, we can build from there and come to understand how speakers can string speech acts together to generate speech activity (discourse) in the form of conversations, stories, new reports and the like. For him, as well, starting with the atomic level we can work down to see best how, for example, the sub-actions of referring work.

More than knowing about the structure we need to see how language works in process. To see about that requires taking account of: (a) the speaker's intention to send a message; (b) his intention to have his intention to send a message recognized by the hearer and (c) the intention to have the hearer recognize that the message being sent is in accordance with the language rules of a shared language.

Characteristics of various speech acts

Having given his readers a general account of speech acts (and language communication), it is quite natural for Searle to start thinking about the differing characteristics of various speech acts. As has been noted already, the philosophic tradition within which he is operating took it as one of its special insights that our natural language can be used for more than just constating (asserting) purposes. Our language is a many splendoured instrument, so Searle now looks analytically at its many splendours.

He does most of his analysis of a variety of the speech acts in terms of four major structural conditions. The first is the propositional content condition (which, recall, comes to us as a joint venture of the referring and predicating acts). Some speech acts, for example promising, require that the propositional content be formed in the future tense. Simon says to Harriet "I promise to help you tomorrow". It would make no sense for Simon to say "I promise to help you yesterday". Other speech acts, like an apology, require forming the propositional content in the past. Simon says to Harriet "I apologize for not coming yesterday to help you". Thus, how the propositional content is formed helps determine what kind of speech act is being issued by a speaker.

The preparatory condition represents the second of the four conditions Searle uses to characterize the various types of speech act. This condition is usually stated in the plural since more than one condition often needs to be specified. Preparatory conditions are those that need to hold before a speech act can be properly issued. As has just been noted, an apology requires that a prior event harmful (or thought to be harmful) to the hearer has already taken place. Congratulations are quite the opposite. Now the hearer has been blessed with some happy event like winning the lottery. But preparatory conditions need not be events. They may concern the social, mental, or physical state of either the hearer or speaker. With a command issued by General Savage, it is required that he outrank those he commands. With a promise, it is required that Simon believe that Harriet wants help in moving her furniture. With a question, it is required that Sam not know the answer to the question he asks of Henry.

The third condition Searle calls the sincerity condition. With Simon's promise to Harriet, the sincerity condition is satisfied when Simon intends to help her. With General Savage's order, that same condition is satisfied if he wants those under him to do what he orders. And with any claim that something is true, the sincerity condition is satisfied when the speaker believes what he claims. The sincerity condition is somewhat peculiar in that, although it is helpful in characterizing speech acts of various kinds, it does not have to be satisfied. The person is likely to be sincere when issuing a speech act, but he does not have to be. Thus an insincere promise still counts as a promise. Yes, says the sailor to his naive young lady, he will marry her. He says that even though, as he makes the promise, he knows that he will be off to sea in a week, never to return. His lack of intent does not represent a defence when she accuses him before the law that he broke his promise. He can't argue that he never really made a promise because he never meant to keep it or because he had his fingers crossed. Similarly if Susie makes a claim that she knows is not true, she has still made the claim. Austin talks of the lack of sincerity in these kinds of cases as speech act abuse (Austin 1975: 15–16). Austin contrasts abuses with misfires. Searle goes along with this contrast. Misfires are infelicities (flaws) in the production of speech acts that actually make them null and void. If the Smith child is kidnapped and then named after one of the kidnappers in an otherwise normal baptismal ceremony, the whole ceremony is null and void because only the Smiths have the authority to permit such a ceremony to take place. One of the preparatory conditions has obviously gone awry here. In a similar vein, John cannot sign a contract selling Henry's car to Mary. Of course physically he can sign the contract, but once it is clear that John was not authorized by Henry to sign, the document with his signature no longer counts as a contract (is null and void).

The last major condition Searle talks about is difficult to characterize. He calls it the essential condition and his usual way of characterizing it is in terms of intentions since, as acts, speech acts are issued intentionally. A general characterization of the essential condition, for Searle, takes the following form: S, the speaker, intends that the utterance of a sentence, T, counts as a token of a speech act of type X. If T is a promise then S intends that the utterance of the promise counts as placing him under and obligation to do some action, A. If T is an order then the utterance of the order counts as placing H, the hearer, under an obligation (some duty) to do action A. Or, described differently, the order counts as S's attempt to get H to do A. In his later writings (1979a: 2; 1985: 87–8) Searle talks about this condition more in terms of the illocutionary point or purpose of a speech act. He usually says that the essential condition or the condition that generates the point of a speech act is the most important of the four.

With these conditions in hand, the analysis of the various speech acts follows seamlessly. To be sure, other conditions need to be cited when a complete analysis of any one type of speech act is forthcoming. Thus, starting with an analysis of promising, as Searle does in *Speech Acts* (1969: 57–61), he first mentions what he calls normal input and output conditions. Input conditions refer to the speaker, output to the hearer. Some of the conditions included under input and output are that both speaker and hearer understand the language being used, both are conscious of what they are doing, neither is suffering from some physical impediment (e.g. the speaker has laryngitis and the hearer is deaf) that might block communication and that they are not engaged in some special activity such as play acting.

Since the input and output conditions are necessary for issuing any speech act whatsoever, they do not help in sorting one kind of act from another. For that, Searle turns to his four "characterizing" conditions which, in summary form, are:

- the propositional content condition (the "what" of a speech act);
- the preparatory conditions (the background of a speech act);
- the sincerity condition (the hearer's accompanying psychological feelings and thoughts);
- the essential condition (what the speaker wants to accomplish linguistically by issuing a speech act).

Referring to these conditions Searle tells us what it means to make a promise. As noted already, the propositional content condition for promising must be in the future tense, that is, the promised act is to be performed in the future. That's simple enough. Such is not the case with the preparatory conditions since there are several for promising. One of these Searle expresses as follows: "It is not obvious to both S [speaker] and H [hearer] that S will do A in the normal course of events" (1969: 59). In other words, there is no reason for the husband to promise his wife to take the rubbish out if he is in the habit of doing so anyway. Another preparatory condition is that the action, A, is preferred by the hearer; and, further, that the speaker believes the hearer would prefer that A be done rather than not. Here Searle is telling us how we differentiate a promise from a threat. Promises of punishment (as in "You will be punished if you don't study hard, I promise you!") are not really promises but ways of emphasizing the dire consequences of disobedience. They are threats clothed as promises.

But there are other preparatory conditions for promising that Searle doesn't tell us about in *Speech Acts*. These relate to the ability, situation and social position of the speaker. If the speaker does not have the ability to move a building, it makes no sense to suppose that he can promise to do so. Nor can Amy promise to buy, today, a present from Paris for her friend Amanda if she has no way of obtaining one. Amy's situation has something to do with when a promise counts as a promise. So does social position. Sam cannot promise Harriet that John will help her move furniture, unless John is his slave, his employee, or John has designated Sam to make promises for him. Sam can promise that he himself can help since he is autonomous and can make promises about what he can do. But he can do so, it seems, only if he is in position to help (not half a world away), if he has the ability to help (his back isn't aching), if it isn't obvious that he was going to help anyway and if it is believed that the promise will help Harriet. So there are a host of preparatory conditions needed for issuing a proper promise.

The third structural category to take account of in this analysis of promising is the sincerity condition. It will be recalled that, in one sense, this condition does not have to be satisfied for speech acts to take effect. Sam may be lying to Henry (not be sincere) but, if all other conditions are satisfied, he has still issued a perfectly good speech act when he says "It's raining outside" even though it isn't raining. The reason he has is that, in another sense, the sincerity condition has been satisfied. Sam has publicly *expressed* his sincerity. He is on record as being sincere; even if he is not. It is the same with promising. Sam has expressed his sincerity to do for Henry what he has promised whether he intends to keep the promise or not.

In spite of these problems with compliance, the sincerity condition is helpful in sorting one speech act from another since it varies qualitatively from one speech act type to another. With promising the sincerity condition has nothing to do with what the speaker believes or is supposed to believe. Rather, it is has to do with intent. The person who made the promise is supposed to have the intent to carry out what he promised. In contrast, with commanding, the sincerity condition is desire. When General Savage issues a command he expresses the desire that his soldiers perform some actions that lead to the success of the unit's mission.

The fourth category in this analysis of promising is the essential condition. Expressing this category in terms of intent as Searle does, this comes down to "S intends that the utterance of T (the sentence) will place him under an obligation to do A" (1969: 60).

Searle's own analysis of promising is more complete than the one presented here. He includes in his analysis a condition, discussed above, that takes account of the speaker's various intentions. For the present purposes, however, enough has been said to show the direction that the analysis takes. It is useful by way of contrast to look at the analyses of two other speech acts: "Hello" and "Please (I beg you) don't shoot me!" The former has no propositional content; nor, according to Searle, does it have a sincerity condition. However it does have a preparatory condition. "S has just encountered (or been introduced to, etc.) H" (1969: 67). The essential condition of "Hello" is that it: "Counts as courteous recognition of H by S" (1969: 67).

"Please don't shoot me!" is somewhat more complicated. The propositional content is composed of the reference (to the speaker) and the predicate (concerned with shooting – at some future time, possibly in the immediate future). There is certainly a sincerity condition present. Presumably the speaker dearly wants to live and thus wants H not to shoot. As to the preparatory condition one can imagine that H has power over S in so far as H is holding a gun to his head. More than that, it must be presumed that H knows how to use the gun, the gun is loaded, etc. As to the essential condition, S's pleading counts as his attempt to get H not to shoot. It counts as a case of pleading, rather than politely asking, because of illocutionary force indicating devices ("Please . . .!" and "I beg you . . .") tell what it is and because of the intimidating preparatory conditions (i.e. the gun to S's head).

Referring

Searle follows a pattern of analysis in his discussions of how we refer and how we predicate that is somewhat similar to his pattern for full speech acts. As noted already, referring and predicating are linguistic acts – although as we will see shortly, since predicating is a peculiar *dependent* act Searle says that it is significantly different from referring. Still, loosely speaking, referring and predicating are sub-acts performed as a part of performing larger, more complete acts as in tennis where laying one's wrist back, bending ones knees, pushing off on one's back foot, looking-the-ball into the racket are all part of the larger act of hitting the ball.

Just like whole speech acts, then, referring requires that normal input and output conditions apply. Thus when referring takes place, the speaker (or writer) must be able to voice (or write) the words used to refer and the hearer to hear (or read) them. Searle adds a second condition, namely that the reference must be part of some larger (otherwise successful) speech act. This condition we have already anticipated. We don't just refer and then suppose that we are communicating successfully with others.

But now Searle adds two other conditions that get to the heart of his account of referring. He says for proper referring to take place: (a) whatever is referred to must exist (the axiom of existence) and (b) the referring expression must either contain what he calls an identifying description of the referent or the speaker must be able to provide an identifying description (the principle of identification). To help understand what Searle is saying, imagine a setting where two strangers are talking to one another. One nods in the direction of a woman and says "That's my wife". In accord with the first of these two new conditions, the reference (within the whole speech act) is successful partly because the "object" referred to exists so that the axiom of existence is thereby satisfied. Following ordinary usage, Searle would say that if the speaker had said "The pink elephants in my room are noisy" reference would have failed. The speaker could not refer because there is nothing there to refer to. In accord with the second of these two new conditions, the reference is successful partly because the demonstrative "that" and the nod together pick out one object out of the total setting that includes an indefinite number of objects. The reference could have succeeded without the demonstrative aids. The speaker could have said "The blue-plaid dressed woman, wearing glasses, with long blonde hair, holding the baby is my wife". Here the description is definite enough (in context) to pick out the object referred to. So in settings like those involving the two strangers, an identifying description necessary for referring gets done by the use of demonstratives, definite descriptions or some combination of the two. It gets done when there is no ambiguity as to whom or what is being referred to. If the speaker had said "The woman with long blonde hair is my wife" but there were two women standing next to one another with long blonde hair, then reference has failed. It is a failure or infelicity comparable to Austin's misfire rather than abuse. Not only does the referring fail, but because referring is an important part of the total speech act, the total speech act also fails.

In his analysis of referring Searle adds still other conditions, ones comparable to those found in his analysis of full speech (illocutionary) acts once again (1969: 95). These include conditions having to do with intentions. Speakers must intend that the expression they use pick out or identify for hearers the object to which they are trying to refer. He also intends the referring expression will do its job in such a way that the hearer will recognize the speaker's intention to refer. Further the speaker intends to achieve this recognition via shared rules of language. Searle gives us some alarming examples to explain the need for the rules condition.

> For example, I may call my hearer's attention to an object by throwing it at him, or hitting him over the head with it. But such cases are not in general cases of referring, because the intended effect is not achieved by recognition on his part of my intentions. (1969: 95)

Searle adds one more condition: viz., that each and every condition he has included in his analysis needs to be done correctly.

It should be clear that Searle is following a pattern of analysis fully in accord with a point made early in this chapter. To get things underway he starts with easy or standard cases or settings. Getting comfortable with these, he typically moves to those that are, for him, not so easy to handle. Thinking about these not-so-easy cases, someone might ask, what about proper names as a device for referring? Certainly proper names are important since they are our favourite devices for referring when we can neither point to objects, nod in their direction nor describe them as they are standing before us. Referring after all is not restricted to what is before us. We can refer to somebody who has been dead for many years or is thousands of miles away.

But these settings where we use proper names pose a problem for Searle because of his principle of identification. Proper names appear to be just labels or tags with little if any sense or connotation. John Stuart Mill and Bertrand Russell (Searle 1969: 163–4) among others argued for such a labels theory of referring. From a proper name such as "Kim", "Kelly" or even "Kelly Stanton" it does not seem possible to obtain a description of the person or object named to identify him, her or it.

Searle deals with this problem by reminding us what happens when Alice asks Bill "Who is Kelly Stanton?" Bill does not respond by saying "He's Kelly Stanton, of course", but instead presents Alice with a description such as "He's the man who got in trouble for not paying his taxes and who lives in that ugly red house on the corner". If that description isn't enough he can add to it. It doesn't matter that Bill identifies Kelly Stanton one way and Charley some other. There need not be an essential definition of "Kelly Stanton" for purposes of referring. Nor need the speaker provide a description of the one referred to on every occasion. Once those chatting about Kelly know who he is, all they need do is use the empty sounding name "Kelly Stanton" to do the referring for them.[3] Yet, should the occasion arise when the hearer doesn't know who Kelly Stanton is, those who know to whom the name refers must be in position to give one or another definitive description. So Searle is able to fit proper names into his analysis of referring that features the principle of identification and fits, as well, his more general account of speech acts.

Predicating

Searle's account of predication follows, in step, his account of referring. It includes mention of input and output conditions, intentions and all the rest. However, three conditions differentiate predicating from referring. The first is simple enough. It says that prior to predicating one must have satisfied the conditions for referring. It makes no sense to predicate that Bill is tall if Bill can't be referred to because he does not exist. Similarly it makes to sense to predicate that Sally is standing between Suzie and Samantha if either or both Suzie and Samantha can't be referred to because they don't exist.

The second condition says "X is of a type or category such that it is logically possible for P to be true or false of X" (Searle 1969: 126). Here "X" stands for the thing referred to. So X could stand for a person, animal, physical object, an action, process and so on. 'P' stands for the predicate. What this condition says then is that if we predicate of X that X is articulate then X must be the type of thing that could be articulate. X can't be a rock or even a cat. So predicating involves knowing a lot about concepts and how they relate to one another, and also knowing a lot about the sorts of things out there in the world.

The third condition is the most difficult to understand. Here is how Searle states it. "S intends by the utterance of T to raise the question of the truth or falsity of P of X" (1969: 127). Again "X" stands for the thing referred to and "P" for the predicate; but now, in addition, "S" stands for the speaker and "T" for a sentence or a larger stretch of discourse. What he means by "raise the question of the truth or falsity of P of X" is not what it sounds like he means. One naturally reads "raise the question" as saying something like "deciding the truth or falsity of P of X". If it were read this way, one would suppose that predicating occurs exclusively within descriptive speech acts (constatives). It is as if predicating takes place in response to questions such as "Is it red, tall and loud (or isn't it)?"

But, as noted already, Searle, Austin, Wittgenstein and others have told us that language can be used to do more than describe (assert, constate) so it is not likely that predicating is limited to just that one basic type of speech act. We predicate when we not only say "The door is shut" but also when we say "Shut the door". There is no problem of predicating with the request "Shut the door" with respect to the first two conditions mentioned above. There is proper reference because we see the door and we point to it. So the first necessary condition is satisfied. The second is satisfied as well because doors are the kind of thing that can be said to be open or shut. We are not asking of the door whether it is sweet or sour; or kindly or not.

What about the third condition? When we say "Shut the door" the door (normally) isn't shut but we are still raising the question of the truth or falsity of the door (X) being shut (P). In so far the door isn't shut now, we can say that it is true that it isn't shut; and it will be true that it is shut when the request to shut it is satisfied. We are still talking about truth and falsity (i.e. raising the question of the truth or falsity of P of X) even if in the process of making the request "Shut the door" we are not asserting anything at all that is true or false right now. So all three conditions for predicating apply to requests just as they do for descriptive speech acts such as "The door is shut". Thus, predicating is evidently not something we do just with assertions (constatives). It seems to have wider application.

However, no matter how widely we predicate we must not forget that predicating takes place within the full speech act. By itself it only brings content to the total speech act. It tells what we are talking about (i.e. the subject matter), but not what we are going to say about that content. It's like saying "The rock red" where it has not been established whether the rock is red, we are to make it red by painting it, we wish it were red or what. To establish what is going on we need to add an illocutionary force to what is being said. If we say "Yes, the rock is red" we know now that it is an assertion or a descriptive utterance. We can, then, determine by looking at the rock whether the assertion is true or false. Similarly if we say "Make the rock red!" we know that it is a request or command, and know that the rock, right now, is not red. So, for Searle, in so far as predicating supplies only the content of the speech act (the subject matter or the what-we-are-talking-about part) and in so far as how that content gets interpreted depends upon the illocutionary force, predicating is *not* an independent speech act. Referring, recall, is. Referring is an independent operation even though in one sense it is also a dependent act that takes place within the complete speech act. It is independent in that it is not affected by the illocutionary force found in the total speech act. We refer in the same way no matter what kind of speech act we issue. But the predicating will be different for an assertion and for a request. With the former we say the thing referred to is red, with the latter it will be red (if we paint it so). If one wishes, predicating may be thought of as a speech act. It is something that we do after all. But since it possesses a form of dependence beyond that found when we refer, Searle says it is not a speech act in the strict sense. To predicate properly we need to know the complete speech act's illocutionary force (what we are doing with language when we speak). Putting it differently, providing the speech act with content is not enough. We need both content and some illocutionary force to understand fully the what it is we do when we predicate.

It should be noted that nowhere in his analysis of predicating does Searle say that to predicate is to refer to something like a universal. For Searle, predicating has more to do with knowing the meaning of a term or knowing how to use it than it does to pointing to anything. Here he is expressing his disagreement with Platonists, of course, but also with Frege and Strawson (Searle 1969: 113) among others. These thinkers seem to want to make a parallel with referring and thus to say that predicating is a special kind of referring to something special outside of language like a universal. It is referring to something that we, in our non-philosophic mode of thinking, would never have thought we were referring to. But to admit that when we predicate we refer to some Idea, concept or whatever is, for Searle, to go against his point that predicating isn't really an independent speech act.

More to say

As it has thus far been recounted, Searle's theory of speech acts in his first book reiterates, systematizes and supplements Austin's exploratory work. It does so by looking at both the structure of speech acts and the processes that allow us to communicate. About the structure he tell us how referring and predicating acts work together to allow us to issue acts possessing propositional content; and how these latter acts unite with what I call illocutionary acts to give full-bodied illocutionary speech acts. Concerning structure, he also tells us (as did Austin) that a distinction needs to be made between the illocutionary effect (and the corresponding illocutionary act) and the perlocutionary effect (and act). It is the former that deals most directly with language. The illocutionary effect has to do exclusively with the rules of language. The perlocutionary effect, in contrast, deals with causes. It is concerned with causal effects that take place after a full-bodied speech act has been issued.

Searle also tells us about the role intentions, preparatory conditions, the sincerity condition and the essential condition play in the process of making communication possible.[4] However, Searle has much more to tell us about speech acts than has thus far been recounted. Towards the end of *How To Do Things With Words* Austin attempts to classify the almost indefinite number of speech acts that he had identified into a few basic types. He felt that there must be some sort of order present in our natural language, and that it was his job to find it. However, he realized that all he had provided his readers was a preliminary version of a classification system, and that much more work needed to be done on it. Unfortunately, because of his early death, Austin never got the chance to do the work of refining his classification system. Others would have to finish the job for him. In one of his most interesting and important articles in his career, titled "A Taxonomy of Illocutionary Acts" Searle takes up that task.

It is to that lead article in *Expression and Meaning* (1979a) that we turn next.

Notes

1. It should be noted that neither Austin nor Searle talk about an illocutionary force indicating act. I do so to show how the structure, the illocutionary force indicating act plus the propositional act, together, help generate a (full) illocutionary act. They talk about illocutionary force indicating devices. Such devices are expressions that indicate whether one is asserting, pledging, congratulating and so on. On my account the illocutionary force indicating act contains an illocutionary force indicating device. So the two terminologies are not incompatible.

2. *How To Do Things With Words* says: "We must distinguish the illocutionary act from the perlocutionary act: for example we must distinguish 'in saying it I was warning him' from 'by saying it I convinced him, or surprised him or got him to stop'"(p. 110). The perlocutionary act is the attempt to convince, surprise, etc. someone, while the effect is actually convincing, surprising, etc. the hearer.

3. Searle opposes the causal theory of reference as championed by the likes of Kripke (1972) and Donnellan (1974). This theory says that a proper name "refers because of a 'causal chain' connecting the utterance of the name to the bearer of the name or at least to the naming ceremony in which the bearer of the name got the name. So the puppy Amelia got her name when my wife and I decided to give her that name after which the name was passed on to our neighbor to our left, who passed on the name to her neighbor on her left so that now when a visitor who comes to know about Amelia through the last neighbor says 'Amelia is a nice puppy' the reference succeeds because of the causal link or chain that takes 'Amelia' back to the 'naming ceremony' my wife and I engaged in" (Searle 1983: 232). First of all Searle says this theory contains descriptivist features so his descriptivist theory can accommodate the causal theory. "The dog (Amelia) named by my neighbor" is one such feature. But second where we know the person or creature named directly (as against knowing about an historical figure) proper names can refer without going through the "chain of command". Instead the reference works because of some description (internal in one's head).

4. A large number of recent articles on speech act theory can be found in *Foundations of Speech Act Theory: Philosophical and Linguistic Perspectives* edited by Savas L. Tsohatzidis (1994). Some of these articles are sympathetic with Searle's account of speech acts, some are not. Authors in this volume include William P. Alston, Steven Davis, John T. Kearns, Tzohatzidis and Daniel Vanderveken. Vanderveken's two-volume *Meaning and Speech Acts* (1990–91) is also helpful (and largely sympathetic to Searle). An earlier work in the area of speech acts is David Holdcrofts's *Words and Deeds* (1978). Aside from presenting his own views on speech acts, Holdcroft surveys the field and so gives the reader a better sense than does Searle in any of his writings what others are saying about speech acts. Unfortunately, *Words and Deeds* was published before Searle's *Expression and Meaning* and so does not take into account some of the more important things Searle says about speech acts.

Chapter 2

Searle's taxonomic theory

Twelve ways that illocutionary acts differ

How, one might wonder, can a *taxonomy* of speech acts be both interesting and important? It might seem more appropriate to call it boring, since the business of classifying any set of phenomena or objects is normally thought of as mechanical and hardly a challenge to the imagination. And it might also seem unimportant since Searle has already put much of his speech act theory in place. Developing a taxonomy for such acts seems, therefore, somewhat akin to engaging in mop-up operations in war rather than in a major battle. I will argue, to the contrary, that Searle's taxonomy is indeed interesting and that he is not engaged in mop-up operations.

Searle begins his search for a satisfactory speech act classification system or taxonomy by identifying no less than twelve ways that speech acts can differ from one another. Some of the ways or dimensions are repeats from *Speech Acts*, but some are new. As it turns out, the old are generally more important than the new. But all need to be identified and understood in order to avoid one or other kind of confusion about how we do things with language. Unavoidably, then, one must march tediously from the first dimension all the way through the twelfth to get a sense of what Searle wants his readers to understand about how to classify speech acts properly. If not boredom itself, the reader might be experiencing an anticipation of boredom at this point. But, keep in mind, patience is a virtue.

Searle characterizes the first dimension as the "Differences in the point (or purpose) of the (type) of act" (1979a: 2). Another term he uses is "illocutionary point" and he adds that it is related to our old friend "essential conditions". Different types of speech acts will have different illocutionary purposes. Some will commit the speaker (as in a promise), others will represent what is true or false (as in a description) and still others will attempt to direct people's behaviour one way rather than another (as in a command). However many illocutionary points or purposes there are, Searle makes an extremely important distinction in the process of discussing this dimension. This distinction marks a significant terminological change in speech act theory so it needs to be attended to carefully. Austin had not made the distinction, and Searle had not made it clear earlier either.

The distinction is between illocutionary force and point. Illocutionary force is like a large batch of paint that results from the mixture of several smaller batches each with its distinct colour, while illocutionary point is one of the distinctly coloured batches. So the illocutionary point contributes to the mixture that makes for the force. But, then, each of the other dimensions also makes its contribution, as will be evident shortly. What the "point" contributes exactly will become clearer after the other dimensions have been discussed. But this much is evident from what Searle has told us in *Speech Acts*. The "point" or essential feature of a speech act (which is governed by the rules of the language) is not to be confused with the perlocutionary (causal) effect. Rather than being concerned with the causal effect of a speech act issuance, it is concerned with the illocutionary effect. Asking about the point of a speech act is like asking: What has happened or changed *linguistically* as a result of the issuance of this speech act? The answer is that the hearers have understood what was said, they've got the message or even communication has taken place. Searle says that the point is *the* most important dimension when it comes to doing something with language.

Searle's second dimension that brings out differences among speech acts he calls the "direction of fit". He speaks of certain speech acts as having a word-to-world direction of fit. This means that the word (really the speech act) in some sense is supposed to fit, match, correspond to, etc. the world. So, when spelled out, word-to-world direction of fit means something like the word (the speech act) matches what is out there in the world. All kinds of descriptive utterances have this sort of fit. The utterance "The rose is red" fits in this way since the rose *is* red and "Aggression leads to more aggression" also fits since aggression (often) *does* lead to more aggression. Presumably scientists, reporters and anyone else interested in making accurate observations will try to maximize the number of claims that fit the world, and keep the number that do not to a minimum. Not surprisingly the other direction of fit is world-to-word. With this fit, the world is supposed to fit or match the words. An example is when an order is issued to shut the door. Presumably with the door open there is a bad fit with the words; but after the subordinate closes the door the fit with the words is good. There are four possibilities with the concept of direction of fit. Some utterances have a word-to-world fit, some a world-to-word fit, others have no direction of fit and some have a dual direction of fit.

The third dimension brings about differences among speech acts that relate to the now familiar sincerity condition. Searle characterizes the dimensions as focusing on "Differences in expressed psychological states". He says:

> A man who states, explains, asserts, or claims that *p expresses the belief that p*; a man who promises, vows, threatens or pledges to do *a expresses an intention to do a*; a man who orders, commands requests *H* to do *A expresses a desire (want, wish) that H do A*; a man who apologizes for doing *A expresses regret at having done A*; etc. (1979a: 4)

By "expresses" Searle means something like "leaves it understood" or "implies" that he is sincere in the appropriate way. It will be recalled that the speaker need not in fact be sincere. Still, although Adam doesn't say so in so many words, he would be misleading others if, in fact, he were not sincere when he says "I promise to be at the party". As such, he could be criticized for "abusing" the rules for making promises.

These first three dimensions are the important ones for Searle. It is with them (plus possibly one other) that he generates his classification system. But, as noted already, it is necessary to understand the others to appreciate fully what is and what is not contained in these first three.

The fourth dimension he characterizes as *"Differences in the force or strength with which the illocutionary point is presented"* (1979a: 5). Here Searle tells us that even though the strength of our utterance varies, the illocutionary point need not. So if Alice says "I suggest we go to the movies" while Adam says "I insist that we go to the movies" [Searle's examples], both are attempting to direct the behaviour of their respective hearer. Again, the point is that even if the strength of the speech act varies, the purpose or "point" of the speech act need not. With both, the speaker is trying to get the hearer to act in a certain way.

The fifth dimension Searle characterizes as *"Differences in the status or position of the speaker and hearer as these bear on the illocutionary force of the utterance"* (1979a: 5). Note here that he is talking about "force" rather than "point" (as he did with the fourth dimension). Whatever the force may be (perhaps some combination of the "point", "strength" and other dimensions) we have the possibility of different kinds of utterances depending on whether the speaker or hearer is more powerful socially. The general, the boss, the professor, the religious leader, the man with the gun will tend to give orders while those who aren't generals, etc. will ask or plead for cooperation. Searle notes that this dimension of difference in speech acts corresponds to some of the preparatory conditions he discussed in Chapter 3 of *Speech Acts*, such as what preferences and beliefs the speaker and hearer bring to the speech act setting and what expectations they have (1979a: 5–6).

The sixth dimension is characterized as *"Differences in the way the utterance relates to the interests of the hearer and speaker"* (1979a: 6). When Suzanne is congratulated, her interests are prospering; when she receives condolences they are not. This dimension too, obviously, relates to preparatory conditions (i.e. conditions with a history to them).

The seventh dimension is characterized as: *"Differences in relation to the rest of the discourse"* (1979a: 6). When Andrew presents an argument and then says "I conclude . . ." or "Therefore . . ." his listeners know that he must have issued some other speech acts already, even though they have been daydreaming and haven't heard what he has said already. At this point, we see Searle engaged, ever so briefly, in the study of philosophy of language on a more macro (or discourse) level rather than on the "minimal" level of speech acts. There will be more to say about discourse analysis in the next two chapters.

Searle's eighth dimension concerns *"Differences in propositional content that are determined by illocutionary force indicating devices"* (1979a: 6). This dimension has already been discussed in Chapter 1 especially in connection with predicating. If the indicating device signals "I predict" the propositional content has to be in the future tense; but if it signals "I am reporting to you from Chechnya", what is being reported is happening now ("I can see the missiles falling to the ground") or has happened in the past ("Yesterday's missiles killed three people").

The ninth dimension concerns *"Differences between those acts that must always be speech acts, and those that can be, but need not be performed as speech acts"* (1979a: 6). Searle says that speakers can issue speech acts that start "I classify this . . ." or "I conclude that . . ." but they can classify things and conclude whatever they like without issuing any public speech act at all. In contrast, one cannot promise, excommunicate, issue orders without doing so publicly (through the use of language and, perhaps, the appropriate rituals).

The tenth dimension is characterized as: *"Differences between those that require extra-linguistic institutions for their performance and those that do not"* (1979a: 7). Those speech acts that require some extra-linguistic institution include excommunicating, declaring war, getting married, baptizing and sentencing someone to a prison term. Those that don't require any institution except for the language itself are promising, describing, asking and the like.

The eleventh dimension deals with *"Differences between those acts where the corresponding illocutionary verb has a performative use and those where it does not"* (1979a: 7). There are performative verbs for stating, promising, concluding, ordering, pleading, etc. But, surprisingly, the verb "boast" doesn't belong in this list. It is not a legitimate use of English to say "I boast that I swam across the English Channel" or "I hereby boast that I hit the longest home run in baseball history", perhaps because boasting is not something people are supposed to do. Nor does it makes sense to say "I imply (allude) that it is raining outside". Stating something openly defeats implying it.

The last dimension Searle characterizes as *"Differences in the style of performance of the illocutionary act"* (1979a: 8). He says about this dimension: "Thus, the difference between, for example, announcing and confiding need not involve any difference in illocutionary point or propositional content" (1979a: 8). Presumably other differences in style are to be found in the contrasts between speaking and writing, between sending a message in code or out in the open and between using academic sounding language and ordinary talk.

For purposes of quick reference here is the list of the twelve dimensions that create differences in illocutionary acts. These differences relate to the:

- point or purpose of an act;
- direction of fit;
- expressed psychological state;
- force or strength of the point;
- status or position of the hearer or speaker;
- way the utterance relates to the interests of the hearer or speaker;
- relationship to the rest of the discourse;
- propositional content;
- requirement that some acts must be speech acts while others need not be;
- lack of or need for extra-linguistic institutions;
- lack of or need for illocutionary verbs;
- style of performance.

Searle's taxonomy

With his twelve dimensions in hand, Searle next looks at Austin's preliminary attempt to classify speech acts. He finds his mentor's efforts wanting. One mistake Austin makes is to focus too much on verbs such as "promise", "announce", "order", "state", "congratulate", "intend" and "shall" when they are used in the first person as in "I promise . . ." rather than focus on the acts themselves. As the list of twelve differences shows, focusing on verbs is distracting in that, for example, it treats "I announce" (difference 12) on a par with "I promise". "Announcing . . . is not the name of a type of illocutionary act, but of the way in which some illocutionary act is performed" (Searle 1979: 9). Promises can be announced openly and loudly, or they can be whispered. But the way we perform our promises doesn't change them into new and different speech acts. Language users just don't make announcements. Rather they issue speech acts of one kind or another and, while doing so, present them in one way or another.

Focusing on verbs gets Austin into still more trouble. He lists "intend" as in "I intend to help you" as a commissive. Commissives represent the first of Austin's five types of basic speech acts. "I intend" has the feel of a commissive (like "I promise") whose whole point

(Searle's first dimension) "is to commit the speaker to a certain course of action" (Austin 1975: 157). Indeed, if someone says "I intend to be there" we are likely to take it as a promise to be there. Still, Searle argues, quite rightly, that "I intend . . ." is not an illocutionary commissive verb at all. It does not indicate a kind of speech act but more a description or report of the speaker's state of mind. "I intend to . . ." is a report. Up front, at least, it says that there is an intention that will lead the speaker to (try to) act in a certain way. As we will see in the next chapter "I intend" can be, and more often than not is, used to do something more than report some fact.

Searle has a variety of other complaints about Austin's classification system. The most fundamental is that because Austin does not identify all the dimensions that allow for speech acts to differ from one another, he fails to develop a systematic way of sorting his various basic speech act types. He appeals to one dimension to identify one kind of speech act and then to a totally different dimension to identify a different kind. It's a bit like comparing types of cars by noting that some are eight cylinder machines, some have power brakes and power steering while others are red. Austin thus gives us a strange and, in the end, very unsatisfactory theory of the basic speech act types.

The second type of speech act that Austin identifies he calls expositives. "Expositives are used in acts of exposition involving the expounding of views, the conducting of arguments and the clarifying of usages and of references" (Austin 1975: 161). This type is thus identified mainly in terms of Searle's seventh dimension (*Differences in relations to the rest of the discourse*). Commissives, as we have just seen, are identified mainly in terms of the first dimension (in terms of point or purpose of the act). At this point we can appreciate more fully Searle's criticism that Austin's classification system has no order to it. It truly does jump around from one dimension to another.

A third type of speech act Austin calls exercitives. These have to do with "the giving of a decision in favour of or against a certain course of action, or advocacy of it" (Austin 1975: 155). According to Searle this type is characterized partly in terms of the fifth dimension (having to do with the social status of the hearer and speaker) and partly in terms of the tenth dimension (requiring extra-linguistic institutions). It is now still more obvious than before that Austin is floundering in his attempt to devise a sensible classification system.

Searle also complains about a fourth type of Austinian speech act called behabitives. "Behabitives include the notion of reaction to other people's behaviour and fortunes and of attitudes and expressions of attitudes to someone else's past conduct or imminent conduct" (Austin 1975: 160). About behabitives Searle says that they "do not seem to me at all well defined (as Austin, I am sure, would have agreed) but it seems to involve notions of what is good or bad for the speaker (my feature 6) as well as expressions of attitudes (my feature 3)" (1979a: 10).

Austin identifies one other type of speech act. "Verdictives consist in the delivering of a finding, official or unofficial, upon evidence or reasons as to value or fact, so far as these are distinguishable. A verdictive is a judicial act as distinct from legislative or executive acts . . ." (Austin 1975: 153). Searle does not comment on this type in relation to his twelve dimensions. But it should be clear that verdictives involve appeals to the seventh dimension (*Differences in relations to the rest of the discourse*), the tenth dimension (requiring extra-linguistic institutions) and perhaps the fifth dimension (status of speaker and hearer). However that might work out, Searle's overall point is that Austin's five types of speech acts form no principled list. There is no organized set of principles to which he appeals to enable us to say why this type of speech act is basic or why that one is not.

As is Searle's custom, he becomes impatient with analyzing other people's work. So he quickly goes on to argue that he can best show his readers what a principled system of basic speech act types looks like by presenting his own list for us. Like Austin's taxonomy, his contains five types. However, of Austin's five, he accepts only commissives. "Commissives . . . are those illocutionary acts whose point is to committ [sic] the speaker (. . . in varying degrees) to some future course of action" (Searle 1979a: 14). Searle's account here is indeed close to Austin's. This is no surprise since of his five types only commissives are characterized in terms of the "point" or "purpose" of the illocutionary act. So Austin got it right to identify commissives as a basic type of speech act, and he got it right for the right reason.

However, going beyond Austin, Searle also characterizes commissives in terms of direction of fit. Commissives have world-to-word direction of fit, that is, they represent an attempt to change the world to match the word. By promising (or vowing), Suzanne commits herself to changing the world in some way in the future. So another feature of commissives, as we have already seen, is that their propositional contents will be about some action or series of actions in the future. Identifying the sincerity condition in commissives as intention completes Searle's account of the first basic type of speech act in his taxonomy. When Suzanne makes a promise, she implies in what she says that she intends to carry it out. He symbolizes his account as follows:

$$C \uparrow I \,(S \text{ does } A)$$

where C is the symbol of commitment, the arrow points upward to indicate that the direction of fit is world-to-word, I stands for the sincerity condition of intent and (S does A) (in the future) speaks to the propositional content.

Promises are Searle's favourite commissives. He writes more about them than all other commissives, probably because they are invoked more than any other. But it is interesting to see how other commissives can be characterized in terms of his twelve dimensions. Vows fit the basic commissive formula along with all other commissives. They differ from promises, however, since they are often invoked in a religious or some other institutional setting (tenth dimension). We often think here of taking vows to become a member of a religious order or think of taking marriage vows. The long-lasting commitments associated with vows may explain why they are sometimes characterized as solemn promises and why they are thought of as more stringent than everyday promises (fourth dimension). To be sure, promises are stringent enough. There is no such thing as a weak promise. In this sense, when Sam says "I sort of promise to be at the party" this can only represent an attempt at humour carrying the meaning of "I may not come". Yet even with their strength, promises are overridden not infrequently when something more serious than keeping the promise unexpectedly arises. In contrast, vows, possibly because of their institutional backing and because they often concern life-long commitments, are overridden with greater difficulty. Swearing, as in "I (solemnly) swear to tell the truth . . ." is similarly more stringent than promising. In a court setting, and therefore in an institutional setting (tenth dimension again), it would not do to hear the witness say later "Yes I swore to tell the truth, the whole truth and nothing but the truth. However, my swearing was overridden by a personal (political, other moral) consideration". It seems that we expect the truth to be told no matter what (fourth dimension concerned with force or strength of speech act).

By now it should be clear why Searle is not engaged in the boring business of simply presenting us with a taxonomy. Beyond doing that, he has presented us with a taxonomic *theory*. It is an interesting theory in that it does not just identify the dimensions of language but orders them by identifying some as more basic than others. It then explains how we get variations in how language is used. The variations on a commissive theme begin to show well how Searle's theory works. Three dimensions play primary roles in identifying which speech acts fall under the commissive heading and, to some extent, in identifying commissives as a basic speech act type in the first place. These are the dimensions of the point of the speech act, the direction of fit and the sincerity condition. The other dimensions play secondary roles. Their job is to encourage variations by allowing numerous "language games" (give one's word, commit, pledge, vow, swear, guarantee, etc.) to be played and, yet, allow all this play to take place under the general commissive banner.

Searle's theory works for the other four basic types of speech acts as well. A second class of basic types Searle calls assertives. "The point or purpose of the members of the assertive class is to commit the speaker (in varying degrees) to something's being the case, to the truth of the expressed proposition. All of the members of the assertive class are assessable on the dimension of assessment which includes *true* and *false*" (1979a: 12). The three (or four) dimension formula now looks like this:

$$\vdash\downarrow B(p)$$

where $\vdash$ stands for the assertion mark, the arrow points downward because the direction of fit is word-to-world (i.e. make the word fit or correspond to the world), B stands for the sincerity condition which is now belief, and p stands for the propositional content. As before there are variations, only now on an assertive theme. Sam's utterance "(I state, affirm, insist, etc. that) the house is still standing" will fit the basic formula in that Sam is asserting something (thus word-to-world fit) and is implying that he believes what he asserts. But in affirming his claim firmly, his speech acts manifest strength (fourth dimension) in his utterance. If Sam had been less sure of himself he might have said "I suppose that the house is still standing". In another setting Sam could be boasting about his great strength or be lamenting the loss of his watch (sixth dimension concerning how the utterance relates to the interests of the speaker or hearer). Assertive utterances can vary with respect to at least two other dimensions including how the utterance relates to the discourse ("I conclude that . . .") and as to whether the act has a corresponding illocutionary verb with a performative use or not (e.g. in the above example boasting does not, but lamenting does), that is, differences with respect to the seventh and eleventh dimensions respectively.

Directives form the third basic type of speech act. "The illocutionary point of these consists in the fact that they are attempts (of varying degrees, and hence more precisely, they are determinates of the determinable which includes attempting) by the speaker to get the hearer to do something" (Searle 1979a: 13). Searle's formula for this type is:

$$! \uparrow W \text{ (H does A)}$$

where the illocutionary point of trying to get the hearer to do something is symbolized by the exclamation mark and the direction of fit is the same as with commissives (i.e. world to – match the – word). The sincerity condition is symbolized by W, which stands for the speaker's wanting action A done. The symbolism for the propositional content shows that it is the hearer who is expected to act.

As with assertives, variations of all sorts are possible when the secondary dimensions are taken into account. The fourth dimension (strength with which illocutionary point is presented) is present when the Samantha demands that Henry leave her bedroom or when Simon meekly asks the clothing store clerk whether she will take back the horrible necktie he was given for Christmas. The fifth dimension (status of speaker and hearer) is present when the general orders the private to pick up the litter on the parade grounds. Other dimensions play their roles here as well. One is worth mentioning since Searle casts some doubt as to whether it plays much (any?) role at all. This is the seventh dimension (related to the rest of the discourse). Searle suggests that this dimension affects assertives more than other types of speech acts. His actual words are: "The features they mark seem mostly to involve utterances within the class of statements" (1979a: 6). But surely moral arguments whose aims are to get people to do things also end, and end quite frequently, with such speech acts as "I conclude". Still other discussions of moral issues include expressions such as "I reply" and "I object" – all expressions Searle uses to help explain his seventh dimension. Whether Searle is right about this matter or not, we see in these examples how the secondary dimensions work alongside the primary ones to allow speakers to generate speech acts with varying forces even while these speech acts each fall within one basic type.

Expressives form Searle's fourth basic speech act type. About these he says: "The illocutionary point of this class is to express the psychological state specified in the propositional content" (1979a: 15). Searle does not mean by "to express" something like "showing your emotions by weeping or shouting with joy". Nor does he mean "to talk about one's emotions". Samantha is talking about her emotions when she says (reports) that she was upset with Kevin last night when he tried to push himself into her bedroom. Here Samantha is issuing an assertive rather than an expressive. However, she does not talk about her emotions when she says "My apologies" or "Good morning" – both, for Searle, legitimate expressive speech acts. In saying what she does, Samantha implies that she has the requisite emotions (of sorrow and of cheer respectively). Without saying so explicitly, she leads others to believe that these are her emotions. Putting it this way makes it sound as if Searle is merely playing with words. But his overall point should be clear. An expressive is not part of an emotional response; nor is it itself an emotional response; nor is it a report of an emotional response. It is a speech act that implies that one has an emotion (which one may or may not actually have), and which normally has a social function of making things go better in our relations with one another.

The formula for expressives is:

$$E \oslash (P) (S/H + property)$$

where E symbolizes the illocutionary point all expressives have in common, $\oslash$ symbolizes that expressives have no direction of fit (users employing them do not seek to describe or change the world), P stands for the various psychological states expressed and (S/H + property) symbolizes that either the speaker or hearer has some property (e.g. has become ill, has won a grand slam tennis tournament, has just come into view of the speaker).

Like the other speech acts, the secondary dimensions allow for variations on a basic theme. Many of the variations are related to the eighth dimension concerned with the propositional content and specifically on the property associated with the hearer (most often) or with the speaker (sixth dimension). Thus if Henry has lost his father, condolences are in order, but if he has won the lottery, congratulations are. However, other dimensions can come into play as, for example, with the fourth dimension (strength of illocutionary point) where only a "weak" or perfunctory apology is in order for accidentally bumping into someone in the hallway.

The last major speech act type Searle calls declaration. Here is how he characterizes this type of speech act.

> It is the defining characteristic of this class that the successful performance of one of its members brings about the correspondence between the propositional content and reality, successful performance guarantees that the propositional content corresponds to the world: if I successfully perform the act of appointing you chairman, then you are chairman; if I successfully perform the act of nominating you as candidate, then you are a candidate; if I successfully perform the act of declaring a state of war, then war is on; if I successfully perform the act of marrying you, then you are married.
>
> (1979a: 16–17)

Declarations represent linguistic magic. No other speech act type has this magic-like power. Promises, as a type of commissive, only promise a change in the world if the promiser has good intentions and is able, later, to perform the promised act. Directives are carried out, possibly, by the hearer later. Successful assertives assert the truth – sometimes. And expressives don't bring about any change. But declarations bring about a change in status or condition just in virtue of being uttered successfully. Given these powers, Searle's formula for performatives looks like this.

$$D \updownarrow \varnothing (P)$$

where D stands for the illocutionary point of the declaration, the double arrow shows that there is word-to-world *and* world-to-word direction of fit simultaneously, corresponding to the declaration's magic-like powers, and the symbol $\varnothing$ shows that there is no sincerity condition is needed. Later Searle (1985: 57) allows for sincerity conditions (of both belief and desire) for some declarations. The symbol P in the formula stands for the propositional content.

Once again the secondary dimensions allow for variation within a basic speech act type. For declarations perhaps the most important is the one concerned with extra-linguistic institutions (tenth dimension). Most declarations require such institutions. Excommunication requires a religious institution, a declaration of war requires a government (or nation state), firing someone (as does resigning) requires a some sort of organization such as a governmental agency or business and even gift giving requires a legal system. One exception to this rule about institutions is when the declaration concerns language. An author can say "By 'democracy' I mean . . ." and thereby makes "democracy" in her writing mean what she says. Clearly another dimension that comes into play is the one concerned with the status of the speaker and hearer. Declarations (of war, for example) are invoked only by those in a special social position (fifth dimension).

Reassurance

Having given us his ordered taxonomy, Searle seeks reassurance. He looks to some features of syntax (of English) in the spirit of Chomsky (Chomsky 1965; Searle 1972) to see if there is evidence for featuring just five types of basic speech acts (Searle 1979a: 20–29). The deep syntactical structure of assertives might very well be different from the syntax of commissives, for example. There need not be syntactical differences to reflect differences on the speech act level. Speech act differences might be reflected someplace else within the fabric of language. Nonetheless, Searle conjectures that it is not likely that basic differences in speech acts will not be mirrored in syntax. So he asks: What is the deep syntax of assertives?

In answering this question he focuses, once again, on paradigm cases. But, still, he does not suppose that what he describes as the syntactical structure of assertives covers all cases. In fact he says that there are two types of assertive sentences (speech acts, when asserted). The following are examples of the first type.

A "I predict it will rain tomorrow."
B "I state (affirm, state) that he is in his room."

Their deep structure can be represented as:

$$I \quad verb \quad (that) \quad + \quad S$$

where "verb" is a stand-in for "predict", "state", etc; "that" is optional, and S stands for the sentence following both whatever verb is in place and the optional "that". Another way to diagram the deep structure is as follows:

$$[I \text{ verb (that)}] + S$$

where the brackets indicate a further optional feature of assertives. We can simply say "He hit me" (i.e. S) rather than "I say he hit me". Presumably with the former we focus more on the event (what happened) rather than, as in the latter, on the speaker.

Searle tells us that assertives sometimes take another form. He cites the following examples.

C "I call him a liar."
D "I diagnose his case as appendicitis."
E "I describe John as a Fascist."

The syntactical form for these assertives is

$$I \quad \text{verb} \quad NP \quad + \quad NP \quad \text{be predicate}$$

In accordance with this form "I call him a liar" reads as follows:

$$I \quad \text{call} \quad \text{him} \quad + \quad \text{him} \quad \text{be a liar}$$

So we have two patterns of syntax for assertives. These patterns should contrast significantly with the patterns of the other basic speech act types. We see immediately that they do at least when we consider commissives. The classic commissive, of course, is a promise such as:

F "I promise to pay you back the money."

The syntactical formula (somewhat simplified) for this and similar commissives is:

$$I \quad \text{verb} \quad (\text{you}) \quad + \quad I \quad \text{Future voluntary verb} \quad (NP)$$

This can be read roughly as:

$$I \quad \text{promise} \quad (\text{you}) \quad + \quad I \quad \text{will pay (you) the money.}$$

Notice that the noun phrase (NP) doesn't necessarily specify that it refers to the hearer. I can promise you to give you the money; but I can also promise you that I will give your needy mother the money (i.e. that some third person is involved in the promising act as recipient). Either way, it is clear that the syntactical structure of assertives and commissives are not alike. For example, what follows the verb (e.g. I *state*) in an assertive is a complete sentence.

Such is not the case with a commissive.

Directives differ from assertives in much the same way, but also differ from commissives in one significant way. Consider the following "paradigmatic" directives.

G "I ask you to shut the door."
H "I order you to leave the room."

Searle's formula (somewhat simplified again) is as follows:

I   verb   you   +   you   Future voluntary verb   (NP)

With commissives the pronoun following the "+" is first person, with directives it is second person. With commissives the speaker has a duty to do something; with directives the hearer is supposed (or is being asked) to do something.

Expressives have their own distinctive syntax as well. Here is Searle's formula (somewhat modified once again) for these speech act types.

I   verb   you   +   I/you   VP   gerundive phrase.

In accord with this formula, the expressive "I apologize for missing our meeting" gets read as

I   apologize   [to] you   +   I   missing our meeting.

The gerundive phrase records the notion that the speaker knows that the hearer knows that speaker missed the meeting. So there is no need for an assertion. Similarly, when I congratulate Andre for winning the French Open Tennis Championship I am not giving him any new information. He knows he's won. Not providing any new information (as an assertive would and not doing anything that might change the situation as a directive or commissive might), there is no need for any direction of fit. Apologies, congratulations, condolences, greetings pretty much leave things as they were. And the syntax of expressives expresses this fact and, in addition, help to show the distinctive nature of these kinds of speech acts.

Declarations pose some problems for Searle. Their syntactical formula is actually the same as the second assertive formula.

I   verb   NP   +   NP   be predicate

Thus "I excommunicate you (from the church)" and "I now pronounce you man and wife" get read as follows:

I   excommunicate you   +   you be no longer member of church;

and,

I   pronounce   you and you   +   you (and you) be wife (and you be husband).

In spite of these syntactical similarities between declarations and some assertives Searle feels that his exercise in syntax has suggested that his taxonomy is on the right track. There are significant differences syntactically that reflect differences on the speech act level. Besides, as we will see in the next chapter, it may be possible to explain away the declaration-assertive problem of shared syntactical structure.

Why is this theory interesting?

What does Searle's taxonomic theory accomplish? Several things. First, it fully accounts for the variability that Austin, Wittgenstein and others found in our natural (ordinary) language by identifying and sorting the various dimensions of difference among illocutionary (speech) acts. In one sense, there is an indefinite number of language games within our natural language. Secondly, in yet another sense, Searle's theory shows that there is order within all the variability. There is not just bunch of unrelated language games out there such as promising, vowing, swearing, ordering, pleading, asking, apologizing, giving condolences, describing, theorizing, baptizing, excommunicating, getting married and then divorced. Rather, all those speech acts fall into a small set of basic speech acts. The illusion that there is nothing there but variability comes about by focusing too much on verbs (as Austin did) and not enough on the whole speech act.

Thirdly, unlike Austin's theory, Searle's systematically identifies the basic speech acts in terms of three of the dimensions of speech act difference: viz., the point of a speech act, its direction of fit and its sincerity condition. One could argue that he uses a fourth dimension to help him do his basic taxonomic work, namely, that having to do with propositional content (eighth dimension). But even if we add this dimension to our "basic" list, Searle is still presenting us with a systematic rather than haphazard account. Fourthly, with its five basic speech acts, the theory presents us with a comprehensive classification system. Whatever natural speakers may say within their language, whether it is a single speech act such as "Good morning" or a string of speech acts forming speech activity (discourse), each and everything said falls into one or more of the types of speech acts that form Searle's taxonomy.

Fifthly, and most generally, Searle's philosophy-of-language taxonomic theory helps us in doing linguistic philosophy. Although doing linguistic philosophy is a bit out of fashion these days, keeping one's eye on language as one philosophizes is still a good idea. Important distinctions can be identified and understood as the result of watching carefully how language works. Searle's taxonomic theory is helpful in this regard. Questions such as "What is a promise?" "How does an assertion differ from a prediction?" and "Are there differences between moral and scientific claims?" can be illuminated by noting what kind of speech acts and sub-speech acts are being uttered. So Searle's presentation of his taxonomic theory is hardly a side show.[1]

Although important in many ways, there are things that the theory does *not* accomplish. Recall what was said about Searle's style of doing philosophy near the beginning of the previous chapter. That style starts by dealing with standard or paradigm cases of a phenomenon. In "Taxonomy" he follows this style. So, by and large, the uses of language he allows his theory to explain are straightforward. He has not told us about a wide variety of nonstandard uses such as metaphor, irony and other such uses where the speaker says one thing and means something else. Nor has he told us about other subtle and complicated uses including some that he calls indirect speech acts. There are also uses where one speech act seems to be two; and two seem to be one. We turn to some of these more complicated, less paradigmatic and fascinating uses in the next chapter.

Note

1. Although Searle's taxonomic theory is more widely accepted than any other, it has received criticism. Usually it comes from linguists who argue that empirical observation of how language is used uncovers complexities that armchair philosophizing about language misses. In this connection see Levinson (1983) and Croft (1994). See also Hancher (1979) for a survey of various taxonomies.

Chapter 3

Non-standard speech acts and speech activity

Double and two-part speech acts

Even in "Taxonomy" Searle does not deal exclusively with standard uses. Consider the umpire's call in baseball: "You're out!" (his example). The runner attempts to stretch a single into a double, but just doesn't make it in time. The umpire's call has the feel of an assertive since, clearly, he is making a factual judgment that the ball got to second base before the runner did. So the umpire is asserting that the runner is out. Yet he also seems to be uttering a declaration since once called out, the runner's status in the game changes not (just) because he is late getting to the base but because he is called out. Here being called out is somewhat akin to being "called out" of the church via the official's announcement that you are excommunicated.

Searle calls "You're out!" and such other speech acts as "You are guilty" (when uttered by a judge after a trial where evidence has been presented) assertive declarations. He even gives us a formula for them as if to suggest that there are inelegant five-and-one-half basic kinds of speech acts rather than five.

$$D \downarrow \updownarrow (B)p$$

The sincerity condition in this formula (of Belief) is due to the assertive portion of what I will call a double speech act. The two-for-one character of this kind of speech act explains why there are two kinds of direction of fit. The downward direction of the arrow is for the assertive portion of this double speech act, while the arrow going both ways is for the declaration portion.

In the end, Searle backs off from treating assertive declarations as half of a new basic type of speech act. In his other writings he talks mostly of five basic types. It's a good thing too because we meet other double speech acts in our language that would increase the number of basic acts to six, six and one-half and so on. Consider Suzanne, a prototypical liberal, who says "I protest the way you are treating the poor". Her protest is certainly an expressive speech act in that it reflects back on the treatment of the poor and expresses her attitude toward that treatment. However, as Searle points out, a protest can be, and we can assume in Suzanne's case is, a recommendation for change. So her protest could be an expressive directive or, if you like, a directive expressive.

Here is another example of a double speech act. The captain in charge of a military unit says to his troops "Let's take that hill!" He is certainly issuing a directive, more specifically, a command. But he does not just say "(You) take that hill" since he is going along with them. Is he then also issuing a commissive, a promise to his troops that he is going to accept the same risks as they? If so, then we have a commissive directive or a directive commissive on our hands.

In truth, combining two speech acts into one poses no serious problem for Searle's taxonomic theory. The two-for-one uses exhibit the theory at work albeit in more complicated fashion than envisaged when, given Searle's style of dealing first with standard cases, he initially presented his theory. Clearly the reason for these uses is that we are linguistically utilitarian. In the heat of battle it would be linguistically awkward, and surely less inspiring, for the captain to say "I order you to take that hill; and, hey guys, I'll (I promise to) go along with you".

This two-for-the-price-of-one type of speech act helps explain the problem uncovered late in the previous chapter concerning the syntax of declarations. It will be recalled that declarations have the same syntax as do *some (a few)* assertives.

$$\text{I} \quad \text{verb} \quad \text{NP} \quad + \quad \text{NP} \quad \text{be predicate}$$

So an assertive such as "I call him a liar" and "I describe him as a Fascist" are analyzed syntactically the same way as classic declarations such as "I appoint you chairman" and "You're fired". The reason these assertives look syntactically like declarations is that they are (also) declarations (Searle 1991a: 94–5). Recall that for someone to say "I call him a liar" is to offer up an assertive with attention focused on the speaker (Searle 1979a: 25). Such an assertive contrasts to simply saying "He is a liar" where the attention is on the person being talked about. But in saying "I call him a liar" and focusing on himself, the speaker is coming perilously close to issuing a declaration. By *calling* the person a liar that person has been so labelled. The very act of calling someone a liar certainly changes the status of the speaker to that of an accuser, and the one talked about to that of an accused, especially if the utterance is made within an official setting such as a court. The man, we say, stands accused as if his status is different from what it was before he was accused. Consider Jack's utterance "I describe John as a fascist" as another example. Actually Jack is more likely to say "I would describe John as a fascist". However it is expressed, once he has "declared" (via a public description) that John is a fascist, poor John is so declared. John may not be a fascist, but he has been declared to be. Such a "declaration" does not quite satisfy Searle's insistence that (most) declarations are issued within the bosom of some institution, but it is close enough for it to earn having the syntactical form of a declaration. So the common syntactical form that some assertives have with declarations may be due to their nature as double speech acts. That is, they represent additional examples of assertive declarations.

At this point it is worth noting how Searle draws criticism because of these double speech acts. Jurgen Habermas argues that Searle seems to be turning all speech acts into declarations and, in so doing, destroying his taxonomy (Habermas 1991: 28). He says that this policy of Searle's "explodes the architecture of the classification of speech acts because declarations would lose their distinctive place in it if they were to explain the performative character of *all* speech acts" (Habermas 1991: 26).

Searle replies by making a distinction between a *performance* and a *performative* (1989b: 536–8; 1991a: 94–5). When Jack says "John is a fascist" and then later says "I say John is a fascist" both of his utterances (speech acts) are *performances*. All speech acts are performances of one kind or another. But only second is a *performative*, and is so in the same way that "I promise . . .", "I order you to . . ." and "I accuse . . ." are. They are performatives because they label themselves (as promises, etc.) but, in addition, they are *also* something else (e.g. commissives). Here is how Searle puts it.

> Every utterance is a *performance* in the sense that every utterance is a speech act, but not every utterance is thereby a *performative*. Within utterances, i.e., speech acts, there is a

sub-class of utterances that are performed by way of using a word that names the very type of act of being performed. These and only these are performative utterances. Thus "I order you to leave the room" is a performative, and it is a performative used to make an order. "Leave the room," on the other hand, is a sentence used to make an order, but the making of an order with this sentence, is not a *performative*, though, of course, it is a *performance.*   (1991a: 95)

What Searle's analysis of double speech acts shows, then, is not that his taxonomy collapses into one type of speech act (viz. declarations) but that certain uses of language are more complicated than even he thought when he wrote *Speech Acts* (1969) and *Expression and Meaning* (1979a). Habermas is thus wrong in supposing that Searle's taxonomy is damaged by Searle's admission that certain speech acts are more complicated than he had supposed they were in his younger days. Here are Searle's comments on these matters.

> I believe that my account of performatives strengthens the taxonomy rather than weakens it. What it shows is that the power of declarations is more extensive than I had originally thought. For example, one can perform an assertive, either by uttering and indicative statements "It is raining," or by way of declaring that one is performing the assertive, "I hereby state that it is raining." In the latter case, one actually performs two speech acts in one utterance: One makes a declaration but one thereby makes a statement because one's declaration creates the statement that one is making. But such facts in no way detract from the validity of, for example, the categories of assertives and directives. Furthermore, we avoid the mistake of supposing that all utterances are performatives; rather performatives, strictly speaking, are included in the class of declarations. It is a mistake, I believe, for Habermas to speak of "the performative character of all speech acts." As I have said above, if this notion is to have a clear use at all, only a very restricted class of speech acts are performatives.   (1991a: 95)

A second type of non-standard linguistic phenomenon that Searle deals with is the opposite of the two-for-the-price-of-one variety. With this type we get one speech act with two utterances. Here we think naturally enough of betting and contracting. Searle says (1985: 197–8) that a bet gets made when Bob and Barry each commits to paying $5 given the outcome of the game. If the local team wins Bob gains $5, if it loses Barry wins. So we have a parallel set of commissives to get the bet "done". Actually, between friends, the betting is somewhat more complicated. Usually the original speech act issued is "I'll bet you $5 they win tonight". If Bob says something like this to Barry, he has committed himself to paying off if his team loses. But the bet, any bet, is conditional on some response from the other party. So Bob is also issuing (making) an offer. He is inviting Barry to take him on. So we have a double speech act (a commissive directive) in Bob's "I'll bet you $5 they win tonight". But now Barry needs to respond. When he says "You're on" he issues a pure commissive (a promise to pay if he loses). So in order to get the bet made, Barry and Bob need to engage in a little piece of speech activity (discourse). Although we may think of a bet as a single act, it comes about only when we fuse two or more speech acts together.

Contracts are both more complicated and simpler than betting. They are more complicated since they usually require speech activity prior to the signing. There is usually much oral discussion and fiddling before the document gets signed. Such prior activity is usually wholly missing when making friendly bets. But once the preparations for signing are made, no one has to issue a directive asking whether the other side will sign. All that work has been done and so the signing itself is, as Searle suggests, an example of the issuance of a pair of parallel commissives. For all practical purposes, both sides commit to the conditions of the contract at the same time.

This contract model fits one interpretation of "getting married" quite well. On this interpretation the wedding ceremony is divided into three parts. There is the preparatory portion where an official (religious leader, government representative, etc.) and the couple engage in speech activity by issuing a series of assertives, directives, commissives, expressives and even some declarations. Then the short and crucial second stage begins and ends with the couple exchanging vows (parallel commissives). The final stage of the ceremony is also composed of all sorts of speech acts but certainly includes some expressives (largely celebratory in nature).

A different model of "getting married" does not treat the exchange of vows, that is, the contract, as the necessary and sufficient conditions for the marriage to take place. Instead the exchange is treated only as necessary. What completes the process is the issuance of a series of speech acts by the official who then, near the end of the process, says "I pronounce you man and wife" (a declaration). Under this interpretation "getting married" is speech activity via a long series of speech acts rather than speech activity via two parallel commissives. However it is described, Searle's taxonomy apparently can account for it since each act within any stretch of speech activity represents an assertive, a commissive, a directive, an expressive or a declaration, or some combination thereof.

Speech activity analysis

But one might wonder whether Searle's taxonomy is really giving a complete account of what we might want to say on the speech activity (discourse or macro) level. Is it, for example, telling us how we string speech acts together to create some sort of order out of what we want to say? Consider the following example. Sam says to Joe "Let me tell you a dirty joke". Joe responds eagerly "Yeh, go ahead". In accordance with Searle's taxonomy, Sam's speech act can be characterized as a (conditional) commissive and a directive. He promises to tell the joke if Joe agrees, and Joe is directed to respond by agreeing or not. Joe responds with an enthusiastic directive for Sam to go ahead. It signals Joe's approval for Sam to tell his joke. The joke follows. Probably the joke itself is composed of a series of assertive acts. At some point, something is said and (the hope is that) Joe laughs.

That is one way to describe what happens. Here is another. The initial speech act Sam utters what can be called a *master speech act* (Fotion 1971; 1979). Although it is a commissive it is a special kind of commissive that tells us how language might be controlled or directed in the immediate future (i.e. in a joke-telling way). Joe's response can be called a *consenter*. It consents to controlling the speech activity in the way that Sam proposes. The joke itself can be called *controlled talk*. It is as if the master speech act and the consenter act as officers whose job is to control the enlisted personnel (the series of speech acts that make up the joke).

Here is another example of this way of describing speech activity. At the dinner table the grandmother issues the master speech act "Let us pray". In Searle's terminology this is probably a directive and a commissive combined. All at the table bow their heads, thereby consenting. The prayer (controlled talk) follows. That talk is probably a mixture of several types of Searlian speech acts. God will be described as the one who created us (assertives) and thanked for the many things He has done for us (expressives). Promises will follow (commissives). Yes, they say, they will do His bidding and will be good. Having suitably prepared the Almighty, a series of requests follow (directives). "Keep us healthy, make the harvest good this year and . . ." In the end they all utter the mandatory "Amen". On the macro level this speech act can be called a *stopper*. In terms of Searle's taxonomy "Amen" is a directive. It tells us to stop praying. It may also, by convention, be a directive to tell us to start eating.

Our use of macro level concepts to control our language use is far more common than might be supposed. Titles of a book or an article, and headings within a piece of writing, all act as master speech acts. Depending on the purposes of their authors, they tell us in more or less detail what we are to expect if we are to read on. When in conversation, we use master speech acts to help our listeners understand better what we are talking about. "Let me tell you what happened to Bill and his wife." Or we use these controlling acts to direct how others speak. "What happened to their daughter Susie after she got married?" Within the conversation we can invoke other macro concepts such as *modifiers* that deflect the conversation in a somewhat different direction. "But now tell me in more detail what happened at that point at the party. What did Johnny say such that Anne felt insulted?" In court, special master speech acts such as "Just describe what happens" are invoked to help make our language use as purely descriptive as possible. It would not do to have witnesses insert their opinions or evaluations into their account of what happened at the scene of the accident. Master speech acts are also invoked in scientific writing and speaking, as in the court, to encourage precise uses of language and to control the direction of what is being said. There is no context of language use where one or another macro concept is not invoked to help control our language use.

But none of these macro level concepts that help us to think about how speech activity is organized and controlled is in conflict with Searle's taxonomy. Indeed, to help explain how master speech acts work, we need Searle's basic speech act categories. Some master speech acts are commissives as is Sam's "Let me tell you a dirty joke". But others are directives as when Joe says to Sam "Tell me a dirty joke". Macro level analyses of speech activity supplements rather than replaces Searlian speech act analysis. The two go hand in hand such that it is fair to say that Searle's theory of language does not suffer from deficiencies as language use moves from speech acts to speech activity.

Indirect speech acts

Searle's taxonomic theory and his more general speech act theory can give an account of still other complicated speech phenomena. Searle writes about one such phenomenon in his well-known article "Indirect Speech Acts" (1979a: 30–57). Samantha and Henry are standing close together on a very crowded bus. Samantha says to Henry "You're standing on my foot". Taken literally Samantha has uttered an assertive. She is conveying information to Henry that is either true or false. It is also information that he does not have, thus satisfying one of preparatory conditions normally needed for making assertions. Having heard and understood what Samantha has said, we can imagine Henry looking down to see exactly where his foot is located and then saying "So I am. How interesting!" Clearly Samantha is not in the business of merely conveying interesting information to Henry. She wants him to move his foot off of hers. So she is indirectly issuing a directive (a request, a demand or some such) by means of issuing an assertive. With indirect speech acts we are in the business of issuing, once again, two speech acts for the price of one.

It is easy to imagine similar examples. Here are three.

(a) "I want that toy!" (Directly this is an assertive about what a child wants, but indirectly it is a directive for the mother to buy the toy.)

(b) "I've told you three times already to shut up!" (Directly this is an assertive about what has been said in the recent past, but indirectly it is a directive to shut up. This one differs from the stepping-on-Samantha's-foot example in that, presumably, Big Mouth already knows about what is asserted. But, then, maybe he needs reminding.)

(c) "There is a bomb under this house and it's about to go off." (Again this is directly an assertive. Actually there are two assertives here so we are dealing with a simple form of speech activity. Directly, interesting information is being conveyed.

Indirectly, those in the house are being encouraged, urged, etc. to leave the house promptly. So indirectly a directive is being issued once again.)

Examples need not follow the assertive–directive mould. Searle gives a classic dining-room example of one such: viz., "Can you reach the salt?" Here we can imagine that the questioner is Dr Phixum, the famous orthopedic surgeon. What he asks might be a test question and the response from his patient could be "Yes, I can today, but I couldn't make such a move three days ago". In this case Phixum's question (as with all questions) is a directive asking for a verbal response of some kind; and the patient's answer is in the form of a short series of assertives and, perhaps, a little demonstration about how well the arm is working. In the macro level terminology introduced above "Can you reach the salt?" is in this case also a master speech act since it leads to a series of speech acts (speech activity) being issued. But if Phixum needs salt for his soup, now the question may serve to elicit a brief assertive response (e.g. "Here you are") but, we hope, one that delivers Phixum the salt (a directive). Or perhaps the salt is passed without comment. So in this setting the pattern of issuance is directive–assertive (optional)–directive.

Here are some other patterns that begin to show how varied and common indirect speech acts are.

(d) "I think he is angry with me." (Directly this is an assertive about what the speaker thinks, indirectly it also an assertive concerned with someone's anger: i.e. he is angry after all.)

(e) "I intend to study harder." (The temptation here is to read this example directly as a commissive. But "I intend . . ." reports the thoughts of the speaker. It says that the speaker has an intention. So directly, this is an assertive. It is a commissive, then, by indirection.)

(f) "I'm sorry I did it." (This one on the face of it looks like an apology, and thus an expressive, but directly it is an assertive about the speaker's sorrow. Indirectly it is indeed an apology.)

Various other indirect speech acts will be cited shortly. But questions arise: how do indirect speech acts work? And can Searle's speech act and taxonomic theories deal with them? Searle addresses these questions. He does so in his indirect-speech-act article best with the "Can you pass the salt?" example. Here is his excruciatingly complex account of how indirect speech acts work.

Step 1: Y has asked me a question as to whether I have the ability to pass the salt (fact about the conversation).

Step 2: I assume that he is cooperating in the conversation and that therefore his utterance has some aim or point (principles of conversational cooperation).

Step 3: The conversational setting is not such as to indicate a theoretical interest in my salt passing ability (factual background information).

Step 4: Furthermore, he probably already knows that the answer to the question is yes (factual background information). (This step facilitates the move to Step 5, but is not essential.)

Step 5: Therefore, his utterance is probably not just a question. It probably has some ulterior illocutionary point (inference from Steps 1, 2, 3 and 4). What can it be?

Step 6: A preparatory condition for any directive illocutionary act is the ability of H to perform the act predicated in the propositional content condition (theory of speech acts).

Step 7: Therefore, Y has asked me a question the affirmative answer to which would entail that the preparatory condition for requesting me to pass the salt is satisfied (inference from Steps 1 and 6).

Step 8: We are now at dinner and people normally use salt at dinner; they pass it back and forth, try to get others to pass it back and forth, etc. (background information).

Step 9: He has therefore alluded to the satisfaction of a preparatory condition for a request whose obedience conditions it is quite likely he wants me to bring about (inference from Steps 7 and 8).

Step 10: Therefore, in the absence of any other plausible illocutionary point, he is probably requesting me to pass the salt (inference from Steps 5 and 9).

(1979a: 46–7)

Several comments are in order about this account. First, its complexity should be no surprise. Recall that accounts of even simple physical motion and simple speech acts are complex. That is, the account is not of the conscious mental activity that we as users of the language go through when we hear "Can you reach the salt?" and then end by passing it. It all happens in a flash since we generally just hear "Can you reach the salt?" as a directive to pass the salt to the questioner. Still the account purports to tell a story about the steps of the process that could be articulated should it be necessary to do so. The steps are thus normally implicit as we hear "Can you . . .?" but think "Pass the salt, please!"

Secondly, Searle says that "Can you pass the salt?" is to be taken literally. It does not mean "Please pass the salt!" Nor does it mean something ambiguous such as "Can you pass the salt?" or "Please pass the salt". It isn't ambiguous since ambiguity would typically lead the listener to be puzzled about how to respond. In response to the unusual circumstances of talking to Phixum, one might seek clarification as to whether he is asking his question as an orthopedic surgeon or as a consumer of food. But Searle's point is that, normally, no clarification is needed and no confusion is present. Normally, one knows what the questioner has asked and, as a result, talks and acts accordingly.

But "Can you pass the salt?" doesn't mean "Please pass the salt!" either. As we have seen, it *seems* as if that is what it means since we infer instantly what it is the speaker wants us to do. But "Can you pass the salt?" has its own meaning as we can appreciate when the patient surprises and disappoints the flavour-starved Phixum when she says "I'm sorry I still can't move my arm" or "Sorry, I can't. I don't have the salt. I think the waiters have forgotten to put it on the table". So although when "Can you pass the salt?" is asked, it is meant as a directive, if appropriate, his patient can respond by talking about her lack of ability to deliver more flavour into Phixum's soup. But in normal circumstances Phixum, as the speaker, is performing two speech acts. He is asking a question about his hearer's abilities (even when he well knows the answer) and indirectly issuing a directive for her to pass the salt.

This business of a double performance is even clearer with Samantha's "You're standing on my foot". Yes, an assertive has been uttered but, by indirection, something more has been uttered as well (in this case a directive, to get Henry's foot off of hers). So an indirect speech act says one thing and, by means of saying it, says something else as well without the presence of ambiguity, vagueness or anything of the sort.

Thirdly, the indirection works because the direct speech act is connected in some important way to the indirect speech act via speech act theory. In the case of "Can you pass the salt?" the connection is the preparatory condition that the hearer is thought to be the kind of creature who has salt-passing abilities. It would not do for Phixum to ask her for the salt by saying "Winston Churchill smoked cigars" or "Who was last year's men's Wimbledon champion?" Out of the blue, either one of these utterances would puzzle his listener, and so neither utterance would likely even suggest to her that she is being asked to reach for the salt. What is needed to make the indirect speech act work is some connection to one of the preparatory conditions (e.g. hearer's or speaker's abilities, the hearer's or speaker's wants, the social setting) or to the propositional content to tie the direct with the indirect (and unspoken) speech act. The following are examples, all Searle's, of this point.

(g) "I would like you to go now." (Here the speaker issues an assertive about her wishes and thereby, along with a suitable context, issues a directive.)

(h) "You could be a little more quiet." (Here the speaker issues an assertive about the hearer's abilities and thereby, indirectly, issues a directive.)

(i) "Would you be willing to write a letter of recommendation for me?" (This example gets a little complicated. The speaker is issuing a directive that asks her hearer to say something about his willingness to write. The hope and expectation is that he is willing to write and will say something like "I am happy to write you a letter". His response is directly an assertive and indirectly a promise to write, that is, a commissive. She is thus issuing a directive to get him to respond to what she has said, but also a directive by way of asking him to write the letter of recommendation.)

(j) "You had better go now." (This one differs from (g) above in not making an assertion about the speaker's wishes. Instead the implication is that there is at least one good reason for the listener to leave although the reason is not stated. Searle seems to take an utterance like this one as an assertive. So this assertive serves as the direct speech act. The indirect speech act is a directive.)

Some examples of indirect speech acts pertaining to the preparatory conditions are peculiar. Consider the very common "Can I help you?" asked of Sally by the always cooperative Sam. The puzzle is why is Sam asking about his own abilities? It certainly would make sense for Sam to ask about Sally's abilities because he might have some question about them. So understandably he could issue an indirect speech act can by asking "Can you do it by yourself?" or "Do you need help?" But to ask about one's own abilities is puzzling. Things get even more puzzling when Sally responds by saying "Yes you can". It is as if she knows more about Sam's abilities than he does. Things seem to be backward.

But in reality they aren't. "Can I help you?" does not just ask about Sam's abilities in the abstract, but about whether his abilities are suitable to whatever problem Sally is facing. If her car is broken down and Sam doesn't know why, Sam can meaningfully ask "Can I help you?" He needs to inquire whether his abilities fit the situation. Sally, realizing that the problem is just a flat tyre and realizing that Sam probably knows how to fix such things, can also meaningfully respond with "Yes you can". So in some situations at least an expression like "Can I help?" can be seen to be directly a directive (it asks Sally to say something) and indirectly a (conditional) commissive.

Fourthly, in part because indirect speech acts are so common, they usually take on idiomatic form. In our example we ask idiomatically "Can you pass the salt?" rather than "Are you at the moment able to pass the salt?" Similarly we say idiomatically "I would like the steak well done" rather than "It would please me immensely to have my steak well done" or "It is the case that I want the steak well done".

Fifthly, in step 2 Searle appeals to the principles of conversational cooperation. He is here borrowing from Paul Grice (1989: 26–31). Grice already anticipated some of the insights concerning speech activity (discourse) discussed in this chapter. Focusing more on conversations as one form of speech activity, Grice says "Our talk exchanges do not normally consist of a succession of disconnected remarks, and would not be rational if they did" (1989: 26). In conversations the hope is that the participants will cooperate. So when one participant in the conversation brings up a certain subject (perhaps by invoking a master speech act) the other will stick to the subject. If that happens, Grice says that we are following what he calls the Cooperative Principle which he states as follows: "Make your conversational contribution such as is required, at the stage at which it occurs, by the accepted purpose or direction of the talk exchange in which you are engaged"(1989: 26). Under this major principle he invokes several so-called maxims such as "Make your contribution as informative as is required (for the current purposes of the exchange)". And "Do not make your contribution more informative than is required". Searle finds it necessary to use this principle and its corresponding maxims to explain how indirect speech acts work. In doing so he appeals to a way of thinking about language use that is close enough to his speech act theory as to not undermine it.[1]

Speaking more generally about indirect speech acts, Searle says that politeness is the main reason we employ them. Directives issued directly often have a sharp edge to them. When speaking to his aide, the general might not want to issue still another order and so says to him "I'd like some ice cream!" or, similarly, the mother might say to her son "Wouldn't you like to help clean the house?" rather than boss him around with "Get to work and clean the house!" In both cases there is an appearance, it may be no more than that, of allowing the "inferior" the option of rejecting the offer to do something. Politeness seems to be at work with "You had better go now!" as well. This assertive (implying that negative conditions truly apply, e.g. it is late, my husband is coming, or your behaviour has been insulting) again gives the listener, at least in theory, the option of rebutting the indirect directive to leave. Because it does and because it allows the speaker to avoid saying "Get out of here!" it does have a more polite or softer tone to it.

But surely indirection has other major motivations behind it. At the concert hall saying to the lady seated in front of you "Lady, your hat is blocking my view of the whole stage" need not, and indeed probably does not, mean to project politeness. Further it serves a double purpose. It not only tells the lady to take her hat off, but tells her why she should. So here indirection allows much to be said in a few words. The same applies with "There is a large rattler near your left elbow". The indirection serves to tell you to move slowly away from where you are sitting and why. Utility seems to be the motive in these cases. At other times indirection is used when we want to be impolite rather than polite. Think here not only of the lady with the large hat, but of the driver who is told "Can't you see you are blocking the road?" Notice how the speaker can supplement his direct speech act with a rich assortment of insults. "You stupid #*#* jerk, can't you see . . .?" Politeness hardly seems to be in the forefront of the speaker's mind in this example. It seems that the varied nature of indirect speech acts allows for more varied reasons for invoking them than Searle allows.[2]

Literal speech

One of Searle's most important distinctions in philosophy of language is between speaker meaning and sentence (or word) meaning. The two meanings come apart with indirect speech acts. Sam says to Hazel "I want you to come with me". His (speaker) meaning is the directive "Come with me". But his sentence meaning, that is, what he actually says, is an assertive about what he wants. Searle's analysis of indirect speech acts is in large part a programme to show how the two meanings can be understood so that from sentence meaning the hearer can work out what the speaker meaning is.

But sentence and speaker meaning can come apart in other ways as well such as when irony is used. In disgust, you say to your tennis partner "Great shot!" when he misses an easy overhead. You say one thing (sentence meaning), but mean just the opposite (speaker meaning). Sentence and speaker meaning come apart as well when we use metaphor. When Sam says "Sally is a block of ice" (Searle's example) what is actually said represents sentence meaning; what Sam means to say about Sally (that she has a cold personality, or worse) is speaker meaning. As he does with indirect speech acts, Searle wants to show his readers how metaphors work, that is, how when we use a metaphor (sentence meaning) we are able to arrive at what the metaphor means (speaker meaning). It is part of his intellectual burden to show that his speech act theory can deal not only with standard uses, but all sorts of uses of language. He wants to develop a comprehensive theory of language.

However, Searle begins his analysis of metaphor by first examining literal speech. He supposes, typically, that we can understand non-standard uses (i.e. metaphors) better when we first understand standard uses (i.e. literal speech). But beyond that, Searle has things to say about literal speech. That speech is important as well, and thus deserves to be analyzed on its own terms. With literal speech, sentence and speaker meaning come together. The sentence says neither more nor something other than what the speaker means it to say. Speakers use literal speech when they say that the dog is asleep; it is raining outside; Susie went to the movies; there are almost three million people living in the Atlanta area; the New York Yankees did not play a game last night; this drug causes liver damage among 3 per cent of those who take it on a regular basis. Literal speech is also being used when issuing directives as when we tell someone to stop making a noise, shut the door, bring the newspaper, or pass the pepper. Literal speech extends to the other speech act types. If you make a promise to meet me in St Louis you (can) mean what you say and no more than what you say. Similarly if you congratulate your opponent for beating you at tennis you are speaking literally as does the king when he declares war on a nearby "enemy" state. Literal speech is everywhere.

Even so, speech where sentence and speaker meaning break apart is also everywhere. Searle's problem thus is one where he must distinguish literal from non-literal speech One solution he considers involves appealing to the concept of context. The idea is that when the two meanings fall apart, being aware of the context in which the utterance is issued enables us to understand what is being said. In contrast, when sentence and speaker meaning come together (i.e. with literal speech) no appeal to the context is needed. If General Savage says he is going to use his artillery on the azalea bushes you, as listener, need to know about the context to work out that he is not going to bombard the bushes with 155mm shells but with water from his hose. However, when he says that there are numerous rocks among the azaleas, no context seems to be needed for you to understand what he is saying because he is now speaking literally.

Searle firmly rejects this way of reading the difference between literal and non-literal speech. It doesn't take a genius to tell why. Recall how important context is for any speech act theorist even when considering paradigmatic (literal) uses. Orders cannot be issued if the speakers do not have the social status to issue them. The same is true of acts of excommunication and war. Apologies require a context having to do with past events, as do congratulations. In the form of preparatory conditions, context is present for promises where we have to presuppose, among other things, that the one promising has the ability to carry out what he commits himself to do and the one promised wants whatever it is that is being promised. Assertive claims as well, at least certain ones, require as context or background that the speaker back what he has to say with evidence.

But context, or background, is more pervasive than the ordinary notion of preparatory conditions suggests. For Searle, our speech is embedded in background. He drives home this point in "Literal Meaning" (1979a: 117–36) with one of philosophy's most important foundational claims: viz., "The cat is on the mat". If this sentence is uttered as the cat lies there on the mat, it would seem that we have a good candidate for a context-free utterance. Of course in one sense "The cat is on the mat" cannot help but be somewhat context dependent since indexical terms in the utterance such as "the cat" and "the mat" refer to this cat and this mat in this context (1979a: 120–21). But Searle is concerned with context beyond reference and attribution, and even beyond having to do with whether the speaker is in position to make the claim he makes. The sense of context he is most concerned with includes gravity where the sentence "The cat is *on* the mat" gets its sense in large part because the cat and the mat exist on a planet where there is a considerable amount of gravity. What would we say if the context were different and the cat and mat, both touching one another, were floating about inside the international space station? Is the mat on the cat? The other way around? Or would we be puzzled about what to say?

Other contextual features do their work in our example of cat and mat. We bring to our utterance a certain understanding what a cat is, and how it behaves; and bring as well similar information about the mat. Having pointed to the richness of the context Searle next asks: Why not make all this context part of the sentence? Some of the context can be brought in. However, after a while, the sentence we want to utter becomes shockingly long and complex. But there is another problem. To bring all these parts of the context into the sentence we have to deal with other sentences that have their own context of use. If we were to insist on making the context completely explicit we would find the process endless. It seems as if we can't get away from context or background. He summarizes nicely what he has to say about literal meaning in the following passage.

> For a large class of unambiguous sentences such as "The cat is on the mat", the notion of literal meaning of the sentence only has application relatives to a set of background assumptions. The truth conditions of the sentence will vary with variations in these background assumptions; and given the absence or presence of some background assumptions the sentence does not have determinate truth conditions. These variations have nothing to do with indexicality, change of meaning, ambiguity, conversational implication, vagueness or presupposition as these notions are standardly discussed in the philosophical and linguistic literature. (1979a: 125)

In this and other passages in "Literal Meaning" he is somewhat shy about telling us how large the class of unambiguous sentences is. He merely tells us it is very large (1979a: 132). Nor does he tell us what kind of literal sentences fail to fall into this class of being background dependent. At one point he considers mathematical sentences as candidates (1979a: 131–2). But he rejects this suggestion and supposes that they too are context dependent. He is thus content to show us that literal sentences are context (background) dependent contrary to what he takes is the prevailing view.

Searle says much more about these matters in his later writings with the introduction of such context-related concepts as Network and Background. So in time (especially in Chapter 6) it will be appropriate to say more. But for now, before turning to a discussion of metaphor, it is enough to mention one other feature of literal speech. For Searle literal speech relies heavily on the notion of similarity (1979a: 81). To say, literally, that Amelia and Lindy are friendly puppies is to say that they have a personality feature like that of many dogs, and some cats and a few humans. As Searle puts it: "To know that a general term is true of a set of objects is to know that they are similar with respect to the property specified by that term" (1979a: 81). Making this point is important for Searle since similarity is an attribute that supposedly is key to understanding metaphors. Supposedly, similarity explains how metaphors work, but not how literal speech works. Searle disagrees. He wants to argue that similarity is found not just in our metaphors but in our literal speech as well.

We are now ready to deal with metaphors.

Notes

1. For more on conversational maxims see Vanderveken (1991). His account shows how these maxims fits in with Searle's speech act theory.
2. For some criticism of Searle's account of indirect speech acts see Bertolet (1994) and Holdcroft (1994). Bertolet argues that the concept of indirect speech act is not needed to account for linguistic phenomena that we call indirect speech acts. Ordinary conversational rules can do the job more economically. Holdcroft points to various complexities in understanding indirect speech acts that, he claims, Searle does (can) not deal with.

Chapter 4

Metaphor and fiction

1 Metaphor

Searle's main interest in metaphor is in how it works. Once we answer that question, he thinks we can answer other questions more readily such as "What is metaphor?" and "Why do we use it?" He begins his discussion by telling us that metaphor is still another type of linguistic use where sentence and speaker meaning come apart. In so far as he begins this way, he is opposed to anyone who tries to understand metaphor by working solely with sentence meaning. It might be thought, for example, that a metaphorical sentence is ambiguous. On this account the sentence uttered has both literal meaning and metaphorical meaning. The job of the hearer is to detect the ambiguity, and then realize somehow that the speaker intends for the hearer to focus on the metaphorical side of the ambiguity. Having focused properly, the hearer's job then becomes to decipher somehow what the metaphor is telling us.

In opposition to this interpretation, Searle argues that there is no ambiguity when we use metaphor. When, after watching Sam eat at the dinner table, one of guests says "Sam is a pig", she is not speaking ambiguously. "Pig" means pig and "Sam" refers to Sam and, further, there is no ambiguity in "is" or "a". Nor is there any ambiguity in "Sam is a pig" as a whole. The sentence uttered means what it says. But as hearers we realize that there is a disjoint between what was said and what presumably the speaker meant to say. Sam after all doesn't look or smell like a pig. Our job is to figure out how we go from sentence meaning to speaker meaning. Understandably, Searle is not content to explain how a metaphor works by appealing to an intuition. Such an account explains nothing. Rather, he supposes that there are principled connections between sentence meaning (S is P) and speaker meaning (S is R) that need to be uncovered just as there is with indirect speech.

As usual Searle begins his analysis with simple cases. In particular, he deals with simple subject–predicate uses that fall nicely into the S is P/S is R mould. Using this mould, he notices quickly a major difference between indirect speech and metaphor. With indirect speech the speaker takes "S is P" literally and seriously. The lady does mean to assert "You are stepping on my foot" by way of getting the gentleman to take his foot off of hers. She means what she says (P), but she also means something more (R). But with metaphor we do not mean S is P. We mean something different, namely S is R.

This makes getting from sentence meaning to speaker meaning more difficult than with indirect speech. But the difficulty is not insurmountable. Suzanne says to Henry, someone she has just met, "Sam is coming to the party". There is no problem here since "S is P" and "S is R" coincide – sentence and speaker meaning are the same. So far she is speaking literally. But then Suzanne adds "You know, Sam is a pig". Now the listener, who knows nothing about Suzanne and the kind of parties she gives, might think that she is still engaged in literal speech. For all he knows Suzanne has strange friends who not only bring their human friends to parties but their pig friends as well. Maybe they bring goats too. It could be, then, that the invited pig's name is Sam. However, the situation is different at another party where only friends and acquaintances from work are invited. Now when Sally says to Hayden "Sam is coming to the party" and adds "Sam is a pig", Hayden knows that Sally is saying something strange with her second utterance. In Searle's terminology she is saying something "defective" such as "an obvious falsehood, semantic nonsense, violations of the rules of speech acts, or violations of conversational principles of communication" (1979a: 105). So for Searle the first step in moving from "S is P" to "S is R" and thereby to come to understand how metaphors work, is to adopt the strategy: *"Where the utterance is defective if taken literally, look for an utterance that differs from sentence meaning"* (1979a: 105). The need to look may be obvious as when one is reading poetry, reading romantic literature or simply dealing with those who think of themselves as literary types. At other times, the need will be obvious simply because the "defective" character of what has been said is so obvious. Yet there will also be times when one realizes that what was said is metaphoric in retrospect.

The second step in dealing with metaphor is to look for a set of strategies for determining what R is, that is, what metaphoric meaning the speaker intends to convey. Here Searle concedes that there is no cut-and-dried formula. In fact, he has a whole set of strategies that he also identifies as principles. Here is a sample of four that gives a sense of how Searle thinks we should proceed to decipher metaphors.

"*Principle 1*. Things which are P are by definition R. Usually, if the metaphor works R will be one of the salient defining characteristics of P" (1979a: 107). His example of P is "Sam is a giant". By definition the hearer can infer that R is "Sam is big". If we follow this principle we can similarly infer R as "Sam flies (is a pilot)" from "Sam is a bird".

"*Principle 2*. Things which are P are contingently R. Again if the metaphor works, the property R should be a salient or well known property of P things" (1979a: 107). Picking on Sam once again, Searle's example of P for this principle is "Sam is a pig". Applying Principle 2 we can infer "Sam is filthy, gluttonous, and sloppy". Similarly we can infer R as "My tractor is swift" from "My John Deere tractor is a deer".

"*Principle 3*. Things which are P are often said or believed to be R, even though both speaker and hearer may know that R is false of P" (1979a: 108). Searle's example for this principle is "Richard is a gorilla". The paraphrase he offers for the metaphor (R) is "Richard is mean, nasty, prone to violence and so on". The metaphor works even for those people who know that gorillas are shy, sensitive and timid creatures so long as they make the "right" associative connections. They are likely to make these connections if they believe that others believe that gorillas are mean, nasty, etc.

"*Principle 4*. Things which are P are not R, nor are they like R things, nor are they believed to be R: nonetheless it is a fact about our sensibility, whether culturally or naturally determined that we just do perceive a connection, so that P is associated in our minds with R properties" (1979a: 108). This principle needs some explaining. Searle argues that some metaphors do not necessarily compare two like things. One example he gives is "Sally is a block of ice". The paraphrase he presents is "Sally is unemotional". But in what sense is being unemotional like a block of ice? Even if we said that she not "hot" sexually this hardly suggests that making love to Sally is like making love to a block of ice. Still, even though there is no real likeness between Sally and a block of ice, we make a (socially generated) connection between Sally and the block of ice. So the metaphor works. Another example Searle gives is "I am in a black mood" with the corresponding paraphrase "I am angry and depressed". In what sense, he asks, is something being black like being depressed? Likeness here is not present at all, or is remote at best.

Searle presents us with four other principles and says that maybe there are more, but the main ones have been already cited. As mentioned, these principles give us a sense as to how Searle approaches the second step in the process of deciphering metaphors by moving from "S is P" to "S is R".

But a third step is needed. The associations our strategies generate in Step 2 may be too rich. If Sam is called a pig, does this mean he has a flat nose? Is fat? Wallows in mud? Makes grunting noises? Is literally thick skinned? Step 3, then, attempts to trim the associations from a long list of possibilities to those that the speaker intends. Unfortunately, Searle doesn't tell us much about this step. Presumably one of the deciphering strategies that could be employed is to match the metaphor to the conversation. If the discussion up to the point of saying "Sam is a pig" has been about sanitation, we are likely exclude "He has a flat nose" as a proper interpretation of the metaphor. In Searle's terminology we would be looking at some of the metaphor's preparatory conditions to help us interpret it.

Another restricting strategy is to know something about the speaker's interests. If she often comments on people's noses, how ugly or beautiful they are, then "He has a flat nose" might be a proper interpretation of "He is a pig". Still another strategy is to keep one's own interests in mind. The speaker may be employing a "designer metaphor" for you and your kind. So if you think of yourself and are known as someone who monitors calories in order to stay trim, then the metaphor "Sam is a pig" might plausibly be interpreted as "Sam is fat". Clearly taking account of your interests (as hearer) or those of the speaker has to do with the metaphor's preparatory conditions.

Regardless of how many steps there are, and no matter how many principles there are within each step, it is important to note that we normally "decipher" metaphors intuitively. It is the same with steps and principles that guide our thinking when we issue simple literal or indirect speech acts. We should not confuse the analysis of the process which gives us our principles and is not intuitive, with the process of how we actually think while dealing with metaphors which often is intuitive. More often than not, we immediately "catch on" when we hear a metaphor being used, which is to say that we've learned to interpret many metaphors so quickly that there is no need to articulate consciously or unconsciously the principles found in Step 2 or 3. Certainly at times we will need to cite or recite the principles. At other times our minds will be blank even after we try to apply the principles consciously. Just as inside jokes "go by us", so it is with inside metaphors. At other times we will misread metaphors. Still at other times we will be "so out of it" that we won't even know that metaphors are at play in the speech activity setting.

Metaphors may be hard to decipher not just because we don't have the right social connections. As the Searlian principles suggest, metaphors are not one specie of animal. The associations they force us to make are not all of the same type. Some are based upon definitions that connect P and R, some on observations of likeness while others, it seems, we associate even though there is no likeness present at all. Still, because associations play such an important role in his thinking about metaphors Searle's theory can be called the associationist theory of metaphor. It can be contrasted to the comparison or similarity theory championed, in one form or another by Aristotle, Paul Henle (1965) and G. Miller (1993). This classic theory, according to Searle, can be criticized on at least three grounds. First, one version says that metaphors compare two similar objects such as Sam and pigs but, as we have seen, some metaphors compare or associate two objects that do not share any meaningful similarities. Secondly, similarity does not differentiate metaphor from literal speech since both appeal to similarity. And, thirdly, the similarity theory attempts to *define* metaphors in terms of similarity. This is a mistake not just because some metaphors are not based on similarity, but because this theory confuses the defining characteristics of a phenomenon with its strategies for deciphering metaphor. Looking for similarities between P and R is in fact a good strategy for coming to understand many metaphors. But that is all it is.

Searle criticizes what he calls the interaction theory as well. The champions of this theory are Monroe Beardsley (1962) and

Max Black (1962; 1993). As Searle sees it, this theory makes a mistake similar to the one made by the similarity theory. The similarity theory has in fact some interesting things to say about strategy, roughly with respect to Step 2 (where one is looking for associations between P and R to help decipher the metaphor). In effect, its mistake is to see Step 2 as the essence of the metaphor. The interaction theory's mistake pertains to Step 3. It talks of the attempt to restrict the comparison between P and R as a process of interaction. Searle doesn't find the concept of interaction a particularly helpful metaphor for understanding metaphor. It suggests a strategy, or series of strategies, without actually presenting us with the details. But the interaction's theory more basic mistake is to identify metaphor with one, and only one, of the three strategic steps for deciphering metaphors. So both the comparison or similarity theory, on the one hand, and the interaction theory on the other tell us only part of the story all the while pretending to tell all of it.

For Searle, then, what I am calling his associationist theory tells a more complete story. It attempts to explain the process of how we decipher metaphors by taking account of their complexity and variability. In so doing, Searle's theory has a messy appearance. With respect to Step 2, for instance, no account is given as to which of the eight or so principles one is supposed to cite in order to decipher a particular metaphor for the simple reason that no account can be given. And, as we have also noted, he actually says little about how Step 3 is supposed to be taken. Still, his theory has some obvious merits. It does, as just noted, deal better with the metaphoric variability than do the competing theories. It does, as well, begin to present us with details about how metaphors work. The details are given in outline form, but they are there in his theory where, in contrast, they are generally lacking in the competing theories. Searle's theory of metaphor also shows how metaphor fits into his larger theory of speech acts by employing the distinction between sentence and speaker meaning, the notions of essential and preparatory conditions, the notion of speech act types (mostly assertives) and context.

One other merit of Searle's theory deserves mention. Containing as it does a variety of principles under Steps 2 and 3, the theory allows for multiple interpretations of any one metaphor. For Tom to say that his CEO is a warrior may mean "You can always depend on him to put up a fight on every issue". That may be one reading.

But other readings might be also be appropriate. "He is a warrior" might also be read as "He is brave" and "He never gives up and he can take criticism" and so on. Using Searle's theory it is possible to think of metaphor the way we think of multiple-choice test questions where one of the answer options is "all of the above". And that is how it should be. We often think of how rich metaphors are. Part of that richness is surely due to contrast between the simplicity of the sentence meaning, on the one hand, and the complexity (of various simultaneous interpretations) of speaker meaning, on the other.

Some further comments about metaphors and other matters

Searle's account of metaphor has no difficulty dealing with more complex metaphors than the ones upon which he focuses most of his attention. With the simple metaphors he has been considering that the metaphoric expression is found in the predicate place of a sentence. "Sam is a pig" and "Sally is a block of ice" are our already familiar examples of this type. But a predicate term can be nominalized so that once Sam is identified as the pig we can say "The pig is eating at the trough" and mean, in a political context, that Sam is piggishly finding that being in office affords him the opportunity to line his pockets. Suddenly we understand why Sam's driveway is blessed with a Mercedes-Benz E-55 and a Jaguar XJR. As Searle points out, we can even eliminate the literal use of "is" and insert a third metaphor into the mix and then say of Sam "The pig grovels at the trough".

It makes no difference to Searle that we are dealing here with a triple metaphor. It likely will make a difference to some hearers. They may find it more difficult to decipher what the speaker's meanings are. But, in principle, the same principles used to decipher simple metaphors can be used to decipher the complex ones. Indeed, Searle sees that his theory's ability to deal with these complex metaphors gives it an edge over the competition. Various versions of both the similarity and interaction theory, he says, presuppose that there is a contrast between literal and metaphoric uses. The interactionist theory, for example, says that there is a kind of linguistic interaction that takes place between the literal and metaphoric sense of the metaphoric expression. But this can't be right since some complex metaphoric utterances have no literal sense built into them at all (i.e. the noun, the verb and the predicate phrases are all metaphors).

So Searle supposes that he has given us an account of how both simple and complex metaphors work. As noted already this account is not really complete especially with respect to Step 3. Still, he has given us enough detail so that we can determine how, in principle, the rest of the theory would look like and work. But beyond talk about metaphors, Searle applies his how-to approach to other uses such as dead metaphor and irony. With the former R has become P. Thus for certain groups who hate the police, they can express themselves by saying something like "The pigs are coming". If, being urban types, they never see real pigs, and if they use "pig" repeatedly to refer to the police, then "pig" and "pigs" take on literal meaning. These expressions for these groups become their name for the police. In the process, they may go so far as to drop the word "police" from their vocabulary.

As to irony, the gap between sentence and speaker meaning is there just as it is for metaphor and indirect speech. But with simple irony at least, the subject of the sentence is *not* described in terms that seemingly do not fit the subject, as is common with metaphor. As I look at Sam and Sally I see that the former doesn't looks like a pig and the latter doesn't look like a block of ice. There is a disconnect here so I assume that the speaker is using metaphor (or that he is crazy). In contrast, with irony the disconnect is more likely to be within the setting in which we find ourselves. The baseball outfielder misjudges the ball. It bounces off his head and falls into his glove. Viewing the scene, I say "Wasn't that a great catch?" The paper read at the conference is long and boring, and I say "Wasn't that interesting?" Or the salesclerk has taken her time and kept her customers waiting, and I say "Thank you for your prompt attention". In all these cases, the disconnect is so obvious that the hearer has to (we hope at least) assume that I mean the opposite (speaker meaning) of what I say (sentence meaning).

In "Metaphor" Searle does not get around to telling us what metaphor means. Still in the process of telling us how to decipher metaphors, and in his contrast of metaphors to literal uses, indirect speech, irony and other uses, he gives us some hints about a definition. Had he given us one it would look something like this. A metaphor is a sentence or a series of sentences which, when uttered, we find: (a) there is a sharp disconnect between sentence and speaker meaning; (b) the disconnect is generated by an obvious difference or clash between the two (or more) objects talked about (e.g. the ship that ploughs through the sea isn't a plough) and (c) the disconnect is nonetheless bridged by associating (most of the time, but not always, via similarity) the two or more objects.

In addition to not giving us a definition, Searle does not tell us much about why our language contains metaphor. Surely what he could, and no doubt would, have said is that metaphors have many purposes one of which is to issue assertives "in a new light". Freud did so when he compared the human psyche to a pressurized plumbing system. So did Newton when he compared objects both larger and smaller than billiard balls to billiard balls. So science and even ordinary folk use metaphors to help us see things in ways that we did not see them before. A second use of metaphor is to help us speak economically. Metaphors help us to do the work of many utterances with one. To return to Sam one more time, in calling him a pig we say that he is (with apologies to pigs) a glutton, filthy, ugly, crude, etc. This piece of work is related to the point made above that metaphors are like multiple choice questions where choosing "all of the above" is a possible legitimate answer.

A third purpose of metaphors is that they help us engage in hyperbole. To call Slim a snake in the grass says that he is not to be trusted and a bit more. A fourth purpose, perhaps sometimes related to the third, is to allow us to speak in a more colourful and less boring manner. A fifth is to help avoid or evade speaker responsibility. In an authoritarian nation it is often useful to use metaphor in order to allow for some play when the authorities suspect that your writing represents criticism of the regime. With metaphor you can deny you meant what you meant in a way that you could not if you spoke literally. In effect, you can deny your speaker meaning and argue that what you said is nothing more than sentence meaning.

Some of these reasons help explain why paraphrasing a metaphor always seems to leave something out. If Slim can be justly called a snake in the grass, it just isn't enough to paraphrase the metaphor as "He can't be trusted". Even adding "and a bit more" doesn't help much since it doesn't tell us what more should be added. We could always add to the paraphrase, "Slim is quick, slippery and dangerous". Adding more helps, but the more we add the more we lose the virtues of economy and hyperbole. But that aside, adding to the paraphrase does not necessarily catch all that the speaker intends to pack into the metaphor. Metaphors are often open ended to the point that even the speaker isn't clear just how much is supposed to be packed in it. It certainly makes sense for Suzanne, when questioned about her piggish metaphor about Sam, to say "Well yes, I hadn't thought about it quite that way, but that is part of what I (could have) meant".

All these shortcomings to our paraphrases do not disturb Searle. He happily grants that paraphrases cannot catch the full sense of a metaphor. He is not in the business of reducing metaphors to paraphrases. The strategies that he identifies that yield paraphrase have another purpose. They point to only part of the "meaning" of this or that metaphor. Their purpose is not to completely grasp and thereby replace the metaphor but to give the hearer a large sense of what was intended by the speaker. That includes what truth the metaphor articulates. Searle's way of putting this point is to say that "The best we can do in the paraphrase is reproduce the truth conditions of the metaphorical utterance" (1979a: 114). To the dummy who doesn't grasp what Suzanne means when she calls Sam a pig, it is enough to rattle off such things as he's fat, filthy, ugly and a slob. She can't, but in addition, doesn't have to, tell the whole story to enlighten her mentally challenged listener.

Searle's view that metaphors can be true or false has not gone unchallenged. It has been suggested that metaphors are not descriptive (assertive speech acts) but, rather, are utterances that are constitutive of our world view. As such, they are better characterized as appropriate or inappropriate rather than true or false (Burkhardt 1990: 325). In support of this challenge it is argued that a metaphor is not a "serious" but, rather, a defective form of predication. Suzanne isn't seriously saying that Sam is a pig and thus should be put in a pig pen with other pigs, and that he should be offered a full stock of pig food.

Searle agrees that it is the defective nature of what Suzanne has said that alerts us to her metaphorical speech. But, if we are so dense as not to see that she is using a metaphor, the wheels of our mind will likely generate thoughts of the form "What she says isn't true. Sam really isn't a pig. I mean . . ." In thinking this way one implies that the metaphor is indeed descriptive, that is, it is in part an assertive, even if a defective one. However, beyond the defective feature of the metaphor, Searle claims that the metaphor purports to speak some kind of truth. The truth is not on the face of the metaphor, but it is there nonetheless. That is what the paraphrase purports to do. It tries to tell us what truth is hidden in the metaphor. And, again, Searle is not committed to the notion that the truth embedded in a metaphor, and in its paraphrase, tell the whole story. On his theory all he needs to say is that truth and falsity form an important part metaphor.

One final point about metaphor. In telling us about metaphors Searle is not in the business of classifying them as are Lakoff and Johnson (1980). That is, he is not concerned to tell us that spatial metaphors ("I have an idea in the back of my mind") are more common or influential than we might suppose, and that they are to be contrasted to so called conduit metaphors ("His words *carry* little meaning") (Lakoff & Johnson 1980: 11). Nor is Searle interested in telling us how important they are our thinking. He leaves these tasks up to others who are more concerned with linguistics than philosophy of language. His concerns are with understanding how metaphors work and how they fit into speech act theory.[1]

Fiction

As we have seen, Searle's interest in philosophy of language revolves around two closely related questions "What is the nature of language? and "How does it work?" The language in question is our everyday, or natural, language. He sees scientific language as an extension of ordinary language so he also has some concern for it too. Yet, mostly his attention is focused on everyday language. Given that interest, and his interest in developing a comprehensive theory of language, he must come to terms with fictional discourse sooner or later.

Fictional discourse poses a special problem for a speech act theorist like Searle. Language is, for him, rule governed. If the users of language follow certain rules they can string together assertives, directives and the other types of speech acts in order to engage in meaningful speech activity (discourse). But with fiction, it seems that the users, novelists for example, violate the language rules regularly especially those governing the issuance of assertives. Searle reminds us what the rules are.

An assertion is a type of illocutionary act that conforms to certain quite specific semantic and pragmatic rules. These are:

1. The essential rule: the maker of an assertion commits himself to the truth of the expressed proposition.
2. The preparatory rules: the speaker must be in a position to provide evidence or reasons for the truth of the expressed proposition.
3. The expressed proposition must not be obviously true to both the speaker and the hearer in the context of utterance.
4. The sincerity condition: the speaker commits himself to a belief in the truth of the expressed proposition.

(Searle 1979a: 62)

All these rules are seemingly violated by fiction writers with the possible exception of 3. The first rule is apparently violated since these writers do not seem to be committing themselves to any truth (concerning the world out there). The second is violated since the writers have no evidence or reasons to cite, while the fourth rule is violated since they are not committing themselves to any beliefs. It is difficult to know what to say about 3. Since truth is not an issue in fiction, it hardly makes sense to apply that rule to fictional discourse. In any case, the seeming violations of the rules of assertion are gross enough to leave any speech act theorist wondering just what is going on in fictional discourse.

In addition to violating a host of rules on the illocutionary act level, fiction writers apparently also violate one of the rules for referring. Recall, that in order to refer, the referent, X, has to be there. "Whatever is referred to must exist" (Searle 1969: 77). This is the so-called axiom of existence. The problem with fiction is that more often than not, X isn't there. To be sure, fiction will often incorporate real referents. Novels like Herman Wouk's *The Winds of War* (1971) and *War and Remembrance* (1978) refer to real events such as World War II, Pearl Harbor, the Battle of Leyte Gulf, real places such as Poland, Germany and Japan and real people such as Hitler, Stalin, Roosevelt, Churchill and Admiral Nimitz. But, as novels, these books also refer to fictional characters such as Pug Henry, his wife Rhoda, their children and their friends. So even in Wouk's novels there seem to be significant violations of the existence axiom, as there are gross violations of that rule in other novels, short stories and other forms of storytelling that have no connection to history or geography.

But are these violations really violations? Searle sets out to answer this question as part of his general account of the logic of fictional discourse. The word "discourse" should not be passed over lightly. It shows Searle once again doing philosophy of language on a level beyond speech act analysis. Terms such as "illocutionary" that are appropriately applied on the speech act level are not necessarily appropriate for the discourse level. He is thus suspicious of any analysis of fictional discourse as "the illocutionary act of telling a story or writing a novel" (1979a: 63). Whatever fiction is, it is not a use of language where a new speech act type appears in addition to assertives, commissives and the rest. Rather, like any other discourse, fiction displays all the usual types of speech acts. Mostly they are assertives (1979a: 65). Understandably so. Fiction writers describe events that take place in their stories They must also give identifying descriptions of their characters; and then describe what the characters do and think. There will also be descriptive accounts of what the characters say and, not surprisingly, what they say may itself be assertorial (descriptive). But the fictional characters may also issue directives. One character in a story may say "Shut the door". Another may make promises. So fiction may look like, although it need not, just like non-fiction. Thus looking just at the text, readers might be hard pressed to tell whether they are reading fiction or not.

But how, then, do the two forms of discourse differ? Searle says that fiction authors are pretending, "going through the motions", or "acting as if" they were making assertions, issuing directives and all the rest (1979a: 65). However, they are not pretending the way liars pretend. Liars are out to fool their hearers and, strictly speaking, they do not pretend to issue illocutionary acts of one kind or another. They actually do issue such acts. A liar who says to his wife that he did not spend time with his old girlfriend during his last business trip has issued an assertive. It is just that in doing so, he has violated the sincerity condition by not believing what he asserts. He knows, but his wife presumably does not, that what he said is false. Fiction writers also issue assertives and other speech acts but they "break" the rules out in the open. They don't try to fool anyone.

Still, even if it is out in the open, fiction writers are pretending; and, Searle says, pretending is something we do intentionally. Then he adds:

> the identifying criterion for whether or not a text is a work of fiction must of necessity lie in the illocutionary intentions of the author. There is no textual property, syntactical or semantic, that will identify a text as a work of fiction. What makes it

> a work of fiction is, so to speak, the illocutionary stance that the author takes toward it, and that stance of the complex illocutionary intentions that the author has when he writes or otherwise composes it.   (1979a: 65–6)

Now that can't be right if Searle means that authorial intentions tell us whether a work is fiction or not. That is, it doesn't follow that if the text itself doesn't tell us what is going on, authorial intentions will. Searle is right in saying that works of fiction are written intentionally. But it is not the complex illocutionary intentions that we fathom in order to identify this as a novel and that as some form of non-fiction. It is not as if we read the book in front of us and then also "read" the author's mind.

We look for any number of linguistic and contextual cues away from the text, and sometimes in the text, to determine what kind of work we are reading. In the case of Wouk's *The Winds of War* we see the expression "A novel" on the cover. As if that were not enough for a novel that mixes real events and people with fictional ones, Wouk feels compelled at the end of *War and Remembrance* to tell us who and what are and are not real (1978: 1125–8). He writes a short essay to explain that a German officer named von Roon is fictional, as are the American submarines *Devilfish*, *Moray* and *Barracuda*. But there are other ways that authors and story tellers signal their intent to engage in fictional writing. They can say "A short story". Notice they need not even call their stories fictional. We assume that stories are fictional unless we are told that a particular writing is "A true story of romance . . ." or something of the sort. Or, contrary to what Searle tells us, authors can signal their intent in the text itself by saying "Once upon a time", "Let's pretend", or by saying something outlandish as Kafka does in *Metamorphosis*. We know, if we did not know already, that Kafka's work is fiction when we are told that the main character has been transformed into a gigantic and reprehensible creature.

Most of these signals informing us of authorial intent were labelled master speech acts in Chapter 3 (Fotion 1971; 1979). Such acts are typically commissives. They commit the speaker in the immediate future to say certain things or say them in a certain way. So when the cover of a book says a "A novel of passion and betrayal" the author (or the publisher) promises to deliver a fictional story that will likely excite and anger us. In effect, master speech acts allow speakers (authors) to tell us publicly what follows linguistically and, in so doing, they reveal speaker intentions. What permits speakers to say things like "A novel" (elliptical for "This is a novel") is that there are linguistic conventions in place for writing novels. Searle expresses this point by using the Wittgensteinian term language game. He has already used the term in his taxonomy article. There he said that there are essentially five language games corresponding to the five basic types of speech acts (assertives, commissives, directives, expressives and declarations). But now Searle is using "language game" on the discourse (speech activity), not speech act, level. The rules of the fiction language game permit some of the referring rules to be cancelled. They also allow some of the rules for making assertions and the other speech acts to be cancelled. Arthur Conan Doyle is not committed to having a referent for the proper names Sherlock Holmes, Dr Watson and the Baker Street Irregulars. And, of course, he is not committed to believing that the assertions he makes about these people are true. Nor is Doyle, or any novelist, committed to realistically reporting what mental powers humans can have. Holmes may be super-human in this regard. Others, in different works, may be physically super-human. In still other works the laws of biology (Kafka again) or physics may be "violated". The game of fiction is very forgiving in these ways. It gives authors much slack as to what they can say (Searle 1979a: 72–4). The slack is such that it may be best to think of fiction not as one but many games. All these games are to be contrasted to other games on the discourse level such as the writing and reading of poems, essays on fiction, history, philosophy and scientific reports, and so on. And all these are to be contrasted to gossiping, chatting, praying, engaging in formal religious services (of various kinds), engaging in governmental ceremonies, and so on.

Although fiction allows its authors much slack, Searle points out that some forms of fiction make demands on their authors to meet the standards of "serious" speech. Thus he points out that the Sherlock Holmes stories need to get certain things right about the relative locations of London, Baker Street and Paddington Station. Wouk, in his historical novels, goes to great length to get the events related to the battle of Leyte Gulf right. There is another sense in which certain kinds of fiction need to get things right. The characters in a novel may all be fictitious, as is, perhaps, where they live. It may be that the whole novel takes place on a fictitious planet so we needn't even concern ourselves with fiction having anything to do with this very real planet. Still the people in the novel may be "metaphors" for real people. So the novel may be making serious assertions with respect to human psychological, interpersonal and social reality.

One may wonder at this point what the rules are that allow fiction writers to suspend some of the rules of normal use of language (of truth telling, evidence, of non-obviousness and sincerity) listed above. Searle doesn't tell us in the sense of providing an explicit set of rules or principles the way he does when he discusses indirect speech and metaphor. Rather he identifies the four normal assertion rules as vertical rules. Then he says.

> I find it useful to think of these rules as rules correlating words (sentences) to the world. Think of them as vertical rules that establish connections between language and reality. Now what makes fiction possible, I suggest, is a set of extralinguistic, nonsemantic conventions that break the connection between words and the world established by the rules mentioned earlier. Think of the conventions of fictional discourse as a set of horizontal conventions that break the connection established by the vertical rules. They suspend the normal requirements established by these rules. Such horizontal conventions are not meaning rules; they are not part of the speaker's semantic competence. Accordingly, they do not alter or change the meanings of any of the words or other elements of the language. What they do rather is enable the speaker to use words with their literal meanings without undertaking the commitments that are normally required by those meanings. (1979a: 66–7)

What he says in this quote fits in well with what has been said so far in this chapter. Because these horizontal rules don't change meaning a work of fiction has, the potential is present for it to look like a work of non-fiction. But the quote still doesn't tell us what the horizontal conventions are.

It is actually difficult to articulate these conventions. However if we watch some master speech acts at work we can get some clues. Strictly speaking master speech acts are not (rule) conventions. Rather they are the speech acts that the conventions permit us to employ when we wish to do so. So when a master speech act says "Let's pretend" we can ask what exactly are we asked to pretend. Clearly one thing is that a young and handsome prince and a young and beautiful princess exist who actually don't exist.

The convention that permits the master speech act to be cited is:

1 *The axiom of existence can be put in suspension for purposes of telling stories, writing novels, etc.*

"Let's pretend . . .", "Once upon a time there was . . ." and less explicitly "A novel" also permit writers to write about events as if they have happened but in fact have not. In part this suspension of the facts is due to the first convention that suspends reference. If the princess doesn't exist then whatever she does in the story is not a report of a fact in the real world. But, in addition, we can pretend in stories that real people did things that they did not really do; and pretend that things happened at real places that really did not happen. So a second convention can be expressed as follows.

2 *The essential rule of assertion that commits speakers (writers) to the truth of the expressed propositions they present can be suspended.*

At least one more rule is needed. It can be called the rule of publicity and can be stated as follows.

3 *Speakers (or writers) must, somehow, express publicly their intentions to suspend rules 1 and 2.*

As has been suggested already in discussing Wouk's novels, 1 and 2 can be suspended to a more or less degree. We as readers are put on notice of the suspensions but are not necessarily put on notice with respect to the degree. Wouk discusses in detail the extent of the suspension he imposes on his works. But on television one often sees on the screen the expression "based on a true story". Aside from misleadingly suggesting that the story to be viewed is true, one has no idea from this deliberately vague master speech act whether one-tenth is true or what. Nor does one know, unless the story is about famous people and events (e.g. the assassination of John Kennedy), which one-tenth of the story is true.

Horizontal convention 3 is what differentiates fiction from lying. By making one's intentions to suspend the normal rules about truth telling and the rest, fiction writers cannot be accused of lying. Rather, they are telling their readers that they are engaging in a special "language game" (Searle 1979a: 67). It is a game, Searle says, that is parasitic on the normal game we play since it is played only against the background of the normal game. We have to have the normal rules in place before we can suspend them.

Jacques Derrida, Jonathan Cullar and others have challenged Searle (and Austin for that matter) about the parasitic character of fictional discourse. Part of their complaint is that the parasitic label is demeaning. With a label like this, fiction can be viewed as inferior, defective, an "add-on" rather than a part of our natural (ordinary) language – and, perhaps, something we ought to get rid of. The other part of the complaint is that normal use and fiction go together. They claim that one cannot be understood as taking place without the other. If anything, things could go the other way with ordinary discourse being parasitic on fictional discourse. Listen to Culler in his response to Searle who says that a promise made by an actor on stage is not possible (we would not understand it) if it were not possible to make a promise in real life.

> We are certainly accustomed to thinking in this way: a promise I make is real; a promise in a play is a fictional imitation of a real promise, an empty iteration of a formula used to make real promises. But in fact one can argue that the relation of dependency works the other way. If it were not possible for a character in a play to make a promise, there could be no promises in real life, for what makes it possible to promise, as Austin tells us, is the existence of a conventional procedure, of formulae one can repeat. For me to be able to make a promise in "real life" there must be iterable procedures or formulae, such as are used on stage.   (Culler 1989: 221)

The key notion in this argument for both Derrida and Culler is iterability. To work, language needs to be able to perform repeatable acts. A promise can't be a promise unless first one and then another promise can be made. The same goes for any speech act. To say "Get out of this room!" makes sense to us because we could say the same thing in similar settings twice, three times, etc. Further the argument says that saying something on stage is a paradigm example of iterability since what the actor says is a repetition. The actor repeats what was written and then, presumably, repeats it in the next performance. Quoting someone is also, for Derrida and Culler, a paradigm kind of repetition. The more iterability, it seems, the better. The suggestion is that there is more of this good stuff in play-acting as a kind of fiction than in real world talk.

Now this argument may simply be deconstructive. Its intent may not be so much to replace the Austin/Searle theory with an opposite theory, but simply to embarrass the former by showing that the opposite theory makes as much sense. Whatever the motive, Searle is not amused. He argues that iterability is a feature that *all* uses of language possess. Any form of language, fictional or not, is rule governed; and what is rule governed is repeatable. So nothing follows about the status of fiction by pointing out that it is rule governed and, therefore, reiterable. Other considerations determine the status of fiction such as the kind of rules and conventions writers of fiction follow. Once we monitor these rules and conventions, Searle claims, we see that fiction involves the cancellation of certain rules of "normal" use. In this sense fiction is parasitic on normal use. The point is a logical one, not one meant to demean the importance of fiction. It certainly is not one to demean fiction or that portion of fiction we label literature. Searle's point about the logical dependence of fiction to normal use is perfectly compatible with the sense that fiction (literature) is a most important vehicle for communicating ideas and emotions of all sorts. It is as if Austin's and Searle's deconstruction critics have misread their use of various metaphors. Austin especially, but also Searle, very likely used "parasitic" in a playful metaphoric mood. Not meaning to be insulting, they were taken as insulting fiction (and literature). A sense of humour might have avoided this misunderstanding.[2]

A philosophy of language overview

John Searle's writings in philosophy of language can be characterized as analytic, systematic, imaginative, wide ranging and, certainly, important. Their analytic character flows naturally from the kinds of questions he asks. His two favourites are "What is its structure" and "How does it work?" Applied to language, he supposes that his questions can be answered best by engaging in analysis on the speech act level. He does not deny that speech acts can be analyzed into parts, the most important of which are illocutionary force and propositional content. Still, since the speech act is the minimal unit of language communication, it is analysis on that level that gives us our first sense of how language actually works. Searle's general strategy is not only to start on that level, but to start with simple so-called standard cases on that level. We must work from the simple and standard cases to the complex and non-standard ones. Having dealt with the former we can go on to analyze and understand non-standard cases such as indirect speech, metaphor and irony. From the simple as well we can go on to study how we string speech acts together to form conversations, reports, stories, novels, prayers and the like.

This stringing together is not done in a haphazard fashion. Language use is rule governed activity. There are rules that tell us how to tell and understand stories. There are different kinds of rules that tell us how to employ and understand other non-standard uses. But the rules found in dealing with the standard speech acts must take precedence. It is on that level that Searle does his most imaginative work. He offers us a portrait of the basic language games we play with language. There are five. We use language in order to assert, commit (ourselves), direct (others), express our feelings and make declarations. That is the whole story. All that can be said, can be said as one or other (or more than one) of these basic speech acts. Both the Logical Positivists, who thought that there was only one language game in town, and Wittgenstein who thought there was a bunch, are wrong. The positivists went astray by letting science hypnotize them. Their admiration for science, especially as the result of spectacular developments in biology and physics in the nineteenth and early twentieth centuries, led them to think that meaningful uses of language are found only in science. Since the sciences issue mainly assertive speech acts (constatives as Austin called them) it appeared that only assertive speech acts are meaningful. In his later years, Wittgenstein, in contrast, became hypnotized by the complexity of language. Every speech act type became a game of its own. The over-simplicity of the positivistic portrait of language led to an overreaction in the form of a chaotic Wittgensteinian portrait. Searle (and before him Austin) restores order by showing us (in his "Taxonomy" article) how all the variations (in the role played by the speakers and/or hearers, in the strength or weakness of the issued speech act, in the style in which the speech act is issued, etc.) can confuse us. If we see many of these variations as secondary features of speech acts and attend instead to the primary features, order is restored. The primary features are the point of the speech act, the direction of fit, the sincerity condition and, perhaps, the propositional content.

After presenting his analyses of the standard uses, Searle moves on to apply his analytic talents to more complex linguistic phenomena. New concepts have to be introduced for these new tasks. Foremost among them are those of sentence and speaker meaning. The former tells us what we hear in words or read from the computer screen. The latter has more to do with what the speaker means to say. The two can correspond when we use language in a literal way. With literal speech we say what we mean and mean what we say. But often, more often than we might suppose, sentence and speaker meaning diverge. We say one thing (sentence meaning) but intend for our hearers to understand us as saying something else (speaker meaning). This divergence happens with indirect speech, metaphor, irony and when we speak in suggestive ways. Searle's analyses of how we do it, that is, how hearers decode sentence meaning to arrive at speaker meaning were pioneering.

Perhaps the work Searle did on the more macro level of language analysis is less pioneering. His attention on the micro level of speech acts was so sustained over 15–20 years that he said less than he might have about language activity (discourse, narratives). But even here, what he did that was original in showing how speech act concepts can accommodate concepts on the speech activity level. Overall, that was his purpose. He wanted to show how all aspects of language could be understood within the framework of speech act theory. Speech acts are the building blocks, speech activity is the resulting building.

Notes

1. A rich source of material on metaphor can be found in *Metaphor and Thought* edited by Andrew Ortony (1993). This volume not only contains a reprint of Searle's article on metaphor but also articles by Max Black, Jerrold Sadock, L. Jonathan Cohen, George Lakoff, Thomas Kuhn, Zenon Pylyshyn among others. Favourable and unfavourable comments about Searle's theory of metaphor are scattered throughout the volume.
2. For a reaction more sympathetic to Derrida see Alfino (1991). Alfino helps put the "debate" between Searle and Derrida/Culler in perspective.

Part II

Philosophy of mind

Chapter 5

Intentionality of mind and language

A shift of attention to intentionality of the mind

The appearance of Searle's next major work was anticipated by several articles (1979b; 1980a,b,c; 1982). He views these articles as preliminary sketches. The full title of the final and fully-formed canvas is *Intentionality: An Essay in the Philosophy of Mind* (1983). The title shows a shift of attention away from philosophy of language to a new subject.[1] He still has many things to say about language, but now what he says has more to do with its status in relationship to other things rather than with the analysis of its details (e.g. its logical structure). In that connection, one of the major purposes of *Intentionality* is to show how language relates to the mind. Whatever Intentionality turns out to be, it will become clear shortly that one way mind and language relate to one another is that both exhibit Intentionality. But, it may be asked, do they do so in the same way? Is one form of Intentionality more basic than the other? Dealing with these and other questions thus shows that the shift to a new subject matter is not so great as at first it might be supposed since one purpose in coming to understand Intentionality is to come to a better understanding of language.

However, a second purpose is to show how the mind should be studied. Searle's view is that much of modern psychology is committed to theories of the mind that hold back progress in that field. In particular he is disturbed by certain theories of psychology that take the computer as the model for understanding the mind. With respect to the computer model, *Intentionality* is more a ground-laying work. Searle criticizes these theories in a more

99

direct and systematic fashion in many of his later works, after he has put his conceptual house (concerning the mind) in order. In *Intentionality*, then, his focus is on telling us in detail what it means for the mind to possess Intentionality[2] and other distinctly mental characteristics.

Intentionality

He begins by saying: "Intentionality is that property of many mental states and events by which they are directed at or about or of objects and states of affairs in the world"(1983: 1).[3] When you hope, you hope for *something*. When you have a desire, you desire *something*. When you believe, you believe *something*. When you see (hear, smell), you see (hear, smell) *something*. It is part of the meaning of being in these mental states that they have an aboutness feature.

As the above quotation suggests, however, not all mental states have the feature of being about something. Some anxiety states do not take objects. Jill can have an anxiety attack, one that has causes, but still one that has no object. Certainly she cannot identify an object to go with her mental state the way Jack can with his fear of the bully down the street who pummels him every time they meet. Although the fear that Jack feels possesses Intentionality, the pain that goes with the pummeling does not. In this respect it is like Jill's anxiety. Clues that pain is not an Intentional state can be found in how Jack speaks. He says "I have a (am in) pain" or "My head and shoulders hurt". There is no pain *of* something the way there is a fear of something. Nor does talk of pain take objects the way talk of seeing, hearing, smelling etc. do. We say we see, hear, etc. something. It makes no sense to say we pain something. Searle uses language analysis much like this to help him nail down the distinction having to do with those states that take objects (i.e. are Intentional) and those that do not. Notice, as well, how he engages in linguistic philosophy (in contrast to the philosophy of language work that he does in *Speech Acts*) in the following passage to help us understand the distinction.

> A clue to this distinction is provided by the constraints on how these states are reported. If I tell you I have a belief or a desire, it always makes sense for you to ask, "What is it exactly that you believe?" Or "What is it that you desire?"; and it won't do

for me to say, "Oh I just have a belief and a desire without believing anything or desiring anything"? My beliefs and desires must always be about something. But my nervousness and undirected anxiety need not in that way be *about* anything. Such states are characteristically accompanied by beliefs and desires, but undirected states are not identical with beliefs or desires. On my account if a state S is Intentional then there must be an answer to such questions as: What is S about? What is S of? What is it an S that? Some types of mental states have instances which are Intentional and other instances which are not. For example, just as there are forms of elation, depression and anxiety where one is simply elated, depressed, or anxious without being elated, depressed, or anxious about anything, so, also, there are forms of these states where one is elated that such and such has occurred or depressed and anxious at the prospect of such and such. Undirected anxiety, depression, and elation are not Intentional, the directed cases are Intentional.   (1983: 1–2)

Searle argues that when a mental state takes or possesses an object, it does so "internally". It is not as if one has a belief and then that independent (or separate) belief attaches itself to some object or other. Rather, the object Intended is part of the belief. If the Intended object were different, one would have a different belief. "I believe in God" and "I believe it is raining outside" are expressions of two different beliefs because their objects are different. Similarly, if the object desired changes from food to sex, one's desire has changed.

Searle thinks of himself here as articulating the "logical" features of Intentionality itself and also the "logical" features of various specific Intentional states. He is not engaged in ontology at this point (1983: 15). Ontology answers the question: What is the mode of existence of beliefs, desires, etc.? His questions concerned with "logic" are instead: What is Intentionality, belief, desire, etc.? His answer goes something like this.

- Intentional states have both a "psychological mode" and (Intentional or representative) content. The former can be belief, desire, hope, fear, etc., the latter pertains to what is believed, desired, hoped for, feared, etc. However, the content of a mental state (like the propositional content of a speech act) should not be confused with the object of that thought. The content is part of the mental state. It is not as if the Intentional state is about its own content. Rather the Intentional state, with its content, is about some object. The thought that FDR was a great American president has the content of FDR being a great president, but the thought itself is about FDR and the things he did that made him great. Thus the belief that FDR was a great president is a full Intentional state with content that is about FDR and his greatness. Intentionality is present within the content in the reference to FDR and in the predication that he is great, but also in the full speech act. The full speech act's Intentionality says, in effect, that it is a real world fact that FDR was great.

- These states have a direction of fit that, not surprisingly, depends upon the psychological mode. Thus if Susan believes it is raining, the direction of fit is mind-to-world; but if she wants her friend to come over to visit her, it is world-to-mind. The parallel of his theory of Intentionality and speech act theory does not escape Searle. He sees that illocutionary forces are like "psychological modes"; and that both speech acts and Intentional states have content and take objects, and that both have direction of fit. But there is still more that Intentional states share with speech acts.

- Intentional states possess what Searle calls conditions of satisfaction or success. Beliefs are satisfied when what is believed is true, intentions satisfied when what is intended is done, wishes satisfied when they are fulfilled. The notion of "conditions of satisfaction" is important to an understanding of Intentionality.

It is a general feature of [I]ntentional states with a propositional content that they have conditions of satisfaction. Indeed, if one wanted a slogan for analyzing [I]ntentionality, I believe it should be this: "By their conditions of satisfaction shall ye know them." If we want to know exactly what a person's [I]ntentional state is, we must ask ourselves under what conditions exactly would it be satisfied or not satisfied.

(1998: 103–4)

Similarly, speech acts possess conditions of satisfaction. Thus, an assertion is satisfied when what is asserted is true, a promise satisfied when it is carried out and a order satisfied when it is carried out as well.

These three features of Intentional states go a long ways toward answering the "logical" questions that concern Searle. Intentional states are just those states that possess Intentional content (pointing to some object or objects) in a certain psychological mode, which mode determines their direction of fit, and whose content determines the states' conditions of satisfaction. Having said this much, Searle adds that the Intentionality of mental states is intrinsic. That is, the mind's Intentionality is not derived from some other form of Intentionality or from some totally different kind of mental state. Rather, its Intentionality is bedrock.

This is not the case with language. Language's Intentionality is derived. Here is how Searle expresses himself on this point.

> Since sentences – the sounds that come out of one's mouth or the marks that one makes on paper – are, considered in one way, just objects in the world like any other objects, their capacity to represent is not intrinsic but is derived from the Intentionality of the mind. The Intentionality of mental states, on the other hand, is not derived from some more prior forms of Intentionality but is intrinsic to the states themselves. An agent uses a sentence to make a statement or ask a question, but he does not in that way *use* his beliefs and desires, he simply has them. A sentence is a syntactical object on which representational capacities are imposed: beliefs and desires and other Intentional states are not, as such, syntactical objects (though they may be and usually are expressed in sentences), and their representational capacities are not imposed but are intrinsic. (1983: vii–viii)

So the close parallelism of language (speech acts) and mental states is explained in terms of the mind, not language. It is not language that imposes Intentionality on the mind, but the other way around. The mind imposes Intentionality on language by intentionally (i.e. purposefully) "conferring the conditions of satisfaction of the expressed psychological state upon" it (1983: 27). Searle does not mean to imply that language does not, in turn, influence how we think. Language takes on a life of its own and, in so doing, helps to mould the mind in how it thinks. Nonetheless, the basic structure of language, its ability to be used to refer, to attribute and to issue full speech acts mirrors the mind. This is why we say that words (language, speech acts) have meaning. Meaning is something we give to entities of some sort or other. But mental states do not have meaning. We don't give meaning to our mental states by having our "soul" or "mind" step back to impose meaning on our beliefs, perceptions, desires, hopes or whatever. Mental states by their nature are Intentional. As noted already, beliefs, desires, etc. are simply not what they are without their Intentionality.

Not surprisingly what Searle says about the relationship between mental states and language has not gone unchallenged. Indeed, some read Searle as abandoning the "linguistic turn" in so far as he says that language's Intentionality is dependent upon the mind's (Apel 1991; Habermas 1991). Others criticize Searle in much the same way without thinking of him to be a turncoat (Alston 1991; Bennett 1991). Presumably the "linguistic turn", as championed first by the Logical Positivists and later by the ordinary language school, gave priority to language over mind. On this view, it evidently makes no sense to say that we can have mental states of knowing, believing, wanting, intending, etc. if we are incapable of understanding some form of language. It is language that structures, forms or "categorizes" the mind; not the other way around.

Searle concedes that this criticism is hard to answer especially since he cannot help but explain the mind's Intentionality without using language (1991a: 94). Here is how he puts this point.

> The reason that it is so hard, of course, is that anything that says has to be said in a language, and any articulation I give of more primitive prelinguistic forms of Intentionality will always be done in language. So, it looks like I am simply using linguistic forms to explicate Intentionality, and thus it looks like the Intentionality is intrinsically linguistic.   (1991: 94)

Then he adds:

> But now ask yourself, "How did the speech acts get this extraordinary shape?" and "Why is it that psychological states have exactly the same shape?" Is it because mankind first learned how to talk and then learned how to experience, feel and think?   (1991a: 94)

He thinks the answers to his questions are obvious. Children, and animals too, have primitive Intentional experiences without the presence of language.

The picture that I have is this: a human child begins with prelinguistic forms of Intentionality. By a kind of boot-strapping effect the child acquires primitive linguistic expressions of that Intentionality. But a little bit of language goes a long way; and the child develops a richer Intentionality which it could not have developed without linguistic forms. This richer Intentionality enables a further richer linguistic development which in turns enables richer Intentionality. All the way up to the developed adult, there is a complex series of developmental and logical interactions between Intentionality and language. Most forms of adult Intentionality are essentially linguistic. But the whole edifice rests on biological primitive forms of prelinguistic Intentionality.   (1991a: 94)

In these early stages of his account of Intentionality, we see Searle outlining the "logic" of mental states as intrinsically Intentional, but also see him anticipating his discussion of the ontology of these states. His version of the ontological question, recall, is: What is the mode of existence of beliefs and other Intentional states? His answer in the introduction of *Intentionality* is worth quoting since it is so succinct, and so anticipates his programme in the area of the philosophy of mind as he develops it later in his career that one can hardly resist quoting it.

In urging that people have mental states which are intrinsically Intentional I part company with many, perhaps most, of the currently influential views in the philosophy of mind. I believe people do have mental states, some of them conscious and some unconscious, and that, at least as far as the conscious ones are concerned, they pretty much have the mental properties they seem to have. I reject any form of behaviorism or functionalism, including Turing machine functionalism, that ends up by denying the specific mental properties of mental phenomena ... I believe that the various forms of behaviorism and functionalism were never motivated by an independent investigation of the facts, but by a fear that unless some way was found to eliminate mental phenomena naively construed, we would be left with dualism and an apparently insoluble mind-body problem. On my view mental phenomena are biologically based: they are both caused by the operations of the brain and realized in the structure of the brain. On this view, consciousness and Intentionality are as much a part of human biology as digestion or the circulation of the blood. It is an *objective* fact about the world that it contains certain systems, viz., brains, with *subjective* mental states, and it is *a physical* fact about such systems that they have *mental* features. The correct solution to the "mind-body problem" lies not in denying the reality of mental phenomena, but in properly appreciating their biological nature.

(1983: viii–ix)

Intentionality and perception

Having outlined his views concerning both the "logic" and ontology of Intentionality, Searle next turns to the details of various mental states. Perception gets its share of attention since he considers this general Intentional mental state to be biologically more basic than such other states as belief (1983: 36). Why he does will become apparent shortly.

The main questions he tries to answers are, once again, the "logical" ones: What is perception? And, what does it mean to see, hear something? His main, or at least initial, concern then is again not ontological. Inevitably, however, his analysis bleeds over into ontology, especially since perception has to do with whatever is out there in the world. Nor is his main concern epistemological (1991b: 188) although, again, there is some bleeding in so far as he says some things that give us clues about how we come by whatever it is we know.

However we label his account of perception, it is carried out in terms of Intentionality. Our natural language suggests as much. As Sally looks out the window she says "I see (perceive) that the aeroplane has landed". Here seeing is like belief as in "I believe that the aeroplane has landed". Both are Intentional in that they cannot be understood without knowing to what they are pointing. Both mental states have the form "x-that the aeroplane has landed". Beyond that, perceptions like seeing, hearing, smelling etc. share with believing that their Intended objects are states of affairs. The aeroplane example helps to show why. What is perceived or believed is expressed linguistically in terms of propositional content. Here is how Searle expresses it:

> The content of the visual experience, like the content of the belief, is always equivalent to a whole proposition. Visual

experience is never simply *of* an object but rather it must always be *that* such and such is the case.   (1983: 40)

Certain language uses suggest that Searle could be wrong about this. Sally might have said, for instance, "I see the aeroplane" where it seems that there is no whole proposition present – just a reference to some object. But Searle insists that language misleads us here. What Sally is telling us, elliptically, is: "I see that the aeroplane is there (in front of me, to the left)". Searle argues that this analysis must be correct because all perceptions have conditions of satisfaction. To perceive something happening or perceive some object is to know what it would take to make it so that the perception is correct (or, expressed linguistically, to make the speech act true). For that to happen, he argues, we must be dealing with whole propositions. In this connection, perception and belief share a common direction of fit. Perceptions to be correct must fit the world as it is; just as beliefs to be correct must fit the world as it is.

In spite of their points of agreements, perception and belief differ in at least one important respect. Perceptions require that what is perceived be there to be perceived. This is a logical point that in part has to do with how our language works. If I say "I see (that) the aeroplane (is in front of me)" but what is there is a bird, I have to withdraw my claim. I now say something like "Sorry, I *thought* I saw the aeroplane". Seeing, hearing, smelling (i.e. perceiving) thus are success words. They have a happy use only when the process involved has gone well. In contrast, although beliefs can be assessed in terms of whether they are true or false (i.e. they have conditions of satisfaction), we can still be said to believe in ghosts even if there are no such creatures. "Belief" then is not a success word. It does not necessarily report success with respect to what it is I believe.

Searle argues, additionally, for a causal connection between what is seen and the process of seeing. So there is a second difference between perception and belief. It is not enough that the aeroplane be there in front of Sally for her to see it. It is part of the conditions of satisfaction that, to be seen, the aeroplane must trigger the perception. Presumably if the aeroplane were actually in front of her, but someone pulled down a heavy curtain between her and the plane and, yet, she hallucinated that the aeroplane was there, we would say that she has *not* seen the aeroplane. It is debatable what Searle would say if Sally saw the aeroplane on television. Indirectly the aeroplane caused, along with other causes, Sally to "see" the aeroplane. We are tempted to say that she didn't really see the aeroplane in spite of the aeroplane's causal work – otherwise why do we say "She saw in on *television*" rather than simply say "She saw it". Searle's position might very well be that the judgment whether she saw the aeroplane could go either way since we are at the borderline again. But borderline cases do not take away the basic logical point he is making that to be seen, heard, smelled, or sensed in some other way, the object sensed must directly cause the perception.

There is one other very important element to add to complete Searle's picture of perception; and thus to mark the contrast between perception and belief in still another way. The content of our perceptions come to us via perceptual experience. We are conscious of our perceptions.[4] When Sally sees her aeroplane, it is there for her to be visualized, heard, smelled and even to be felt as it sends vibrations through the building where she is standing. Sally, the rest of us humans, and animals like chimps, dogs and cats need not have been constructed the way we all are in order to perceive things. It is possible to talk about perception where there is no perceptual experience. Searle is adhering here to what he calls an empirical ontological point, not a logical one. But in fact we humans, and many other animals, are wired with consciousness and so Searle makes it his business to try to understand how that aspect of our perceptual life works.

So far, here is where we stand with respect to the Searlian account of perception. Those creatures that can perceive have conscious perceptual experiences that contain (Intentional) content. That content sets the conditions of satisfaction for the perceiver. These conditions tell us what standards have to be met for an experience to count as a perception. One of these conditions is that the Intentional object (or event) exist and another is that the (perceived) object cause the perceptual experience. On this account, the perceiver perceives the object (the real one out there) and not the visual experience. So Searle's account most emphatically is not, in any form, a sense data theory of perception. We don't observe or "have" sense data; and we do not infer what is out in the world via any such philosophical fictions since the perception as a whole is Intentional as well (i.e. it is about what it is we perceive). At this point, Searle confesses (boasts?) to being a kind of naive realist where whatever sorts of things are out there pretty much come to us the way we perceive them.

This is not the complete picture of perception by any means. For one thing, it does not take into account the role of context (what Searle calls Network and Background) in perception. For another, it does not explain how causes operate in a perceptual setting. I am holding the discussion of these concepts until later when they can be dealt with in a more direct and systematic way. Instead, then, of dealing with these concepts now, I next turn to a discussion of action.

Intentionality and action

If perception represents one of the biologically primary forms of Intentionality, action represents the other form. Understandably, then, Searle strives to show his readers how our actions fit into his theory of Intentionality. But before doing that he finds it necessary to talk about *intentions* since actions and intentions are intimately connected.

One cannot act without having either a prior intention or what Searle calls an intention-in-action. Prior intentions are just what they sound like. If I form an intention to take the refuse out in fifteen minutes, then, if in fifteen minutes I take out the smelly stuff, I am acting on a prior intention. But I needn't have a prior intention to act intentionally. I can act intentionally if I do so with just an intention-in-action. I can slap you in the face, throw the ball or pick up a book without a prior intention. Yet what I do is done intentionally, albeit spontaneously.

Like perception, action can be analyzed in terms of the by now familiar family of concepts pertaining to Intentionality. Presumably the conditions of satisfaction for my prior intention to take out the refuse have to do with actually taking it out. Presumably, as well, we can identify direction of fit, but now in opposite direction from what it was with perception. For action (and intentions) the world is made to fit the thought; rather than the thought the world. There is even a parallel with perception with respect to cause. With perception, part of the conditions of satisfaction is that what is perceived causes the perception. With action, the intention plays a similar role. For an act of a certain sort to be an act it must be the result of the prior intention (along with an intention-in-action), or the intention-in-action alone. Otherwise it is just an event or an occurrence. If Sam intends to raise his arm to ask the speaker a question but, a moment later, his arm moves up (as if he were raising it) because he suffers from a spasm, he has not performed an act. He certainly has not done what he intended to do even though to Sally, who knew of his intention, it would seem as if he had.

The parallel with perception continues when we consider our conscious experiences. With perception we have perceptual experience. With action we have what Searle calls the experience of action. This experience isn't necessary, for it is possible to act intentionally without it. Presumably this happens when Sam is walking (intentionally), but is focused on the curvaceous Sally who is walking a few steps ahead of him. He may at any moment have an experience of walking if he has to climb some steep steps to keep up with the fast-moving Sally. Otherwise he is on "cruise control" in so far as his walking is concerned, and thus not in any way consciously aware of his own walking. But normally various kinds of experiences accompany our intentions either before we do something or as we do it. And at least part of what these experiences are about is their Intentional content. We are aware of what it is we are doing which means that we are aware of the conditions of satisfaction (success) of the actions we intend to do.

So, putting the various portions of Searle's theory of action together, we have the following picture. When Sally has a prior intention to go to class she is, typically, aware of her intention. Being aware means that she knows what it takes for her intention to be carried out successfully. As she arrives in the classroom she knows that she has carried out her intention if the prior intention has caused her to have an intention-in-action, which intention-in-action also plays a causal role in getting her into the classroom. One can add here that her prior intention, and then later her intention-in-action, have a direction of fit where the world is made to match her intention.

Having given an account of simple (intentional) actions such as raising one's arm and walking to class, Searle is concerned to show that his Intentional theory of action can account for more complex actions, those that exhibit the so-called accordion effect. Here is his example of such a complex action.

Consider Gavrilo Princip and his murder of Archduke Franz Ferdinand in Sarajevo. Of Princip we say that he:
pulled the trigger

> fired the gun
> shot the Archduke
> killed the Archduke
> struck a blow against Austria
> avenged Serbia. (1983: 98)

If asked, and if he were willing to talk, Princip might very well have said something like "My intention was to kill the Archduke". The conditions of success of his actions are clear. He would succeed if the Archduke dies as a result of his intention which includes of course the intention to pull the trigger, to shoot straight, etc. He might also further explain his intention by adding that "My intent was to kill the Archduke and thereby to strike a blow against Austria and avenge Serbia". We can, Searle says, start in the middle and "extend the accordion up or down by earlier or later members of the sequence of intentions" (1983: 99). Of course the accordion effect has its limits. Presumably it wasn't part of Princip's intent to start World War I. Nor did he intend to get over ten million people killed in that war. Still, Searle notes, Intentionality and intentions can, as the Princip story shows, extend far beyond the trigger finger.

Searle is anxious to extend his theory of Intentionality still further. He does so by comparing actions and perceptions with desires and beliefs. The former pair of mental states, he tells us, exhibit causal self-referentiality. This means that our perceptions and actions identify their own causes. What we perceive counts as such when the perception's Intentional content tells us that the perception must be caused by the specific outside condition (or object) we perceive. And what we do counts as an action when the action's Intentional content tells us that the action must be caused by the intention in question. Through causal self-referentiality both our perceptions and actions are tied closely to reality. In contrast, because beliefs and desires lack causal self-referentiality I can, as it were, believe or desire almost anything. Searle says:

> Biologically speaking, the primary forms of Intentionality are perception and action, because by their very content they involve the organism in direct causal relations with the environment on which survival depends. Belief and desire are what is left over if you subtract the causal self-referentiality from the Intentional content of cognitive and volitive representational Intentional states. (1983: 105)

John Searle

Theory of causation

Given the central role of cause in his analysis of perception and action Searle finds himself having to answer two questions. The first has a long history. It asks: How can causes do their work between minds and bodies? It is all well and good to talk about how the red billiard ball causes the blue one to move; but how does a physical body move a mind and a mind move a body? To talk as Searle does of something mental such as an intention having a causal influence on one's body sounds mysterious enough to require a serious explanation.

The second question asks: How can an account of mental causation be made consistent with the generally accepted account of causation that goes back to Hume? Hume argued that cause is a correlation between two events and that we learn about this correlation by constant association. Searle asks: Is this really the way mental causation works?

He begins answering these question by contrasting third person with first person explanations. Third person explanations are the kind with which followers of Hume are most comfortable. In psychology they are thought of as objective accounts such as when stimulation type A is seen as regularly leading to behaviour of type B. We then explain why Sam exhibits type B behaviour by saying that he received A type stimulation, and add that A leads to B. In contrast, Searle presents us with the following example of a first-person explanation.

> suppose I am thirsty and I take a drink of water. If someone asks me why I took a drink of water, I know the answer without any further observation. I was thirsty. Furthermore, in this sort of case it seems that I know the truth of the counterfactual without any further observations or any appeal to general laws. I know if I hadn't been thirsty right then and there I would not have taken that very drink of water.
>
> (1983: 118)

There might be Humean-type causal laws that Searle could appeal to in order to explain why he picked up the glass of water and drank it. Deprive Searle of water for fifteen hours and we can fairly well predict that he will drink the glass of water offered him without hesitation. But, Searle tells us, his first-person explanations do not appeal to any law implicit in this prediction. Rather it

112

appeals directly to experience. Searle feels thirsty. But that thirst is not just a thirst, it is a thirst for water in his mouth and down his throat. That is, it is a thirst represented in thought as having Intentional content that identifies the thirst's conditions of success (satisfaction). The thirst, then, acts as a cause but also as an identifier of the effect. It tells us that the thirst makes the satisfaction of the thirst happen.

Cause and effect, for Searle, then, is just the business of making something happen. Here, once again, is Searle's way of expressing some of these ideas as he talks about raising his arm.

> In such cases we directly experience the causal relation, the relation of one thing making something else happen. I don't need a covering law to tell me that when I raised my arm I caused my arm to go up, because when I raised my arm I directly experienced the causing; I did not *observe* two events, the experience of acting and the movement of the arm, rather part of the Intentional content of the experience of acting was that that very experience was making my arm go up.
>
> (1983: 123)

Something makes something else happen with perception as well, only now the direction of fit is opposite so the cause and effect is reversed. The flower perceived (seen and smelled) by you and me makes certain experiences happen to each of us. Like those experiences when we act, perceptual experiences have Intentional content which content informs us of our perceptions' conditions of success. So the experience is both an effect (was made to happen) and an indicator of what it takes to make the perception veridical. To be sure, mistakes are always possible. We both might think we see (have an experience of seeing) the flower but in fact are hallucinating. Our doctor might very well have given us a mind-altering drug. However, barring the corrections in judgments we make when we learn we were drugged, we assume that we did see a flower when we thought we did.

In his account of action and perception, Searle has already begun to answer the two questions posed at the beginning of this section. The first asks: How can causes do their work between minds and bodies? His answer is that the first-person approach shows us how. We are biologically constructed to directly apprehend effects that we bring about through our actions, and effects on us brought about by objects we perceive. The second asks: How does Searle's account fit into the accepted Humean account of cause and effect? His answer is that in a very important sense it doesn't; and it needn't. Searle's account of causation rejects Hume's theory that cause and effect comes to us by regularities at least in so far as the Intentional part of our life is concerned. Our direct awareness of cause and effect (how things are made to happen) by-passes the need for discovering cause and effect through regularities in these matters. However, Searle concedes to Hume's theory that regularities play a part when we are concerned with causes and effects between events that have nothing to do with our experiences.

It works something like this. You as a child learn to manipulate a rock. This already involves trial and error; and repetition – since it takes you already beyond the direct cause and effect relationship you have with moving your arms, legs or any other part of your body. You also learn in this same way that by means of hitting the vase with a rock (Searle's example) the vase will break. It doesn't take you long to detach yourself from the rock and vase completely and learn that if the rock falls on the vase on its own (having rolled down the hill) it will break the vase.

When he turns to a discussion of the ontological status of cause, Searle is not so clear as he usually is. On the one hand he says:

> Just as I can directly experience a red object by seeing it, so I can directly experience the relation of one thing making another thing happen either by making something happen as in the case of action or by something making something happen to me as in the case of perception.   (1983: 123)

Here it sounds as if cause is out there in the world. Indeed he says in a somewhat earlier passage that he is a causal realist and:

> if we believe as I do that "cause" names a real relation in the real world, then the statement that that relation exists in a particular instance does not by itself entail a universal correlation of similar instances.   (1983: 121)

Yet in other passages he talks about cause as if it were just a part of experience and not something (separate) that is experienced. Thus he says:

> On my account the Humeans were looking in the wrong place. They sought causation (force, power, efficacy, etc.) as the object of perceptual experience and failed to find it. I am

suggesting that it was there all along as part of the content of both perceptual experiences and experiences of acting. When I see a red object or raise my arm I don't see causation or raise causation, I just see the flower and raise my arm. Neither flower nor movement is part of the *content* of the experience, rather each is an *object* of the relevant experience. But in each case causation is part of the content of the experience of that object. (1983: 124)

I would suggest that a plausible account of what Searle is saying is that there is a separation between the experience of causation and causation. We experience causation in an Intentional mode but what we experience is not the whole of what cause is. Of course we don't "see" cause the way we see flowers and we don't experience causation the way we do the raising of an arm. But cause is a real relation "out there" which we experience directly when we are concerned with Intentionality. It is the same relation when Intentionality is not an issue (e.g. snow sliding down the mountain when the temperature rises), but that our experiences in coming to know about cause and effect in these settings are different. Searle's criticism of the Humeans is then not that they are all wrong about cause and effect, but that they are concerned exclusively with only one way of knowing about this relationship. Their story would be complete if they took, as Searle has, Intentional causation into account.

There is more to be said about causation (in the next chapter). However before continuing that discussion some new concepts need to be introduced.

Notes

1. There is some unfinished business with the publication of *Foundations of Illocutionary Logic* in 1985 (co-authored with Daniel Vanderveken). This book is about getting the details of speech act theory right, rather than getting on to new ideas.
2. Searle capitalizes "Intentionality" (of our psychological states) to distinguish it from intentionality in the sense of "I intend to be at the party". I will follow that practice in this work even though Searle does not do so in some of his later works.
3. It is noteworthy that in his review of *Intentionality* (1984) Richard Rorty takes little interest in the main subject matter of the book. He says "There is not much point in asking, 'Does Searle get Intentionality right?' for most of us have no particular intuitions about aboutness-as-such, and would not

know what to measure a theory of Intentionality against". Instead, he turns his review in other directions, including those having to do with Searle's quarrels with Dennett and others who deny the importance of Intentionality, consciousness and the family of mental concepts that Searle is so fond of. It is as if Rorty is telling his readers: Why should we bother with detailed analyses of obsolete and unimportant concepts?

4. See Armstrong for a contrary view. He says "I do not think that there are any phenomenal properties linked with perceiving, or indeed, any other mental state or item" (1991: 155). What we perceive (the content) differentiates one experience from another; not perceptual experience as such. He says: "... the only qualities involved in perception are those involved in the intentional content of the perception. These qualities are qualities of *external objects*" (1991: 155).

Chapter 6

Network and Background in mental states and language

Network

A very important portion of Searle's story concerning mental states and language has yet to be told. Although this portion is intrinsic to the whole, it can best be told as if it were separate. Loosely speaking this portion has to do with the setting or context. Mental states, Searle insists, are not formed in an atomistic setting. Typically we do not have mental states that can be fully understood – indeed understood at all – in isolation from other mental states. Similarly, speech acts are not issued in isolation. Typically they are formed in a setting of other speech acts, mental states, and physical and social conditions.

Here is a variation of the example Searle presents to introduce us to what he will call the Network portion of the context. You develop a desire to become the political leader of your country (to become its president, prime minister or whatever). You express this desire linguistically by announcing your candidacy to your fellow party members and the public. But you and we can only understand what you are thinking and saying if we assume that there are political parties in your country and you are a member of one of these parties; if a process for running for office is in place; if there are rules (laws) that tell us that it is appropriate for you to run for office at this time; if you are eligible to run for such office and so on. In other words, you don't just run for office but you do so in a setting of well understood practices and beliefs. Without a Network, your expressed desire to run for office is a meaningless gesture. It would be as if you announced that you were running for the office of chancellor in Germany just after the start of World War II.

The presence of the Network is not restricted to social and institutional settings such as running for political office, getting married and signing contracts. Scientific and other observational claims also get their meaning in a Network. "Her temperature is 98.6 degrees Fahrenheit" is not just an isolated belief or claim. It is embedded in our knowledge of the behaviour of mercury under different temperature conditions, our sense of what temperature or heat is, how we take the temperature of a living human, the operations of the human body etc. The Network, then, is composed of an almost indefinite number of Intentional states or claims that nest individual mental states and/or claims and, thereby, help give them meaning. That is, it is only when these states and/or claims are properly nested that we can determine their conditions of satisfaction (success). But there is more to the context for Searle than the Network.

Background

The best way to show what more there is, is to return to Searle's article "Literal Meaning" and his cat-is-on-the-mat example (1979a: 117–36). Recall that Searle suggests that "The cat is on the mat" is a good candidate as a context-free utterance (1979a: 120–21). If any example should make "atomists" happy about truth claims, this one should do it. But consider that when we believe the cat is on the mat we assume we are not in space where it might become difficult to tell whether the mat is on the cat or the cat on the mat, and that gravity is doing its work to keep the cat in place. We also assume that mats, although not rigid themselves, act as if they are when placed on a rigid floor, that cats don't change into flowers every morning and into soup in the afternoon.

In "Literal Meaning" Searle also considers directives (and desires that correspond with them) such as "Give me a hamburger, medium rare, with ketchup and mustard, but easy on the relish" and the context in which such an utterance is normally found.

> I will remark first of all that a prodigious amount of background information has already been invoked even by the example as so far described – entire institutions of restaurants and money and exchanging foods for money, for a start; and it

is hard to see how the sentence could have quite the same obedience conditions if these institutions did not exist, or if the same sentence were uttered in a radically different context, if for example the sentence were uttered by a priest as a part of a prayer or tacked onto the end of his inaugural swearing in by an incoming President of the US. (1979a: 127)

Some of these background conditions he admits might be better thought of as part of the Network rather than the Background. Although he concedes that there is no sharp line separating the two, Network might apply better here since these conditions are near the surface of our consciousness. They form a cluster of utterances (or beliefs) that, by definition, possess Intentionality. In contrast, Background presumptions are pre-Intentional. They are so fundamental to our thinking that we normally do *not* articulate (in Intentional terms) what influence they have on us. Contemplating his hamburger further Searle says:

Suppose for example that the hamburger is brought to me encased in a cubic yard of solid lucite plastic so rigid that it takes a jack hammer to bust it open, or suppose the hamburger is a mile wide and is "delivered" to me by smashing down the wall of the restaurant and sliding the edge of it in. Has my order "Give me a hamburger . . ." been fulfilled or obeyed in these cases? My inclination is to say no, it has not . . . because that is not what I meant in my literal utterance of the sentence . . ." (1979a: 127)

Of course the literal utterance could be modified to say "Give me a hamburger . . . not in lucite and not a mile long". But it is not likely to be. It would be presumed that, if anything, the hamburger is contained in a sack rather than in lucite and is sized for eating. These presumptions are so much taken for granted that they are rarely, if ever, stated. Searle gives some other examples of background presumptions that have their effect on us in one setting or another.

elections are held at or near the surface of the earth; the things people walk on are generally solid; people only vote when awake; objects offer resistance to touch and pressure. (1983: 142)

Some of these examples fall under the heading that he calls local Background. They are coloured by cultural factors and include our reactions to cars, doors, and, Searle's favourite example, bottled beer. Deep background examples have to do with how we react to such objects in the world as air and gravity. Presumably all humans operate in their lives under the influence of these deep Background conditions.

But, as already noted, if the Background is pre-Intentional and not typically talked about or known cognitively, how do we come into contact with it? How does it influence us? Searle's answer is in terms of knowing how. We can talk about the solidity of a table and treat it as a belief (knowing that it is a table), but its solidity is best seen as influencing us in terms of how we deal with tables in our daily lives. If we know that we can place computers, books and pencils on tables, lean on them, eat and work on them, and even stand on them on occasion, then we have a knowing-how understanding that the table is solid. We don't have in addition a belief that the table is solid. It is solid in so far as we know how to deal with it as solid. He nicely summarizes this point about knowing how in the following passage.

> The Background is a set of nonrepresentational mental capacities that enable all representing to take place. Intentional states only have the conditions of satisfaction that they do, and thus only are the states that they are, against a Background of abilities that are not themselves Intentional states. In order that I can now have Intentional states that I do I must have certain kinds of know-how: I must know how things are and I must know how to do things, but the kinds of "know-how" in question are not, in these cases forms of "knowing that".
>
> (1983: 143)

So far, then, Searle's account of the influence of context on us looks like this. When most speech acts (possessing derived Intentionality) are issued, they are embedded in a Network of other speech acts or thoughts. These other speech acts or thoughts possess Intentionality. In theory a few speech acts may not be embedded in a Network (e.g. "I am in pain") but even they suffer further embedding in the Background. The Background's influence on us is pre-Intentional so we come to know of it primarily in terms of our reactions rather than through cognition.

Together the Network and Background make it possible us for us to determine the conditions of satisfaction (success) of the speech acts we issue. Notice how this works in the following series of speech acts issued by our friend Sam.

A "Joe is running."
B "The engine is running."
C "The car is running."
D "Joe is running his father's business."

According to Searle the meaning of "running" in A to C is the same. Sam is using the same word and using it literally in each case. To deny this is to multiply meanings of "running" to the point of absurdity (1983: 145–8; 1991d: 291–2;1998: 107–9). But if the meaning, the semantic content of "running" is the same, why is it that we need to do different things to determine when each of these assertive speech acts is true or false? The answer is that the Network and Background of each is different. Our assumptions about humans running are different from those about engines running; and these two in turn have different assumptions from a car running. We can appreciate this even more if we consider how we would be puzzled if we heard Sam say:

E "The building is running."

The problem here is not that we fail to understand the meaning of the words. There is no problem with the semantic content of Sam's utterance. Rather, we don't know what the context of the utterance is as we do with D ("Joe is running his father's business"). Buildings don't normally run. The Network and Background related to buildings don't allow for that sort of activity. Hence our puzzlement. With E we either assume that Sam is, once again, on drugs and thus behaving and speaking in strange ways, or we start thinking he is speaking metaphorically (e.g. telling us that the lifts in the building are running smoothly and that the electrical and plumbing systems are also functioning well) as in "The building is running well".

Searle concedes that it is not easy to talk about the Background because, in part, we just don't normally talk about it – we take it for granted. It is not even obvious that our everyday language is geared to talk about the Background in a clear fashion. As a result there can be a certain lack of clarity about the Background's (and the Network's) status (Searle 1983: 153–4; Stroud 1991: 251–2). Is the Background something out there in the world, that is, is it some sort of metaphysical entity? Is the Background a relational something between us and what is out there? Or is it something mental?

When talking about the Background as "context" or "setting" it is indeed tempting to think of it as something out there, as a metaphysical notion. Or perhaps the temptation is to talk about it as some combination of entities independent of us and certain kinds of social constructs. Searle finds some merit in this latter way of talking. The Background certainly has something to do with where we find ourselves while eating, driving, buying a refrigerator, using a computer or whatever.

But Searle finds more merit in thinking of the Background as mental. Why? Recall that the Background manifests itself in us as abilities, capacities and dispositions. Although the Background has to do with where we are (out there), it is how we react to what is out there that matters. You and I "assume" that the ground is firm enough for walking and running. Otherwise we don't venture onto it. You and I "assume" that the car we just bought won't change into a pile of dirt in an hour or two. Otherwise we wouldn't spend good money buying or repairing it. We also "assume" the money itself won't change into a cluster of roses. Although the Background has to do with what is out there, it is our reaction to the world out there that constitutes what Searle means by Background. In this sense he can say, paradoxical as it may sound, that the Background is in our heads.

It is perhaps better to say that various Backgrounds are found in our heads (Searle 1991d: 291). Of course talking this way could create a problem. If each of us had a different Background (which, of course, we do up to a point) we would easily lapse into solipcism and communication would be impossible. Each mind to itself! But happily the world out there is one we share. We all walk on a planet with a certain amount of gravity, we walk upright, we breathe air, we have physical structures that share many qualities and the beer we drink stays generally in the barrels, bottles and cans that beer manufacturers put it in. So although each of us has his own Background in his own brain, the various Backgrounds have enough in common to make communication and social activities among us possible.

Implications

The doctrines of Network and Background have implications for Searle beyond those having to do with how we understand language. First, these doctrines affect how we view one of the classic questions in philosophy of science discussed in the previous chapter. According to Searle, the classic view of how cause and effect work presupposes a general principle, a hypothesis or a theory about regularity. Supposedly, according to Mill, among others, this general principle helps us to justify the process of induction. In other words, on this account, we need to have an (Intentional) belief about regularity in the universe to fully justify how we make science work.

But Searle says that if I investigate the causal relationships between two phenomena by employing a trial and error procedure, I do not need to have a belief about the regularity of nature in place. Our presumption about regularity is not a belief but part of the Background.

> trial and error only has its point against a Background presumption of general regularities. I don't hold a *hypothesis* that the world is such that causal relations manifest general regularities, but rather a condition of the possibility of my applying the notion of making something happen is my ability to make some distinction between cases where something really made something happen and cases where it only seemed to make something happen; and a condition of the possibility of that distinction is at least the presumption of some degree of regularity. In investigating the distinction between apparent and real cases of causal relations, as in any investigation, I adopt a certain stance. Having that stance will not consist solely in a set of beliefs: the stance is in part a matter of Background capacities. In investigating how the world actually works with causes and effects the presumption of regularities is part of the Background. (1983: 133)

So there is no additional principle of regularity above the particular causal laws we uncover when we engage in scientific activity. Rather, there is the presumption of regularity without which the notion of cause and effect (making something happen) would make no sense. It follows from Searle's views that it also makes no sense to try to justify the concept of making something happen in terms of regularity. Regularity is distinct categorically from making something happen. It is pre-Intentional while cause and effect talk is Intentional. The pre-Intentional cannot be given an analysis in terms of Intentionality without distortion.

For Searle, the Background assumption of regularity probably goes beyond our concern with issues in philosophy of science. Although he doesn't say so explicitly, this Background assumption works its effects on all of life. Consider how any of life's activities would be impossible if this assumption were not in place. In everyday life we expect to wake up and be where we were when we went to sleep. Unless we are travelling, the regularity of things is taken for granted. We expect our keys to be where we put them last night. We don't expect them to move or transform themselves into books, chairs or dogs. The furniture, the house we live in the street near our house we expect to be roughly the same tomorrow as they were yesterday. We expect to have the same friends and enemies tomorrow as we did yesterday and so on. If life did not have regularity we would not know what to make of it.

Searle provides us with a similar analysis of ontological issues – a second area where the doctrine of the Network and Background has implications. As noted already (Chapter 5), Searle says he is a realist. There are people out there in the world doing things as well as cars moving about, buildings, houses and mountains standing still, rivers flowing and all the rest. But our belief in the reality of all these things is not really a belief. Realism is not a hypothesis or a theory to be justified by presenting evidence or arguments.

> There can't be a fully meaningful question "Is there a real world independent of my representation of it?" because the very having of representations can only exist against a Background which gives representations the character of "representing something." This is not to say that realism is a true hypothesis, rather it is to say that it is not a hypothesis at all, but the precondition of having hypotheses.   (1983: 159)

So in spite of his contextual leanings Searle counts himself as a realist but one who admits he cannot prove his "position". We are committed to realism, instead, by how we react to things in the world. If one acts as if the house one lives in, the beer one drinks and so on are real then they are. I will have more to say about Searle's realism in Chapter 11.

The third area where we find the doctrine of Network and Background has implications is concerned with how we understand rules and, in turn, with how learning takes place. There are of course various kinds of rules. There are rules pertaining to skills as when one learns to play a game such as tennis and is told to hold the racket in a certain way, to turn one's side to the net when hitting the ball from the back court, to bend one's knees and to keep one's wrist stiff. There are also rules having less to do with skills as with adopting a set pattern of behaviour. These might be invoked at work where a rule might say you must come to work on time, not leave early, take a break for no more than five minutes, dress in a certain way, keep your distance from members of the opposite sex, and so on. Ethical or moral rules are like these work rules in that they too encourage us to adopt patterns of behaviour.

Searle does not disparage the role of rules in our lives. He cites their role especially in the early stages of the learning process. Rules are useful for beginners. Our teachers invoke rules to teach us to play tennis and ski. In so far as they do, they are involved in issuing speech acts that possess Intentional content. Once we hear and understand their speech acts we invoke the rules in such a way that the invocation plays an Intentional causal role in controlling our behaviour. Yes, I am supposed to bend my knees and keep my rear end low when hitting the tennis ball. And, yes, I do bend my knees and keep my rear end low. And, yes, the ball successfully goes over the net out of my opponent's reach.

The question that interests Searle is: What happens next? What happens after the knee bending has been successfully practised a hundred times or so? One thing that is clear is that the rule no longer has to be invoked so frequently. On one interpretation the rule still does its work but now does it on the unconscious level. It is as if the rule is still there, is still being invoked but being invoked silently and automatically. The idea seems to be that if the rule weren't doing its work, we wouldn't be successfully bending our knees and keeping our rear ends low. Knowing how to behave, that is, having the skill, demands that the rule still be in place even if one were no longer aware that it is.

This is *not* Searle's account. For him rules do not become internalized but instead they disappear. Their place is taken by capacities, abilities, skills, or what have you, that are "realized as neural pathways (1983: 150).

> "Practice makes perfect" not because practice results in a perfect memorization of the rules, but because repeated practice enables the body to take over and the rules recede into the Background. (1983: 150)

Actually they don't recede, they are replaced. In playing a game like tennis, Intentionality and intentions may still be present. Presumably the player still can move the ball intentionally (and with Intentionality) first to the opponent's backhand, then to the forehand and then to the backhand again, thereby running the opponent to exhaustion. However, the way the player hits the ball no longer involves the intentional invoking of rules (and Intentionality) because rules are no longer needed. The settled neuronal patterns now take over.

The situation may be more complicated than that. It is possible for the rules to be still in place in the Network and thereby be present unconsciously – or perhaps it is better to say are present not-consciously. Presumably that can happen at an intermediary state when the player does things right often, but not often enough. But with more successful practice the non-conscious rules fade away eventually, and the neurons and the other parts of the body take over (as Background).

Presumably Searle's account of how rules work can be applied to adopting a set pattern of behaviour that has little to do with developing a physical or mental skill. In ethics we cite rules, like we do when learning physical skills, for purposes of teaching. And like the physical skills we also cite rules as reminders to stop the learner from backsliding. But the rules can be moved to the non-conscious level of the Network when there is good progress in establishing a set pattern of behaviour (such as telling the truth). But beyond that, the rules can become irrelevant for a person whose behaviour truly becomes habitual and thus comes to be called virtuous. Saints only need rules to teach others about right and wrong. For controlling their own lives, they can get along quite well without rules.

Searle's account of how we use rules and the role of the Background in making them eventually irrelevant helps to show how the conflict between the advocates of rules in ethics, on the one side, and the advocates of the virtues, on the other, is not really a conflict. A conflict gets generated only when one side or the other insists that its way of characterizing what ethics is about is the only way. Advocates of the virtues might argue that since acting properly in ethics is a matter of acting from a sense of character, that is, from habit, rules are of no importance. Virtue thinkers might go on to say that rules have little or no role at all to play in ethics. And of course they would be right if they were thinking only

of angels and their close associates – as we have seen, angelic people, like natural athletes, don't need moral teachers to teach them
the Ten Commandments or any other set of rules – but they would
be wrong if they thought that rules have no role to play with those
who have yet to achieve angelic or near angelic status.

On the other side rule advocates make a mistake when they
think that the virtues have little or no role to play in ethics. The
virtues play at best a secondary role when we are first learning
how we should act or first learning about the kind of person we
want to be. But rule advocates might even deny this. They might go
on to argue that we cite rules on the conscious level and then cite
these rules later on the unconscious level.

Searle rejects both the virtue theorist's and the rule advocate's
stance since each tells us only part of the story. Searle thinks his
account, which has a strong place for the Background in it, tells us
more than that. It tells us the whole story, one where both the
rules and virtues play their separate roles in ethical life.

Chapter 7

Rediscovering the mind

Searle's incredulity

Searle's *Intentionality* (1983) looks both backward and forward. It looks backward by telling us about language, his old interest. It tells us that Intentionality found in language is derived from Intentionality found in the mind. Humans impose Intentionality on language, but find it naturally in the mind. So *Intentionality* helps to complete Searle's views in philosophy of language. But it also looks forward in that it anticipates some of the controversial things he says in philosophy of mind in *Rediscovery of the Mind* (1992a) and in other writings.

It is interesting that Searle does not quite understand what some of these controversies are about. As he sees it in *Rediscovery*, many of his views in philosophy of mind are so obviously true that it is hard to imagine anyone disputing them. Searle is incredulous about the reactions of some philosophers and scientists to his views concerning four features of the mind. First and foremost among them is his view about the importance of consciousness for the studies of philosophy of mind and psychology. It seems obvious to Searle that conscious mental phenomena such as pains, feelings associated with being touched, visual experiences, beliefs, intentions, various emotional feelings and the like need to be accounted for in these studies (1989a: 193–4). It puzzles him, therefore, when those he labels logical behaviourists seem to deny the importance and even the existence of consciousness.

Searle associates logical behaviourism with such writers as Carl Hempel (1949) and Gilbert Ryle (1949). He characterizes these writers as saying that "it is a matter of definition, a matter of logical analysis, that sentences about the mind can be translated without any residue into sentences about behavior" (1992a: 33). But these classic writers in analytic philosophy are not the only ones guilty of ignoring or discounting the notion of consciousness. Identity theorists (Place 1956; Smart 1959) argue that mental states are identical with brain states, and then go on to generally ignore what might be said of mental states by talking about brain states almost exclusively.

Functionalists similarly ignore mental states (Lycan 1987; Van Gulick1995). They translate sentences containing mental terms such as "believe" and "see" so as to get along without these terms. If an ordinary thermostat had mental experiences, a functional account would not mention these experiences but rather would explain them, or simply talk, in terms of how the thermostat works. The account would go something like this. When the mercury in the thermostat is placed in a warmer environment than it was moment before (input condition), it expands and thus gives us a "warmer" measurement of temperature (output condition). The cause (heat or cold) brings about an effect (expansion or contraction of the mercury). To know how the thermostat works, it is enough to know about certain cause and effect relationships. The same is true with humans according to the functionalist account. With them, it works something like this. To say that Sam hates Butch is to say that when Sam receives Butch like stimuli (causes), he is prone to react by throwing things, using foul language, having his blood pressure rise, and so on. Talking about mental states is, thereby, by-passed in favour of presenting causal kinds of explanations.

Writers committed to the doctrine that Searle calls strong artificial intelligence (AI) similarly by-pass consciousness in describing and explaining psychological phenomena (Chomsky 1986; Fodor 1975; Marr 1982; Newell 1982). These writers are taken by the analogy to the computer. For them, the mind is to the brain as a computer program is to the computer hardware in which it is instantiated. Thus, the job of psychologists is to focus attention on the mind as a program. These writers say that we need not worry about the hardware (the brain), although we can if such worry proves fruitful. But in so far as the mind as a program is the centre of attention, and the processes inside of us (such as long-term and short term memory) are identified and described, there is no need to be concerned about various forms of consciousness and how they work. Once we come to know about the mind as a program, according to the strong AI doctrine, we will know all we want to know about understanding and predicting human behaviour. Consciousness is either superfluous (epiphenomenal) or can be ignored, as if it did not exist.

At least one other group of writers by-pass, downplay or deny the existence of consciousness. These are the eliminative materialists (Churchland 1981; Stich 1983). These writers often are seen as downright deniers. They attack the family of mental concepts such as belief, pain, emotion, etc. by claiming that together they help form what they call a theory of folk psychology. They see this theory as on a par with theories held by ordinary people and early scientists about physical phenomena before modern physics came on the scene. In time, of course, the older theories, with their attending concepts like absolute space, phlogiston, rocks striving to reach the centre of the planet, etc., died out and were replaced with modern theories and new concepts (e.g. such as mass, acceleration, electron, and photon). So the eliminative materialists argue that folk psychology with all (most?) of its attending concepts should (will?) be thrown in the dust heap of old and bad theories.

Searle replies to the eliminative materialists, but really all of those who discount the role of consciousness, by denying that the family of consciousness concepts forms a theory. These concepts might be used to develop a theory but, in and of themselves, they merely represent a cluster of descriptive concepts. Indeed, these concepts are central to understanding mental phenomena. They need to be accounted for and explained, not discounted or explained away.

If consciousness is the first obvious feature that needs to be emphasized in the study of the mind, the second is the mind's subjectivity. By subjective Searle means something ontological rather than epistemological. Mental states have an "irreducibly subjective ontology" (1992a: 19). It is an objective fact that we have subjective experiences. Such experiences have a first-person character such that only the person who has a conscious state can know about them directly. This subjective status of mental phenomena helps explain why so many thinkers practise their discounting strategies when it comes to dealing with consciousness. They look at consciousness from the epistemological point of view only. Further, they are convinced that science can only deal with objective phenomena. Thus, if anyone argues that mental phenomena are subjective, the "discounters" reply by saying that such a confession shows that the mind cannot be studied scientifically. To the extent that psychology involves the study of subjective phenomena, to that extent it is oxymoronic.

But Searle counters that such a judgment is premature. The mistake made by the discounters is to assume "same-behaviour-ergo-same-mental phenomena". By studying just behaviour they cannot help but conclude that humans and robots both have minds if, indeed, they both behave in the same or similar way. They also cannot help but ignore the subjectivity of the mind since they insist that they cannot study it objectively. But, says Searle, if we operate on a "same-cause-same-effects" principle instead, and if we take biology into account we can begin to think about studying the mind scientifically. We know that humans, dogs and cats have (subjectively) conscious experiences because we look at how they behave and also how they are constructed. We see that dogs and cats have eyes, ears, skin and noses that all work like our eyes, ears, skin and noses. We look at robots and see they do not have eyes, ears, skin and noses that work like our eyes, ears, skin and noses. So we draw the obvious conclusions. These other animals are conscious the way we are, but robots are not.

Neither dualism nor monism

This leads to the third obvious (for Searle) feature of mental phenomena. One of science's basic strategies is to explain phenomena occurring on the macro level in terms of ones occurring on the micro. We give accounts of physical things such as tables, chairs, aeroplanes and trousers eventually in terms of atomic and subatomic particles. Biological phenomena are explained in a similar fashion. Digestion which takes place in the stomach is explained, in part, by the action of cells located there; and these cells are accounted for, in turn, in terms of smaller cells and so on. It is the same with consciousness. Consciousness represents the macro level (Searle 1983: 265–71). The operations on that level can be explained, be accounted for or caused by the brain according to Searle. This is an empirical claim for him, a claim for which he thinks there is ample evidence. Here is how he expresses it:

Consciousness, in short, is a biological feature of human and certain animal brains. It is caused by neurobiological processes and is as much a part of the natural biological order as any other biological features such as photosynthesis, *digestion, or mitosis.* (1992a: 90)

The picture he draws about these goings-on is one of cause and effect where complicated processes in our nervous system have evolved so that they create consciousness in us. Consciousness and its subjectivity are emergent features of what happens on the micro biological level(s) (1992a: 14–15). Implied in this claim is that the existence and nature of the emergent features could not have been predicted (in advance) through knowledge of the micro level. So the various conscious states represent higher order functions of the brain, just as digestion represents higher order functions of the stomach. Searle concludes his thoughts about these matters as follows.

The fact that a feature is mental does not imply that it is not physical; the fact that a feature is physical does not imply that it is not mental. Revising Descartes for a moment, we might say not only "I think therefore I am" and "I am a thinking being," but also *I am a thinking being, therefore I am a physical being.* (1992a: 14–15)

Although Searle thinks of his thesis as uncontroversial, he has found controversy nonetheless. Opponents to his thesis point to a major difference between the emergent character of consciousness and other emergent features. The emergent feature of being a smooth table is still a third-person objective feature just as are the atoms and electrons. The emergent feature of digestion is also an objective feature just as are the cells in the stomach (found on the micro level). But the emergent feature of consciousness is a first-person subjective feature. It supposedly arises from the third-person objective micro features of the brain. This sounds mysterious to say the least. How could such a switch from third-person to emergent first-person features happen? How can this emergent gap be bridged?

I will deal with Searle's response shortly. In the meantime, notice how our doubts about bridging encourage a reaffirmation of views contrary to Searle's. On the one side, some critics will take a dualist stance. To be sure, many of these critics are substantival dualists in the spirit of Descartes and the Christian tradition, and so argue that the body is a substance with its properties and the mind is also a substance with its. Searle has little patience with this version of dualism arguing that it just doesn't fit well with our scientific knowledge. He is more concerned with the so called property dualists with whom one might think he would have a good deal of sympathy (Nagel 1974; 1986; McGinn 1991; 1999). This position, and also the most general dualist position that he labels conceptual dualism, hold that mental and physical properties exclude one another. That is, these forms of dualism are committed to what Searle calls the exclusion principle. To claim that belief is a mental feature or property is to claim that it cannot be talked of in physical terms. At the same time, to identify a so-called mental property such as a learned response or a feeling in terms of neuronal connections or some "cognitive program" is to deny that one can think of it as truly mental. These dualists, then, are in the thrall of the gap between the mind and the body. The unique emergent features of the mind encourages them to think that what Searle is telling us doesn't make sense since for him the mental is physical. For them, in contrast, to talk of mental phenomena as also being physical phenomena is, once again, to talk oxymoronically.

Surprisingly, the materialist response on the other side is similar. In a sense materialists are dualists as well since they also accept the exclusion principle. They believe that mind and material talk have nothing to do with one another. These materialists part company with the dualists, however, simply by giving up on the mind (consciousness and all the rest) since the subjectivity of the mind, its first-person character, does not lend itself to scientific study. Better to work with the body, and forget all that subjective stuff, since only the body can be dealt with on a third-person objective basis.

It is clear that Searle sits uncomfortably between the two sides, with each side demanding that he confess his sins. But Searle insists that he is not the sinner. It is his opponents who have sinned by trying to frame him into an outmoded and wrongheaded conceptual scheme. The basic scheme causing most of the problems is conceptual dualism. As noted above, this is the most general dualist doctrine encompassing all forms of dualism and even materialism. It holds that mental concepts exclude physical ones, and vice versa.. In contrast, Searle claims that the physical world is able to manifest itself subjectively. For him, it is a fact of nature that when the nervous systems of certain complex organisms developed in certain ways, those systems yielded various states of (subjective) consciousness. So consciousness is a natural phenomenon. If, then, it turns out that this position is not easily, or not at all, describable in terms of the classic positions in philosophy of mind and science, so much the worse for these classic positions.

The causal roles of mind

There is a fourth thesis to Searle's theory of philosophy of mind that he finds obvious. The mind has causal powers. Patients may believe they are receiving medicine to relieve their ills when, in fact, they are receiving a placebo. Nonetheless, it is well known clinically that many of these placebo patients get physical relief. Beliefs apparently can cause physical changes. On a more conscious level, almost anyone can trigger physiological changes of the appropriate kind by dwelling on the thought or a vivid image of a juicy steak, a cold Coca Cola or an attractive and unsuitably undressed member of the opposite sex. Further, mental thoughts can trigger gross bodily changes as when tennis players decide to serve wide on their opponents in a tennis match and then do so. Searle diagrams these causal patterns in *Intentionality* (1983: 270) as follows. The diagram is somewhat modified. In the upper left-hand corner Searle mentions only intention-in-action. I have added "and/or mental states" thereby generalizing his account.

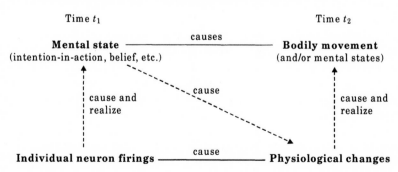

This is a crude diagram but it helps give an overall sense of what Searle is saying. It shows that the biological mechanisms on the lower level of the diagram have their causal effects on the upper level *not* over a period of time (Searle 1995b: 218). The emergent changes on the upper level are simultaneous with respect to what happens (vertically) below. Such is not the case when the mind affects the body on any level. Here cause and effect act over time, both when the mind brings about physiological changes (on the cell, muscle, etc. levels) or bodily movements. Think here of the juicy steak again. The thought of the steak triggers salivation, etc. These kind of changes are like billiard-ball cause and effect changes. The red ball hits the blue one and, *then,* the blue ball moves.

As modified, the diagram also shows how it is possible for a mental state to cause another mental state as when a visual experience causes people to change their beliefs. "If I had never seen it with my own eyes, I never would have believed it would rain today." The mind-to-mind cause and effect relationship seems like the conjurer's trick. How can one mind-state directly affect another mind-state in *Searle's* account of things? Perhaps substantival dualists would have no problem answering this question. Since, for them, the mind is a substance or entity operating in its own sphere, indeed operating exclusively in that sphere, only the mind would seem capable of effecting mental changes.

But Searle denies he is a dualist of any sort. He insists he is not even a property dualist. Recall that a property dualist claims that the mental and the physical represent two irreducible kinds of properties that seemingly run on separate tracks (Searle 1992a: 54; ibid. 1995b: 221). So when Searle says that one mental state brings about another mental state, he cannot mean that this happens directly. He must mean that one mental state (which remember is a macro biological condition that manifests itself in first-person subjectivity) affects physiological changes (represented in the diagram above as moving from the upper left to the lower right and taking place over time); which changes, in turn, bring about another macro mental state (going from lower right vertically to upper right and not taking place over time). Thus the perception that it is raining does not directly lead to the belief about the rain. We talk, misleadingly, as if it happens that way. "I saw it rain (it hasn't rained for over three months), now I believe it." But the way it happens is that the perception causes physiological changes in the brain and perhaps in other locations in the nervous system, and that these changes, in turn, alter our belief from "It isn't raining" to "It is".

Features of consciousness

In outline, then, Searle's theory of philosophy of mind involves four claims – all of them obvious to him but, yet, all of them contested by some group of thinkers or other. To repeat, these four claims are that:

- we and many other creatures have varied conscious states;
- although these states can have objective status epistemologically, they manifest themselves ontologically as first-person subjective, not third-person objective, states (as do other states familiar to science);
- these states have biological causes and are themselves biological;[1]
- these states are not idle epiphenomena since they have causal impact.[2]

Beyond outlining his position on the mind, Searle needs to present us with the details. That is part of the job of anyone working in the area of philosophy of mind. But beyond even that, Searle thinks that a more detailed account is required to help show why what he finds obvious about the mind is not obvious to Dennett, Churchland and others working in their tradition. These thinkers act on certain misconceptions that lead them down the path of saying foolish things about the mind and, worse, of adopting practices damaging to the study of psychology and the other sciences related to psychology.

What are the characteristic features of consciousness? There are many (Searle 1992a: Ch. 6). Working as it were from the inside first and then gradually moving to the outside, there are two closely related, but not identical, features: viz., Intentionality and subjectivity. You see *the table*, John hates *Joan*, Adam is aware *of the ghost in the machine* and so on. The Intentionality feature of our conscious experiences points to something real or unreal, concrete or abstract. Sometimes this feature of the mind is expressed linguistically as consciousness *of* something whatever that something might be. But, as we saw in Chapter 5 of this work, that way of expressing things can be misleading. A doctor can ask a patient "Are you [first-person subjectively] conscious *of* any pain?" This makes it seem as if the pain is one thing and our consciousness of it another, much like a tree is one thing and our consciousness of it is another. However the doctor could have asked "Are you in pain?" or "Do you have any pain?" and, thereby, less misleadingly suggest that the awareness and the pain are indistinguishable and that no Intentionality is present. The same can be said about "That tickles" and "That [the rubdown] feels good". The subjective state in each of these cases may have a cause (the doctor pushes here and causes the pain, the good friend tickles a foot and the masseur rubs the back) and each experience may have a location, but these experiences themselves have no Intentionality.

There are some other non-Intentional first-person states that point to a third "close-in" conscious feature of the mind. An experience, whatever it is, can be tinged with pleasure or "un-pleasure". Here Searle is thinking of various ways that an experience can be tinged including ecstasy, enchantment, enthusiasm, amusement, boredom, irritation and disgust.

Mood is the fourth non-Intentional feature of consciousness. It overlaps the pleasure/"un-pleasure" dimension but differs from it mainly in being more pervasive, more long lasting (more dispositional). When Sam is depressed and Susie cheerful they are that way all day or, possibly, that way for days, weeks or longer.

The fifth close-in and pervasive feature of consciousness is familiarity. Familiarity is not a separate feeling or experience so Searle talks of it as an "aspect of familiarity". Perhaps another way to talk about this feature is in terms of a sense of familiarity. However it is characterized, it has to do with what we take for granted when we walk into the bedroom and everything is as it was before, or when we put on our clothes but hardly notice what we are doing. Unfamiliarity hits us when something to which we are not paying particular attention looks awry. The clock is not in its usual place, the dresser is in disorder, the shoe does not fit the way it has been fitting all along (it got wet during yesterday's rain) and so on. Although he doesn't say so, one would suppose that familiarity extends beyond Intentional states to non-Intentional ones. I am not just familiar with my family, the house, the car, the street, my office and so on but also with the certain pain I have in my shoulder and the anxiety attack that comes over me from time to time for (seemingly) no reason at all.

Familiarity is related to another – sixth – feature of consciousness viz., aspectuality. Actually Searle does not list it as an independent feature so much as a feature attached to Intentionality. All Intentionality is aspectual. By this he means that since conscious experience comes to us always from a point of view, each of us focuses on a different aspect of whatever it is we are attending to. I see the house from my perspective which is somewhat to the right of where you are standing. Consciousness of something is always consciousness of it *as* such and such. Looking at the apple I see it as a round object as if it were a baseball. Later I look at it as a beautiful object and later still as sometime to satisfy my hunger. Aspectuality extends beyond perception. I can view a theory as an explanatory device, as something quite elegant or as something to help organize my thinking. Searle expresses these ideas by saying "Every Intentional state has what I call aspectual shape"(1992a: 131).

Moving now gradually away from the close-in features of consciousness there is the feature, the seventh, that Searle calls overflow. As I notice the Jaguar XJR stopped in front of me waiting for the red light, my mind overflows to thoughts of my friend who has a car like that one. From there, my thoughts move to the friend's divorce and from there to a concern for his former wife who is not well. After the light changes, my thoughts overflow in the direction of avoiding an accident to recalling an accident that happened last week on Interstate Highway 75 and so on.

Searle identifies unity as a eighth feature of consciousness. A series of conscious states (overflow) are often tied together into one package. Winding up to serve the tennis ball, hitting the ball and following through after the ball has gone over the net are all part of one service experience. This unity over a span of time Searle identifies as horizontal. There is also vertical unity. At any one moment as I serve the ball I sense the sun in my eyes, my body stretching and the wind in my face. So unity is possible both horizontally and vertically in one experience.

Whether unified or not, a ninth feature of consciousness is that it possesses "a strictly limited number of modalities"(1992a: 128). Here Searle is referring to the various input capacities humans have. We can receive signals via the five senses (sight, touch, smell, taste and hearing), bodily sensation ("proprioception") and also what he calls the stream of thought. These modalities put us in touch both with our Intentional (e.g. perceptions) and non-Intentional states (e.g. pains). Included under the heading of the stream of thought are our emotions, as when I feel a surge of anger after being insulted and humiliated. Non-verbal thoughts are also included under this heading as when I sense the other driver begin to drift too close to my car and I instinctively react by pulling away from him.

The tenth and eleventh features are almost indistinguishable. The one Searle calls "The Center and the Periphery", the other "The Figure-Ground (Gestalt Structure of Conscious Experience)". The centre has to do with that to which you are attending. You are thinking of meeting your old friend at the airport while, on the periphery of consciousness, you are driving to the airport without giving your driving much thought. You are focusing attention on your friend, not your driving. Yet, on the periphery, you are aware of where you are going and that a red lights bids you to stop at this moment. Similarly, at another time, you bounce the tennis ball on the court without fully thinking of what you are doing while you focus on the kind of spin you will put on the ball and the location of the serve so that you will jam your opponent when he tries to return it. Talk about figure and ground has also to do with focusing attention on one thing, yet all the while being aware of other things. You see the Picasso without being aware of how it is framed. Later you think "The painting had these and those features. But what colour is the frame? Indeed, is it framed?" Your lack of attention to the background keeps you from recalling what you saw. If there is a difference between the periphery and the (back)ground it may be that some of the latter is so much a part of the fringes of conscious experience that there is a question whether we can speak of being conscious of the background at all.

The twelfth feature of consciousness takes us even further beyond the fringes. This feature Searle calls the Boundary Conditions. Part of the Boundary Conditions are probably what Searle calls the Network and even possibly the Background. These conditions are not part of consciousness in the sense that we are aware of them but conditions that put consciousness in a setting. About these boundary conditions Searle says:

> In the course of reflecting about the present, I have at no point had any thoughts concerning where I am located, what day of the month it is, what time of year it is, how long it is since I had breakfast, what my name and past history are, which country I am a citizen of, and so on. Yet it seems to me, all of these are part of the situatedness, part of the spatio-temporal-socio-bio-logical location of my present conscious states. Any state of consciousness is in that way characteristically located. But the location may itself not be at all the object of consciousness, not even the periphery. (1992a: 139)

Here is a list of the twelve features of consciousness that Searle has told us about so far.

1. Intentionality. (This feature itself has a feature: viz. aspectuality.)
2. Subjectivity. (If any is, this is the essential feature of consciousness.)
3. Pleasure/Un-pleasure
4. Mood.
5. Sense of Familiarity.
6. Aspectuality.
7. Overflow.
8. Unity.
9. The limited number of modalities.
10. Figure-Ground (This and its twin feature 11, as well as the aspectuality of Intentionality, unity and familiarity, help to give structure to consciousness. So structure could be thought of as another of consciousness's features.)
11. Center and Periphery. (This one may be indistinguishable from 10.)
12. Background Conditions.

The thirteenth feature does not have the look of a feature. Searle calls it "The Connection between Consciousness and Intentionality". As its name suggests, it has more to do with how two features relate to one another rather than being a new feature on its own. Actually, Searle is talking about connections, not a connection. Here are his words on the matter. He prefaces them with the comment that the claims he makes about these connections need to be proven or substantiated somehow. "Only a being that could have conscious intentional states could have intentional states at all, and every unconscious intentional state is at least potentially conscious" (1992a: 132). We will see in the next chapter how he makes out these strong claims. We will also see how Searle uses these claims to cudgel those whose views about the mind and consciousness differ from his own.

However, before moving onto this discussion, one other feature of the mind deserves attention even though Searle does not actually place it in his list to make the total fourteen. Humans, as distinct from most other animals, have the ability to be self-conscious. Searle does not mean that we are self-conscious in terms of when we embarrass ourselves by doing something stupid at the dinner table in front of those we are trying to impress. His meaning of self-conscious is that we are reflective. Thus, if we wish, we can turn our attention away from all those things, processes, events, etc. out in the world toward our own mental states. We can not only have pains that we experience subjectively, but we can turn our attention to the pain and then remark to a doctor that it doesn't hurt so much now as it did yesterday. Indeed, we can. turn our attention to any mental state. Linguistically we can talk about the attention we give to this and that state by saying such things as "I am not angry" and "I had a thought yesterday about how to solve our problem". So Intentionality is a feature that can point both outside ourselves and "inside".

Granting that we are self-reflective, Searle is anxious to deny that he is a champion of the doctrine of introspection. We do not need to have, nor do we have, any special ability or power to "look" into the mind. The mind is self-conscious (reflective) roughly in the same way that it is conscious of matters on the outside. Self-consciousness is basically no different from non-self-consciousness. That being so, it is not surprising that if we can make mistakes in judgment with matters outside the mind we can also make mistakes on the inside. Those who hold to the doctrine that gives special introspective powers to the mind might deny this. They might argue that self-conscious knowledge is privileged. We have, thus, special authority that allows us to know what goes on in our mind.

Searle expresses disagreement with this doctrine by pointing out, as many others have done, that self-deception is both possible and quite common. Susie thinks she is in love with Sam, even though others can see that she is really in love with Sam's brother Sunny. Joanne says and thinks she is a liberal, but others can tell she really is more conservative than she admits. Adam has convinced himself that he really wants to help the poor but is, in fact, helping them because he wants to impress his girlfriend Anne. Self-deception cases are easy to find especially when we are concerned with long-term mental states (dispositions) such as beliefs and a variety of emotional states (such as love, admiration, hate and envy). Motivational states, although they may or may not be long term, are also prone to self-deception.

Searle even gives us his own account of how self-deception comes about. One way is through inattention. We are busy attending to things in the outside world. When the objects of our Intentional states are matters having to do with work, sex objects, food and so on, we simply find that we don't have time to attend to our mental states. So we make mistakes. We make comparable mistakes about the outside world when we spend most of our time attending only to one part of it (one's business interests) to the neglect of another part (one's family interests), or when we constantly engage in self-conscious or reflective activity and, as a result, neglect the outside world.

A second kind of mistake is made more deliberately. Searle gives the examples here of being ashamed for being angry or for hating someone or some class of people.

> In such cases, the agent simply resists consciously thinking about certain of his psychological states. When the thought of these states arises, he immediately thinks of the converse state that he wishes he in fact held. Suppose that he hates the members of a minority group, but is ashamed of this prejudice and consciously wishes that he did not have this hatred. When confronted with the evidence of his prejudice, he simply refuses to admit it, and indeed, vehemently and sincerely denies it. The agent has a hatred together with a desire not to have that hatred, that is, a form of shame about that hatred.
>
> (1992a: 147–8)

Searle is content here to point to the conflict of emotions to explain why his agent directly denies his complicity. He does not identify any unconscious mental defense mechanism to explain further why this denial takes place. We will see in the next chapter why he is reluctant to invoke these mechanisms to explain most anything.

One can imagine another strategy related to Searle's second kind of mistake. Instead of engaging in direct denial the agent simply "changes the subject". Rather than simply doggedly and directly deny what is true, Searle's agent could avoid discussing what is embarrassing by dwelling on other matters. If thinking about certain things is painful, then one thinks about things that are not. If Susie has just dumped Sam for Adam, then Sam might do well to dwell on any thoughts that do not connect to Susie. Or he might "change the subject" by immersing himself in his work and thus avoid any form of self-conscious pity.

A third source of error is misinterpretation (Searle 1992a: 148). The example Searle gives is of a man who sincerely thinks of himself as being in love with a young woman, but is only infatuated with her. Here is his account of how this form of mistake takes place.

> Crucial to this sort of case is the operation of the Network and the Background. Just as a person may misinterpret a text by failing to see how the elements of the text relate to each other, and by failing to understand the background circumstances in which the text was composed, so a person may misinterpret his own intentional states by failing to see their interrelationships and by failing to locate them correctly relative to the Background of nonrepresentational mental capacities. In such cases we do not have the traditional epistemic model of making incorrect *inferences* on the basis of insufficient *evidence*. It is not a question of getting from appearance to reality, but rather of locating a piece in a puzzle relative to a whole lot of other pieces. (1992a: 148)

What kind of pieces are we supposed to look for to help us understand this kind of mental mistake, and why are the pieces so hard to find? In part the answer to the latter question is likely to be inattention, once again. Adam, is so smitten by his "love" Anne that he doesn't, indeed probably can't, focus on anything else. But, being so smitten, what kinds of pieces from the puzzle is he failing to put in place? Searle doesn't tell us except to say they are somewhere in the Network and Background. Initially, it might be supposed that some of the missing pieces have to do with Anne. But that is not likely since if Adam is mistaken about Anne, his mistake is probably due to insufficient evidence rather than based on something having to do with the Network and/or Background. He only finds out later how selfish she is. So the pieces of the puzzle more than likely have to do with Adam himself rather than anybody or anything else. His own sexual tendencies, some of his preferences for and fears of women, his past history in reacting towards other women and his fears about making commitments would all form part of his personal unconscious Background and Network.

Whatever status these Background pieces to the puzzle have, for now, Searle has made a clear case for what I am calling the fourteenth feature of consciousness. Self-consciousness is a no-frills feature. It does not use any special introspective powers to "look" into the mind, and it is not incorrigible. It makes mistakes of many kinds. It is true that some self-conscious (first-person) reports are incorrigible. We cannot be mistaken about "seeming" claims such as "It seems – looks – red to me". Assuming we are using our native language correctly, mistakes are out of the question because a distinction between appearance and reality cannot be made with these kinds of claims concerned as they are with appearance only. But claims like these aside, self-consciousness is nothing special. It directs attention to mental states in the same way it does other states and it sometimes makes mistakes as do other Intentional states.

So the self-conscious feature of consciousness shouldn't pose any special problems for a theorist like Searle. It isn't as if he is drawing picture of consciousness with features so special and powerful as to legitimately raise the suspicions of materialists, functionalist and other opponents of Searlian theory. Nonetheless, his opponents are suspicious because they take his theory of consciousness, especially that part having to do with self-consciousness, to have just the powers that he denies it has (Dennett 1991). Searle protests against these suspicions:

> several recent attacks on consciousness, such as Dennett's (1991), are based on the mistaken assumption that if we can show that there is something wrong with the doctrine of incorrigibility or introspection, we have shown that there is something wrong with consciousness. But nothing could be further from the truth. Incorrigibility and introspection have nothing to do with the essential features of consciousness. They are simply elements of mistaken philosophical theories about it.
>
> (1992a: 149)

But it is time to turn to a discussion of how consciousness is connected to Intentionality and the related principle that Searle calls the Connection Principle. This principle tells us that unconscious Intentional states have that status only if they are connected somehow to consciousness Intentional ones. As already noted this discussion is important for Searle because he uses it to cudgel his opponents who postulate the existence of unconscious thoughts and processes that cannot be in principle connected to consciousness. But this discussion is important for another reason. Knowing the connection between consciousness and Intentionality is key to his theory of mind because of all the features listed above, these two are the most important to his theory. The others are secondary in that they tell us how and in what way consciousness and/or Intentionality manifest themselves. The aspect of familiarity, for example, has to do with the familiarity we have with this or that conscious Intentional (and sometimes non-Intentional) experience. In the same way overflow has to do with how conscious (mostly) Intentional experiences move from one object of experience to another. So Searle can't avoid discussing in detail the connections of consciousness and Intentionality and also the connections between unconscious and conscious thought. Avoiding such discussion would be tantamount to not telling us about the heart of his theory. So, now, in the next chapter, we move to that discussion.

Notes

1. Latter-day identity theorists continue to dog Searle's trail with respect to this claim (Bechtel & McCauley 1999). They do so with some difficulty. It is easy enough to establish an intra-level identity. I can discover that the person I know as Captain Smith, who I always see in uniform on the military base, is identical with the tennis playing Bill that I know at the club by, among other ways, tracking him as he changes from his uniform into his tennis clothes. But the claim that conscious states on the macro level are identical with certain neuronal states on the micro level is not so easy to establish. The problem is not just that the two sets of inter-level phenomena differ radically from one another. Rather it is that even if conscious states correlate highly with certain neuronal states all one has is sets of correlations. This poses a problem for Searle as well. He needs to show that these correlation claims can be turned into causal ones. As difficult as performing this task is, it is even more difficult to establish that the correlation relationship is really one of identity. One way to get around this difficulty is to treat the identity relationship as a hypothesis and then claim that doing so is a fruitful move for science. This pragmatic move keeps the identity theory alive pending results. A causal theorist like Searle could counter with his own pragmatic move. He could claim that his theory postulating causal relationships between the micro level and the macro level is more, or equally, fruitful scientifically. Not that Searle need make such a move since he could (and tries) to show directly that the relationship is causal (through counter factual claims). But if he did make such a move, he could at least blunt identity theory claims simply by suggesting that the identity theory's pragmatic claims are no better than those of his own theory.

2. Here Searle is in opposition to Frank Jackson (1997), who otherwise might be thought to be an ally. Jackson calls himself a "qualia freak" but also says he is an epiphenomenalist. He argues that evolution is no argument for supposing that our qualia have causal powers. Bears, he tells us, have developed a *heavy* fur coat that of course keeps them warm. But the heaviness of the coat has no survival value – indeed its weight slows the bear down and works against its survival. He also argues that just because we seem to think that our hunger, for example, causes us to go eat does not prove that hunger has any causal efficacy. Both our hunger and our food-

seeking behaviour might have underlying (physiological) causes. Owen Flanagan, in his *Consciousness Reconsidered* (1992), presents a cautious but throughout attack on epiphenomenalism. See especially Chapter 7. In that chapter he argues that consciousness manifests itself in many creatures on this planet and this suggests that consciousness must be something other than an idle (epi)phenomenon (1992: 133–4). He also argues, as does Searle, that consciousness shows up in just those situations where organisms need it the most (for adaptive purposes) as when facing an oncoming car on the highway.

Chapter 8

Cognitive psychology and the unconscious

Background

In Chapter 7 of *The Rediscovery of the Mind* (1992a) Searle remarks on a curious reversal. Before psychology became a free-standing science, and in that science's early years, consciousness seemed unproblematic. Such early psychologists as Wundt (1912) and Titchener (1896) took it for granted that the business of psychology was to study the conscious mental processes. They did not deny that these processes were problematic in that the laws of consciousness had not yet been found. But, for them, it was unproblematic that consciousness was the subject matter of their science. This was so obvious that the expression *conscious* in conscious mental processes almost seemed redundant. Mental processes, at least the interesting ones governing our perceptions, thinking and emotions, were simply assumed to be conscious.

Freud helped change all that (1949; 1959; 1966). He did not deny the importance of consciousness but he did show that there is more to psychology than is on the surface. Beneath the surface, in the unconscious, there are powerful emotionally charged thoughts (e.g. loves and hates) and equally powerful mental processes (e.g. various defence mechanisms). As a result of his work, the question of the relationship between what is and is not on the surface had to be taken more seriously than before.

Behaviourism, a movement in psychology that started about the same time Freud was doing his work, did not initially concern itself with the unconscious. In contrast to Freud, this movement, led initially by John Watson (1913; 1919) and later by the likes of

B. F. Skinner (1953), attacked the notion of consciousness. For behaviourists, psychology needed to be put on a firm scientific basis; and for that to happen, first-person subjective claims (concerning consciousness) had to be ignored. Only public third-person objective claims were to be permitted. Laws of psychology would be a matter of connecting the input conditions (stimuli) with the output conditions (responses). If a behaviourist were experimenting in the area of learning, he might present his subjects with various perceptual stimuli that would act as clues to help them find their way through a maze, provide them with some motivation (by offering food after experiencing a measurable amount of deprivation) and then wait to see how his subjects responded. Neither consciousness nor unconsciousness mattered under this model of doing psychology.

However, not all behaviourists followed this model. Clark Hull (1943) and his many followers were willing to talk about inputs and outputs, but also about what they called intervening variables. Unlike Watson, but especially unlike Skinner, they were willing to theorize about processes inside the organism (variables intervening between the stimuli and responses). On the inside there are habit strengths (learning patterns), drives (motivations) and inhibitions. Behaviour (output) could now be thought of as resulting from a combination of external stimuli and internal factors. It is at this point that the notion of unconscious processes enters into behaviourism. The internal factors or intervening variables could (although they need not) do their work without the subject knowing that they were. However, within Hullian theory, it was possible to know about these factors and their effects on behaviour. Researchers could observe how many hours someone has been deprived of food or sex, and then speculate about the inner conditions. That sort of cautious speculation was acceptable since, after all, it was done on a third-person objective basis. Speculating about consciousness was another matter. That sort was still forbidden since consciousness makes its contribution to life on a first-person subjective rather than a third-person objective basis.

Followers of cognitive psychology took the next step. They were less shy than the Hullians about speculating on what was going on inside the organism. Indeed, for them these "inside" activities, dispositions etc. came to be synonymous with what was meant by the mind. There was still an interest in the outside inputs and how they might affect behaviour and, of course, there was still an interest in monitoring outside behaviour itself. There was also, for some but not for others, an interest in the brain and the rest of the organism as to how they might play causal roles in affecting behaviour. But it was mind viewed objectively, even though it was "hidden inside", that was held to be the key to understanding cognition and other psychological phenomena. Here is Searle's characterization of how most cognitive scientists view their stance on these matters.

> Neither the study of the brain as such nor the study of consciousness as such is of much interest and importance to cognitive science. The cognitive mechanisms we [the cognitive scientists] study are indeed implemented in the brain, and some of them find a surface expression in consciousness, but our interest is in the intermediate level where the actual cognitive processes are inaccessible to consciousness. Though in fact implemented in the brain, they could have been implemented in an indefinite number of hardware systems. Brains are there, but inessential. The processes which explain cognition are unconscious not only in fact, but in principle. For example, Chomsky's rules of universal grammar (1986), or Marr's rules of vision (1982), or Fodor's language of thought (1975) are not the sort of phenomena that could become conscious. Furthermore these processes are all computational. The basic assumption behind cognitive science is that the brain is a computer and mental processes are computational. For that reason many of us think that artificial intelligence (AI) is the heart of cognitive science. There is some dispute among us as to whether or not the brain is a digital computer of the old fashioned von Neumann variety or whether it is a connectivist machine. Some of us, in fact, manage to have our cake and eat it too on this question, because we think the serial processes in the brain are implemented by a parallel connectivist system (e.g., Hobbs, 1990). But nearly all of us agree on the following: Cognitive mental processes are unconscious; they are, for the most part, unconscious in principle; and they are computational.   (1992a: 197–8)

Searle says he disagrees with almost everything this paragraph says (1992a: 198). We will see why shortly. But, Searle's views here aside, the paragraph shows clearly how cognitive scientists view the unconscious as unproblematic in the sense that it is clearly *the* subject of study for them. Again, they grant that they do not know as much about the unconscious as they would like, but as a third-person (objective) subject matter it is in principle unproblematic for them. It is less problematic than first-person, subjective consciousness even though it seemed just the opposite to many of the earlier psychologists.

This reversal of what is problematic bothers Searle. He thinks that the wrong views of the cognitive scientists rest heavily on a misunderstanding of what it is for something to be unconscious. We can anticipate part of what has gone wrong here by reminding ourselves of Searle's connection principle. That principle, recall, says that the unconscious is parasitic on the conscious. What is unconscious must in principle be raisable to the conscious level. But citing the principle is not evidence for Searle's position, but merely a statement of it. So if the connection principle is to hold, and thus serve as a wedge to dislodge the cognitivists from holding many of their claims about the unconscious, Searle needs to present us with an argument of some sort. This he does. However, his argument is less a proof that his conception of the unconscious is correct, and the opposition's incorrect, than it is a presentation of his own position as a plausible alternative.

He begins his presentation by making a distinction between intrinsic Intentionality and as-if Intentionality. As we have seen already, most conscious mental thought exhibits intrinsic Intentionality. It is the nature of these states that they take objects. The man sees the car, hears the car, feels the car as he touches it. As-if Intentionality is not real Intentionality. When we say that the ball desires to fall to the centre of the earth we don't really mean (or we shouldn't mean) that the ball really has desires. Likewise, when we say that the plant deliberately positions itself to be exposed to the sun we don't mean that the plant really deliberates. Nor do we mean what it sounds like we mean in saying that the thermostat senses the rise in temperature in the room. As-if Intentionality can be extended to everything. Thus if we treated as-if Intentionality as the real thing we could apply mental concepts to anything and everything. That conclusion Searle takes to be absurd (Van Gulick 1995; Searle 1995b: 225).

But the real thing, intrinsic Intentionality, applies only to the mind. One important feature of intrinsic Intentionality is its aspectual shape. The Intentional or aboutness feature of the mind is always about certain aspects of whatever the mind intends.

Recall (from the previous chapter) that one perceives the apple as a round ball, or as something to eat or as something nutritious or thirst quenching – or perhaps as some combination of some of these aspects. But one never perceives the apple in all its aspects. Presumably the mind cannot focus on all the aspects (assuming all of them could be, in theory, identified) at once.

Searle insists that both intrinsic Intentionality and aspectuality apply to unconscious thoughts. People's unconscious fear of their big brother is of their big brother; and that fear relates to certain aspects of their big brother – his big muscles, his big shoulders and his bad temper (not his big nose and big ears). In these two senses, our unconscious thoughts are no different from our conscious ones.

Searle next argues that *"The aspectual feature* [of the mind] *cannot be exhaustively or completely characterized in terms of third-person, behavioral, or even neurophysiological predicates. None of these is sufficient to give an exhaustive account of aspectual shape"* (1992a: 157–8; 1989a: 199). Neurophysiology can, of course, give *rise* to intentionality and aspectuality. This is to say that neurophysiology has the causal powers to bring about these emergent features of the mind. Further, it may be possible, if science developed to a certain point, to predict (infer) which intentional and aspectual features will emerge in this person at this particular time and which will emerge in that person at that time. But neurophysiology itself does not possess these two features. It possesses only features such as patterns of neuron firings and the like. It certainly does not possess mental features of any kind including aspectuality.

But, then, Searle asks, where are we to find the unconscious? It is certainly silly to suppose that there is a mental chamber someplace inside our heads where unconscious thoughts and processes are imprisoned. Nor, for Searle, does it make sense to suppose that the unconscious is part of the brain's programme in a sense similar to that of the hardware on my computer which is modified by various programs such as *Windows*, *Word Perfect* and *Quicken*. I will have more to say about why talking about a programme is not an acceptable explanation for Searle when the discussion turns directly to his objections to the cognitive sciences. For now, though, and briefly, Searle argues that talk of programmes has no explanatory value since it anthropomorphizes the brain. To say that the mind is a programme of the brain is to turn it into an inner person – a homunculus. Either the brain turns out to be a person with its own mental abilities or there is, either inside the brain our outside of it, a homunculus doing all this unconscious thinking. Neither alternative seems palatable. Searle concludes:

> The only things going on in his [some man's] unconscious brain are sequences of neurophysiological events occurring in neuronal architectures. At the time when the states are totally unconscious, there is simply nothing there except neurophysiological states and processes. (1992a: 159)

If there is nothing but the brain and conscious mental processes, then how can Searle talk about unconsciousness at all? He does by holding that unconscious thoughts (and processes) must be candidates for conscious experiences – hence the connection principle. Thus an Intentional unconscious mental state is a neurophysiological state that has the special capacity to produce a conscious state. The unconscious state may in fact not surface: there may be reasons such as brain damage to keep that from happening. But if a state has the status of being unconscious it must, according to Searle and his connection principle, be able to surface.

So that is Searle's argument for the connection principle. It probably convinces the converted only, since it depends heavily on concepts such as aspectual shape that are inherent to his own theory of philosophy of mind; and foreign to most opposition theories. In part, this is why I said earlier that this particular argument should not be viewed as a proof but as a presentation that shows the connection principle, and the larger theory that goes with it, as merely plausible.

However, Searle has another argument which sometimes is implicit in his presentations and at other times explicit (1984: 51). He appeals to Occam's Razor. He argues that his theory of the unconscious explains the unconscious in the simplest terms. Someone like Freud talks of the unconscious as if it had ontological status and causal powers all its own. It is almost as if the unconscious is a wild and crazy person inside of us who operates somewhere between the neurophysiological level on the one hand, and behaviour and consciousness on the other. Freud evidently felt he had to postulate something like this underground creature in order to explain such phenomena as repressed feelings we have toward our parents, siblings, etc. But Searle argues that he can account for these "underground" phenomena without postulating either a hidden person inside of us or a dark and hidden chamber. All that we classify as unconscious, he argues, is registered in the brain. There is no need to appeal to The Unconscious to explain what is unconscious.

Nor is there a need to raise the unconscious to the level where it becomes more important than consciousness. On Searle's interpretation that is what Freud does. He quotes Freud on this matter and then comments as follows.

> Here is what he [Freud] says: All mental states are "unconscious in themselves." And bringing them to consciousness is simply like perceiving an object (1915, reprinted in 1959, vol. 4, esp. p. 104ff.). So the distinction between conscious and unconscious mental states is not a distinction between two kinds of mental states, or even a distinction between two different modes of existence of mental states, but rather all mental states are really unconscious in themselves (*an sich*) and what we call "consciousness" is just a mode of perception of states that are unconscious in their mode of existence. It is as if the unconscious mental states really were like furniture in the attic of the mind, and to bring them to consciousness we go up in the attic and shine the flashlight of our perception on them. Just as the furniture "in itself" is unseen, so mental states "in themselves" are unconscious. (1992a: 168)

So Freud not only populates his ontology with The Unconscious but he also gives this underground explanatory tool special status. It is as if he gets carried away by his own discovery and, as a result, begins to explain consciousness away. As we will see immediately below, some cognitive scientists do much the same thing according to Searle.

The cognitive sciences

In presenting us with his theory of the unconscious, as a bonus we have been given an outline of how Searle criticizes certain theories within the cognitive sciences. He says that these theories wrongly deflate the status of consciousness and inflate the status of the unconscious. But a more detailed analysis is needed to appreciate the full scope of his criticism and to see whether it is fair or not. Initially it seems unfair. If one peruses much of the literature in cognitive psychology, one is struck by the non-deflationary status of consciousness. There is a large body of literature pertaining to memory (Bransford & Johnson 1972; Brown & Kulik 1977; Loftus & Palmer 1974; McCloskey et al. 1988; Tulving 1985), attention (Norman 1981; Reason 1984; Treisman & Gormican 1988), imagery and perception (Marcel 1983). Much of this work starts with consciousness. Memory for some significant event is tested, or the testing deals with stories one has heard. If attention is the focus of research, the subjects might be distracted in some way to see how difficult it is for them to maintain their attention. Or, if the research deals with perception, the subjects might be tested with respect to how well they perceive as the experimenter manipulates the background. Much of this research, then, is descriptive of conscious experience.

Beyond that, it is often concerned with identifying various types of whatever phenomena are under study. If memory is the subject of study, the researchers might go on to identify various kinds of memory. Tulving (1972), for example, distinguishes between episodic memory (of events), semantic memory (of words and concepts), and Anderson (1976) adds the notion of procedural memory (of knowing how to do things).

So far, so good. Searle should be content with these brands of cognitive psychology even if their work shows that the consciousness (the mind) does not have to be rediscovered by Searle in the year 1992 AD. Consciousness (the mind) was already known to be there by many psychologists who themselves rediscovered it, presumably, after it had been buried by the behaviourists and their kin during the first half and the middle of the twentieth century. Searle probably would concede as much even if, at times, he seems to be tarring and feathering a whole generation of cognitive psychologists and cognitive scientists. The most he can rightly claim is that some wayward types have done their best to keep the concept of consciousness buried or to treat it like a neglected child.

But, then, if the sin committed by cognitive scientists by way of deflating the role of consciousness is not so great as Searle sometimes suggests, what about the sin of inflating the role of the unconscious? Indeed, the unconscious plays an explanatory role for many cognitive scientists. It is their explanatory weapon of choice. It is allegedly not only a powerful weapon, but also a secret weapon. As such, it is tempting for cognitive scientists to employ it to impress lay people by saying in effect "We know something that you ordinary folk know nothing about". So cognitive scientists have much invested in this weapon. It would be surprising, therefore, if they would not be upset when someone like Searle comes along with the threat to take it away from them. How does Searle go about doing this? Here matters get complicated since, as we have seen already, he is not opposed to the concept of the unconscious as such – he is only opposed to certain versions of it. Nor is he opposed to the cognitive sciences. Indeed he confesses to have been a practising cognitive scientist for some time now (1992a: 197).

To see more clearly where the disagreement between Searle and his cognitivist opponents lie, it is best to start with an easy example of an appeal to the unconscious that Searle himself cites. In *Intentionality* he talks of learning how to ski (1983: 150). The novitiate takes lessons and, in the process, is given a set of rules to follow. She is told repeatedly by her instructor to: "Lean forward", "Bend the ankles and the knees", "Keep your centre of gravity low", "Spread your skis just so far", "Keep your weight on the downhill ski", "Start on easy slopes", etc. At first, the novitiate recites the rules to herself, and so the conscious awareness of the rules plays a causal role in the learning process. As Searle puts it "Each of these [rules] is an explicit representation, and, to the extent that the skier is seriously trying to learn, each will function causally as part of the Intentional content determining the behavior".

Let us assume that the student is a fast learner. She cites the rules, starts to lean forward, bends her ankles, etc. on a regular basis and, then, in time, finds that rule recitation is no longer necessary. What happens to the rules? If we hadn't already read the previous chapter, we would likely suppose that they had become internalized. That, presumably, is what some (most?) cognitivists would say. The rules go to the unconscious. Searle, as we now know, would disagree. Here is how he expresses his disagreement.

> As the skier gets better he does not internalize the rules better, but rather the rules become progressively irrelevant. The rules do not become "wired in" as unconscious Intentional contents, but the repeated experiences create physical capacities, presumably realized as neural pathways, that make the rules simply irrelevant. "Practice makes perfect" not because practice results in a perfect memorization of the rules, but because repeated practice enables the body to take over and the rules to recede into the Background.   (1983: 150)

Searle is here giving us an explanatory promissory note rather than an explanation. After all if he were to allow only for a neural explanation as to how our skier's behaviour has changed, no one could deliver such an explanation to us. Neuroscience is not yet ready to tell us that it is these specific changes in the neural pathways that make the difference between before and now. That sort of explanation would be comparable to the one biologists give when they appeal to auxins to explain why plants grow in the direction of the sun. That would be the kind of causal explanation we would ideally want. So in telling us that it is no good appealing to unconscious rules, Searle appears to be saying that we must settle for no explanation at all, at least for now.

But in fact Searle's explanatory account is not quite so austere. It is true that neuroscience knows next to nothing about what has changed on the neural level to explain how our skier looks so smooth and strong on the slopes today, whereas last year she was a candidate for a skiing disaster. But it is also true that we know (so Searle tells us repeatedly) that the neural changes for a better skiing experience "house" the habits the skier has acquired. Evidently the good new skiing habits are the behavioural manifestations of these neural changes. So we can explain the changes as to how our skier skies by saying that she has all the right habits (skills). As Searle suggests, these skills are not just found in the neural pathways but in the muscles and other parts of the body as well. The body, then, acts as if it were unconsciously following the rules whereas all it is doing is acting in accordance with them (i.e. mimicking rule-following behaviour). Another way of expressing this is that the habits are unconscious, but they are not in The Unconscious.

Searle's account of the skier's development clearly fits in with his connection principle. That principle, recall once again, says that if an experience or thought is to have unconscious status it must in principle be able to surface. Unconscious habits surface in either of two ways. First, when our skier backslides into her old pattern of crashing into trees, she recites the rules (if she is still alive). She can do this by actually reciting them (e.g. "Bend your ankles") or by describing how she was skiing before backsliding (e.g. "I was bending my ankles"). Secondly, the unconscious habits can surface not by recitation, but by practice. The skier can take herself onto the slopes and very self-consciously do what the rules say she should do.

So there is no problem for Searle in talking about the unconscious when the subject matter is skiing, golf, tennis, chess, knitting and other such skill activities. Nor is there any problem with most Freudian-like examples of the unconscious. If it is possible in principle to dredge up to consciousness one's unconscious hate for one's father, then Searle's connection principle is safe. So long as we realize that the unconscious hate is found within the brain and not in The Unconscious or The Mind, there is no problem at all.

But what of the following kinds of cases having to do with memory? Various "cognitivists" – Tulving (1986), Anderson (1976) and Squire (1987; Squire & Kandel 1999) among others – argue that memory is not a single system where we file away our thoughts. Each in his own way argues for several memory systems. Squire, for one, argues for the existence of short term and long term memory systems. We see our short term memory at work when we remember the telephone number just long enough to dial it. Squire divides long term memory first in terms of declarative and procedural memory (1987: Chs 10 and 11). He further divides declarative memory into episodic and semantic. The former is concerned with remembering events such as what happened at the last company Christmas party and the accident on the ski slopes on the last day of last year. The latter is more general memory. It is memory of analytic truths such as cubes have twelve edges and uncles are males. It is also memory of empirical relationships such as that objects accelerate when they fall, and very few people live beyond the age of 100 years. Procedural memory has to do with skills. I remember how to ski even though I haven't been on the slopes for years; and how to speak German even though I haven't talked to a speaker of that language in years as well.

These memory systems are identified in a variety of ways by cognitive researchers. For example, word association experiments (Tulving & Thomson 1973) show that memory for pairings of words not normally associated with one another (e.g. house and bugs), and thus that come to be associated episodically in the experiment itself, operate differently from memory for pairs already closely (i.e. semantically) associated with one another (e.g. bark and dog). Other studies show that when older people lose memory most of the loss is "episodic". The same can be shown with patients suffering from amnesia. For our purposes it does not matter whether these kinds of evidence are sufficient enough to justify postulating these particular and the other memory systems. Our concern is with the status of these systems no matter what exact form they take. So when "cognitivists" claim that one kind of memory system is distinct from another, what kind of claim is being made?

One kind is that these systems represent unconscious mental activity. If this is what they claim, Searle could object since the presence of these systems would challenge his connection principle. Unlike the hate that a Freudian patient might have for his father, these systems cannot be dredged up to consciousness through therapy or any other way. We can talk about these systems as the "cognitivists" do and, as I am doing now, but the systems themselves cannot be experienced directly in consciousness. Searle might then object even more if these systems were thought of as not only unconscious but as being in The Unconscious or in The Mind. His sense of explanatory sparseness would seem to be necessarily offended by such an overly ontologically rich account.

But "cognitivists" could be making another kind of claim, one not so rich ontologically. Here is what that might look like.

> Memory systems talk is just another way of talking about brain activity. The neural firings and structure of the brain are such that they manifest themselves as episodic, semantic or whatever kind of memory. None of these forms of memory exhibit any inherent intelligence. Nor need they be thought of as having been produced by an intelligent creature and thus represent some sort of internal programme. They are just the way they are, and not some other way, because of evolution. "Cognitivists", then, are surmising about these systems based primarily on behavioural experiments. It would be nice if we could supplement this research with sophisticated brain research. That would give us greater assurance that we got the systems right. But, clearly, given our present technology, that is not possible. So we must work with what we have in order to identify, as best we can, the nature of these memory systems. That is, although this "cognitivist" or "behavioural" approach represents a second best effort, it is legitimate in its own right and very likely will yield, and already has yielded, useful information about memory.

What might Searle say about all this? He could, rather reflexively, reject it. If these memory systems are thought of as unconscious thoughts and if they cannot, in principle, surface to consciousness, then they represent direct challenges to his connection principle. But Searle makes a distinction that leads him, in fact, not to reject the above mental/biological account of memory. The distinction is found in the ambiguity of "mental process", On the one side, this concept can mean "process with mental content". Here, presumably, we have processes such as the citing of rules governing grammar, vision, reasoning, etc. If these processes are in the deep unconscious they would indeed violate the connection principle. On the other side, "mental process" can mean "process by which mental phenomena are related" (Searle 1992a: 239). These processes contain no mental content. Rather, like the various kinds of memory identified by Squire and others, they form what might be called the structure of the brain (manifested as memory). Making these, and similar structural distinctions, has nothing to do with actually processing mental thoughts in accord with the computer model that the cognitive scientists are so fond of. So for Searle these structural concerns [my terminology] are not subject to the connection principle one way or the other. They have nothing to do with deep unconscious thoughts but represent processes that fall under the heading of what Searle calls the non-conscious. Non-conscious processes are strictly not in mental line of business. Rather they represent the structure that makes it possible for us to have conscious (mental) experiences.

The connection principle as a screening device

In essence the connection principle is a screening device. But so far it has screened out nothing. It has told us that certain Freudian-like thoughts (e.g. John's hate for his father) pass through the screen and that memory systems of the kind discussed above should not be placed against the screen to see if they can pass through it or not. But Searle clearly intends his principle to do some important screening work.

He shows us what it can do in his discussion of Irvin Rock's study of perception (1984). Rock says *perception* is "intelligent".

> I mean to say that it is based on such thoughtlike mental processes as description, inference, and problem solving, although these processes are rapid-fire, unconscious, and non-verbal . . . (Rock 1984: 234)

Then he adds:

> "Inference" implies that certain perceptual properties are computed from given sensory information using unconsciously known rules. For example, perceived size is inferred from the object's visual angle, its perceived distance, and the law of geometrical optics relating the visual angle to object distance.
> (1984: 234)

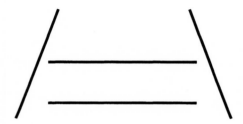

Searle takes what Rock is saying and applies it to the Ponzo illusion (above). Rock, Searle says, would explain the illusion by saying that the perceiver follows two unconscious rules and makes two inferences (1992a: 232).

> The first rule is that converging lines from lower to higher in the visual field imply greater distance in the direction of the convergence, and the second is that objects that occupy equal portions of the retinal image vary in perceived size depending on perceived distance from the observer (Emmert's law). On this account the agent unconsciously infers that the top parallel line is farther away because of its position in relation to the converging lines, and second, he infers that the top line is larger because it is farther away. Thus there are two rules and two unconscious inferences, none of whose operations are accessible to consciousness even in principle.   (1992a: 232)

Searle, of course, cannot accept this account since it directly violates his connection principle. However, he is unable to provide us with an actual biological model to explain the illusion. The technology is simply not in place to do the job. So he provides us with another example, where the technology is in place, to help us see what a proper explanation should look like. With this example we have to imagine that cognitive scientists are trying to explain how our vision remains stable even though we are driving in a car over a bumpy road. Their account could very well appeal to the conscious rule "Keep your visual attention on the road". But it could also likely appeal to a deep unconscious rule that Searle expresses as: "Make eyeball movements in relation to the eye sockets that are equal and opposite to head movements to keep the retinal image stable" (1992a: 235).

It is this sort of appeal that disturbs Searle. In part, the reason is that this rule and its application requires that something or somebody inside the head exhibit intelligent behaviour. Information is taken in and processed through the rule under a variety of conditions – not only when the road is bumpy but when dusty, wet, narrow, and during the night, and so on. It is almost as if this imagined cognitivist account requires that there be some intelligent creature inside the head. It is as if there is an anthropos inside the anthropos.

The problem, Searle says, is that this account is false. It is an account comparable to one we give when explaining why plants turn toward the sun. They do so not because of some intentional-like account that says they want to survive but in terms of the secretion of a auxin, a type of hormone. He says "The variable secretions of auxin account for the plant's behavior, without any extra hypothesis of purpose, teleology, or intentionality" (1992a: 229). So, now, concerning our vision as we drive over bumpy roads, Searle says:

> What actually happens is that fluid movements in the semicircular canals of the inner ear trigger a sequence of neuron firings that enter the brain over the eighth cranial nerve. These signals follow two parallel pathways, one of which can "learn" and one of which cannot. The pathways are in the brain stem and cerebellum and they transform the initial input signals to provide motor output "commands," via motorneurons that connect to the eye muscles and cause eyeball movements. The whole system contains feedback mechanisms for error correction. It is called the vestibular ocular reflex (VOR). The actual hardware mechanism of the VOR has no more intentionaliy or intelligence than the movements of the plant's leaves due to the secretion of auxin. (1992a: 236)

He then adds:

> Instead of saying:
> Intentional: To keep my retinal imagine stable and thus improve my vision while my head is moving, I follow the deep

unconscious rule of eyeball movement.

We should say:

Hardware: When I look at an object while my head is moving, the hardware mechanism of the VOR moves my eyeballs.

Functional: The VOR movement keeps the retinal image stable and this improves my vision.

(1992a: 236)

The functional account that he adds above he explains as follows. Such an account "is not a separate level [of explanation] at all, but simply one of the causal levels *described in terms of our interests*" (1992a: 237). So in mentioning the VOR, the functional-level account is dependent on the biological. It gives an explanation of image stability as if the VOR were acting intentionally, but in fact this is only a manner of speaking. If the basic causal account were either not in place or there to be discovered in the future, the functional account would have no useful role to play in explaining anything.

This points to the problem with the deep unconscious intentional account. The appeal to a deep unconscious rule is supposed to stand on its own. It is supposed to have its own causal powers that either make the "hardware" level irrelevant or that downgrade the importance of the hardware level. It, supposedly, explains how we achieve visual stability. But Searle argues that such an account cannot do the job in principle. This is because the kinds of deep unconscious concepts employed by many cognitive scientists to explain what is going on in our heads are not intrinsic to us.

Intrinsic properties are best understood by their opposites. Terms like "house", "car", "thermostat", "picnic" and "baseball game" name features of things or events that can be understood only relative to ourselves. They are observer (or better yet, user) relative concepts that name features of the world that are understood only by reference to those who use the objects mentioned or engage in the activity in question. These concepts contrast to "rock", "star", "density of the gas", "hurricane", "neurons" and the like. These name things or point to features in the world that can be understood without reference to a user or an observer.

Searle argues that "computer" is an observer-relative concept. Something is a computer because we assign that status to it. We discover out in the world that something is a computer only after it has been called or used as a computer by someone. If, now, we are concerned to identify what is inside the human head it won't do to say "There is a computer brain in there". Saying that doesn't describe what is inside intrinsically. What we want instead is an account in terms of "neurons", "neuron firings", "clusters of neuron firings" and so on.

Searle's big arguments

Searle sees this criticism of the cognitive sciences as serious. It shows that they are fundamentally misguided to the point that they are harming the development of social sciences, especially psychology. Actually Searle supposes that he has several serious arguments against various versions of the cognitive sciences. I will package these arguments together by, first, presenting and then assessing each of these arguments. I will begin with the argument just presented which I will call, unfelicitously, The-Brain-is-not-a-Computer Argument.

As we have seen, this argument says that the "computer" is a user-relative concept and as such cannot be employed to describe the brain. The brain needs to be described in terms of its intrinsic features. Cognitivist objectors could, of course, say that the brain-is-a-computer claim is only a metaphor, one useful for helping us organize our thinking about our thinking. But Searle quite rightly argues that this is not the intent of many of his cognitivist objectors. They mean to be giving an account that actually describes how we think and how these ways of thinking causally produce behaviour. This certainly seems to be what Chomsky, Dennett, Marr and Fodor are doing. They explicitly talk about the presence of deep unconscious rule-following that can only mean that they are taking the brain-is-a-computer talk seriously. So they, and perhaps other cognitivist scientists, have a problem in the face of Searle's objection. The only way they can deal with it is to admit the user-relative nature of the computer concept and then go on to identify the user as some agent or homunculus in the head. But this leaves them open to the charge that they are anthropomorphizing the brain – a charge Searle is all too happy to level against them.

However even if we agree with Searle that his the-brain-is-not-a-computer argument damages those cognitivist theories that are seriously computer based, we must remember that this damage does not extend to all work done in the cognitivist tradition. Consider once again the distinction discussed above between long term and short term memory. Cognitivists can, and often do, talk about how the brain processes sort our thoughts into one or the other of these categories. Such talk suggests that they are indeed thinking of the brain (or the mind) operating much as a computer does. But, as noted above, these scientists need not talk or think that way. What they may, or at least can, be doing is using the short term and long term memory distinction as a very general way of talking about how the brain is structured. Short term memory might, then, be thought of as a crude biological term that refers to a portion of the brain that holds certain inputs in place (via various kinds of neural firings) for a short period of time only. Perhaps these memories are held in the brain not so much by some part of the brain but by firings from various parts. Long term memory would then be said to hold thoughts in place in different portions of the brain or in different ways. However that might work, the point is that some cognitivist-like concepts would apparently escape Searle's the-brain-is-not-a-computer criticism. Even if scientists as yet have not identified where these memory processes are located in the way they have for certain processes and abilities like learning, emotions, vision and the like, it still makes sense for them to speculate about memory. So long as the model for these speculations is biology, and not the computer, they are not obviously illegitimate. Searle's criticism perhaps destroys or harms much theory in the cognitive sciences but not so much as it sometimes seems. Searle, recall again, says that he too is a cognitivist scientist. His concern is to destroy that portion of the cognitivist model that portrays the mind as a computer – no more, no less.

The second major criticism Searle levels at his cognitivist opponents I will call the Aspectual Shape Argument. Recall that for Searle aspectuality characterizes all intrinsic Intentional experience. We don't see or think of the apple in all of its aspects, but only some. We don't think of all aspects of democracy when discussing political theory but only one or two. But, as we have seen, this feature of aspectuality poses a problem for those who posit deep unconscious thoughts that can, in principle, never become conscious. If these unconscious thoughts are mental, the question is: How do they acquire their aspectuality? Conscious thoughts that become unconscious (i.e. recorded for Searle in the neuronal structure of the brain) can take their aspectuality "down" to the neuron level with them. But deep unconscious thoughts that never were, and can never be, conscious are another matter. It is not clear how aspectuality would assert itself even if the deep unconscious thoughts were sponsored by an internal agent (a homunculus). It certainly wouldn't help to characterize deep unconscious thoughts in third-person terms since, after all, aspectuality is by its nature a first-person phenomenon.

So, once again, Searle presents us with an argument that places much of cognitivist talk in jeopardy. Like the-brain-is-not-a-computer argument, the aspectual shape argument's attack focuses on cognitivism's explanatory tools. Both arguments attack the credibility of middle level concepts, falling between the level of biology and the conscious level, that are supposed to present us with the keys to explaining human psychology. However, the keys – deep unconscious thoughts – are stated in such vague terms that Searle is tempted to say not that they are just false but that they lack credible meaning. For him, it makes no sense to compare the brain to a computer when such a comparison does not describe the brain intrinsically. It also makes no sense to say that the mind (or the brain) contains deep unconscious thoughts that lack aspectuality and therefore do not behave like other thoughts.

But even if these unconscious explanatory tools had more meaning than they do and were less mysterious than they are, Searle would still object to them. He does so by appealing to Occam's Razor. His Occam's Razor Argument is simply that much of the middle explanatory level (where the cognitivist unconscious concepts are found) is superfluous when we realize it will be replaced sooner or later by a biological account. Here is what he says about this matter in connection with his attack on Chomsky's theory of universal grammar.

> Specifically, the evidence for universal grammar is much more simply accounted for by the following hypothesis: There is, indeed, a language acquisition device innate in human brains, and LAD constrains the form of languages that human beings can learn. There is, thus, a hardware level of explanation in terms of the structure of the device, and there is functional level of explanation, describing which sorts of languages can be acquired by the human infant in the application of this mechanism. No further predictive or explanatory power is added by saying that there is in addition a level of deep unconscious rules of universal grammar, and indeed, I have tried to

suggest that the postulation is incoherent anyway. For example, suppose that children can only learn languages that contain some specific formal property F. Now that is evidence that the LAD makes it possible to learn F languages and no further evidence that the child has a deep unconscious rule, "Learn F languages and don't learn Non-F languages." And no sense can be given to that supposition anyway.   (1992a: 245)

The three arguments together help to establish the connection principle. That principle makes sense since computer-based deep-unconscious thoughts makes no sense. Thus, their inability to connect with the conscious level is not so much due to their deepness, profundity or to their mysterious nature but to their non-existence. What can connect are thoughts that were already on the conscious level but, for some reason or other, are now embedded in the neural structure of the brain. There is the brain and consciousness. That is all.

This leads to a discussion of the fourth, and last, major criticism of the cognitivist sciences. For Searle, the problem is that for many cognitivist scientists the connections they aspire to discover are not to consciousness but to something else. Their picture of what should be happening in their sciences can be characterized as follows.

There are inputs (stimuli) that are processed in the permanently subterranean realm and, then, there are behavioural outputs. We either ignore consciousness or discount it. Yes, of course, consciousness is there. We would be fools to deny it. But consciousness plays little or no role in our third-person objective science. Our method demands that we follow this stimuli-process-behaviour model of looking at things. Our method is our message.

As we have seen, sometimes Searle greets this message with exasperation. It is so obvious to him that consciousness plays an extremely important role in our mental life that it seems wrongheaded from the outset to ignore it. We must explain consciousness, rather than explain it away, but we must also explain how one conscious state can help bring along another one. So it is understandable that Searle has still another argument to show just how wrong the opposition is. That argument is his famous Chinese Room Argument.

With this argument we are to imagine a room in which resides an isolated individual who has at his disposal an extremely powerful syntactical program. This enables him to respond in Chinese to questions asked him in Chinese. He does this even though neither he nor his computer know the meaning of the Chinese symbols being manipulated. That is, they have no idea what the Chinese symbols refer to. However, together, they are able to respond in such a way as to make it impossible for those on the outside of the Chinese room to distinguish their responses from those that a native Chinese speaker would give if placed in the room all alone. In other words, what we have in the Chinese room is an instantiation of the strong artificial intelligence (Strong AI) position that says that the mind is a computer program – also known as computer functionalism.

What the Chinese room scenario is supposed to show is that something very important has been left out of the picture of the mind as it is drawn by AI. About this Searle says:

> neither the person inside [the Chinese room] nor any other part of the system literally understands Chinese; and because the programmed computer has nothing that this system does not have, the programmed computer, qua computer, does not understand Chinese either. Because the program is purely formal or syntactical and because minds have mental or semantic contents, any attempt to produce a mind purely with computer programs leaves out the essential features of the mind. (1992a: 45)

Certainly something seems to be left out by those versions of the strong AI and functionalist positions that equate the mind with the brain's computer program. What they leave out are consciousness and Intentionality. Against these positions, the Chinese room argument has some force since one would suppose that they should at least speak to these phenomena. Searle's argument is that in so far as they concern themselves with program talk, that is with syntax, they do not.

Searle argues that it does no good to enrich the argument by putting the person inside a robot instead of a room (1984: 34–5). Let us call this the Chinese Robot/Man Argument. Unlike the man in the room the robot has "sensors". It can "see", "hear", "touch" and even "smell" objects in its immediate environment. Let us assume that it is sophisticated enough so that when it "sees" an object in its path that would cause it to stumble and fall, it sends signals in Chinese to the man inside. The man then translates the message in such a way so as to "tell" the robot to alter its path and thus avoid falling. Does the man understand what is going on? In so far as all he is doing is processing Chinese symbols (and peering outside to see what is going on), he is still operating syntactically, not semantically, and therefore has no understanding. "Sensing" is not sensing, and "acting" is not acting.

But, now, change the argument to the Chinese Robot Argument. Take the man out of the loop. Again, the robot "sees" the object in its path, processes the information in Chinese (or English for that matter) and then moves aside to avoid "harming" itself. Is anything being left out in explaining the behaviour of the robot? Certainly consciousness is, for the simple reason that the robot is not conscious. But nothing else is left out. The account that we could give of the robot's behaviour, by knowing how the computer inside it works, how its arms and legs work etc. would be complete. We would be satisfied in explaining the robot's behaviour simply by giving such an account.

In a sense we would be satisfied in giving much the same sort of explanation for the man inside the robot in the Chinese Robot/Man Argument. What the man is doing inside the robot is the same as what the robot is doing by itself. Both are manipulating symbols on the syntactic level. Neither knows the meaning of what is being manipulated, that is, neither is semantically engaged in manipulating the symbols. Among other things, neither knows how to use the symbols to refer to anything and thus does not know whether this Chinese symbol is being used to refer to the big rock standing in the robot's path (Jacquette 1989; Searle 1989c).

In contrast if a normal human being, our friend Sam once again, walks in the same path as the robot he will see the rock, understand what it is and understand as well that if he continues walking straight toward the rock untoward things will happen. If Sam could understand Chinese he would process what is happening in his head with "meaning" in a way that the man in the Chinese room could not. With Sam there is consciousness, Intentionality, intentional behaviour and the rest.

Searle's claim, then, is that if we thought we could explain human psychology (behaviour included) just in terms of the Chinese Room Argument scenario we should realize how much we are leaving out. But if that is what we think, we are like the proverbial boxer fighting with one hand tied behind his back. Of course Searle's opponents are tempted to fight with one hand because they do not want to have anything to do with the subjective reality of experiences like Sam's. And of course they believe that subjective reality cannot be studied because they oppose with objective (third-person) reality. It is as if the other hand is uncoordinated and just gets in the way in the fight, so it is best to tie it up.

In countering with his Chinese Room Argument, Searle is telling us of the high costs of fighting with one hand. He is not against fighting with the "third-person" hand. There is nothing inherently wrong with doing studies in the old stimulus–response way. But there is no reason to stop there. We can study ontologically subjective phenomena in an objective way. If we do we are more likely, according to Searle, to see psychology and the other social sciences flourish more than they have in the past.

Part III

Philosophy of society and other matters

Chapter 9

Social reality

Introduction

Searle has a penchant for asking and answering certain kinds of questions. His favourites are "How does it work?" and "What is its structure?" Others have a penchant for asking what they consider to be deeper or prior philosophical questions such as "Does it exist?" or "Is it real?" as in "Do mental events (or the world, ethics, etc.) exist?" In order to answer his own questions Searle is willing to assume, at least at the outset, that he knows the answers to these deeper questions. "Yes of course I have a mind, so do you; and that is not a bunch of sense data of a car out there, but a real car." Beyond that, he thinks that answering the deeper questions at the outset is likely to lead to philosophical disaster in the form of scepticism or solipcism (Baggini 1999: 38). So when Searle turns his attention to the social sphere in his next major work (*Construction of Social Reality* (1995a)) it is not surprising to see him asking his kind of questions first. What sorts of structure do we find in this sphere? How do social concepts work? We know they are there and we know they work, but how can they work given that we live in a world we know is made up of atomic particles?

> How can there be an objective world of money, property, marriage, governments, elections, football, games, cocktail parties and law courts in a world that consists entirely of physical particles in fields of force, and in which some of these particles are organized into systems that are conscious biological beasts, such as ourselves? (Searle 1995a: xi–xii)

That Searle has turned to questions pertaining to social reality should be no surprise. His early work in speech act theory is thoroughly enmeshed in social concepts. To issue a command is to do something in a social setting. If the commander is not a social superior to the one commanded, then the command is not really a command. Similarly, to excommunicate someone, declare war, fire someone from their job, resign from a job, sign a contract, make a treaty or a will, and get baptized, married or divorced all involve issuing speech acts that require social institutions. For Searle, even if his only concern were to understand more fully how language works, some understanding of social reality would be necessary.

However, his interest in social reality goes beyond making language intelligible. He wants to present us with a more complete portrait of reality. Part of the portrait is already complete. It shows that mental reality emerges from physical reality (Chs 7–8 in this work). But now he wants to show us how social reality emerges from the mental reality. When complete, the portrait will show that there is no trichotomy of the social, mental and the physical. There is also no dichotomy of the mental and the physical. As we will see, for Searle, there is only one seamless reality. We will also see that while he deals with what he conceives to be the relatively neglected field of social reality, he also deals with the "deeper" questions in his own good time. Finally, we will see why it was important for him to answer questions about language and the mind first, before dealing with those concerned with social reality and the so-called deeper questions.

Preparation

Answers to questions about how social reality works and how it is structured are not easily uncovered. Preparations are required. Not surprisingly, for Searle, these preparations have been in the works for a long time. Most of the concepts he needs to prepare the way are found in his earlier studies concerned with language and the mind. Searle says that he needs only three concepts – the first and third clearly coming from his past works. These concepts are: (a) the assignment of function, (b) what he calls collective intentionality and (c) constitutive rules.

However, to explain these concepts, he needs to employ two additional sets of concepts that are also largely products of his earlier works. The first of the two explanatory concepts is really a double set having to do with the concepts of ontology and epistemology, on the one hand, and objectivity and subjectivity, on the other. Ontology deals with entities or groups of entities that exist. Some of those entities like mountains, rocks, clouds, dogs and electrons exist objectively while others like pains and tickles exist or manifest themselves subjectively. They both are real but the former group is known publicly (on a third-person basis) while *some* in the latter group are known privately (on a first-person basis). In contrast, epistemology deals not with entities (and their existence) but with judgments about entities. Some of these judgments are objective as in "That mountain is 7,000 feet tall" and "Mr Smith slipped on the ice and broke his leg". Although pains and pleasures are subjective ontologically, judgments about them can be objective. Such is the case with the judgments "He is in more pain today than yesterday" and "Searle likes skiing". In contrast, what is ontologically objective can be talked about subjectively as in "That is an ugly mountain". But it is also possible to make subjective judgments about what is subjective ontologically. This is the case with "Of all the pains a person suffers the worst is caused by dentists" and "That was a wonderful experience".

We met these two sets of distinctions (ontology/epistemology and objective/subjective) initially in Chapter 7 of this work in connection with Searle's philosophy of mind writings. The next distinction (from Chapter 5) should be familiar as well since a version of it comes from these same writings. Searle distinguishes between intrinsic and derived Intentionality. Humans, as creatures of the universe, have certain features that make up their nature; and one such feature is Intentionality (i.e. aboutness). Humans see, hear, know about, have opinions about, worry about, get angry at, remember, etc. all kinds of things. They have these Intentional powers on their own. They do not gain Intentionality the way language does. Language's Intentionality is imposed upon it by humans. So language's Intentionality is derived not intrinsic.

Searle now articulates a more general sense of this distinction. He distinguishes between intrinsic and observer relative features of things. His terminology varies. He sometimes talks about observer (user) independent and observer(user) dependent features. Terminology aside, the basic idea is this. Some things possess features quite independently of anyone who might observe them. As Searle puts it, the mountain would be there and be 7,000 feet tall even if humans didn't exist to see it or to measure its height. The stars would be there too, and were there, before humans came to observe them. Certain features possessed by objects and events in the universe have, then, a status independent of observers. Searle grants that the judgment about the mountain's 7,000 foot height is not completely observer independent. "Foot" defined as "12 inches" and "inches" defined in this or that way are themselves human concepts. We invent them to help us think about things out there. But aside from this linguistic dependence, observer independent features have no connection to humans. Mountains don't exist because humans want to climb them – or explore, ski, admire, or paint them. Rather we climb them because they are there (in the first place).

It is different with some other objects and features of the world. To say that Amelia is a dog is to utter an observer independent judgment. It is also epistemologically an objective judgment. In contrast, to say Amelia is a pet is, again, to utter one that is epistemologically objective, but observer dependent. Being a pet cannot be known by a more careful scrutiny of Amelia's chocolate coloured coat, her brown and blue eyes, long eyelashes, long ears, wagging tail or any other part of her anatomy – or her behaviour for that matter. Being a pet involves knowing that she has a relationship with her owner; and that relationship involves knowing something about the intentions, desires, etc. of the owner. Pets, then, because the concept of pet can be understood in part in terms of mental concepts, are ontologically subjective objects. Similarly, as we have seen, a computer is a computer only when an "observer" or user is put into the loop who has intentions to use the machine in one way or another. So computers are also ontologically subjective entities. Without the user all we have is a machine made from a chip, a motherboard, a hard drive, wires and other electronic paraphernalia. To be labelled a computer, the equipment bought at Computer Heaven must have someone in the loop who built it for or uses it for, among other things, word processing.

Putting the two clusters of concepts together here is what they look like in schematic form. In the schema 'OD' stands for observer dependent, while 'OI' stands for observer independent. Notice that there are two distinct kinds of entities in the Ontology/Subjectivity cell. The first kind contains entities such as pains that are purely individualistic while the second contains entities such as cars that are more social in character.

	Objectivity	Subjectivity
Ontology	dogs, trees, rocks, mountains, clouds, oceans, etc.	pains, tickles, thrills, anxieties, fears, desires, etc; plus, cars, fountain pens, pets, spoons, language, jelly, etc.
Epistemology	"I am in pain" (OD) "Amelia is a dog." (OI) "Amelia is a pet." (OD) "The tree is 100' tall." (OI) "Our bench is that tree over there." (OD) "We'll make lots of money from that lumber." (OD) "My car is fast." (OD)	"Amelia is a beautiful dog." (OD) "The jelly tastes good." (OD)

As the schema shows, being observer (user) dependent does not prevent a feature from being judged or talked about objectively. That Amelia is a pet can be verified by observing both Amelia and some human interacting in a parental and, one hopes, a playful manner. Similarly, coming to know objectively that the tree over there is our bench involves observing both the tree and our use of it as a place for sitting. For the present purposes the main difference between making objective judgments like "Amelia is a dog" and "Amelia is a pet" is that the latter, involving reference both to Amelia and her "keeper", is more complex. As we will see, the objectivity of observer dependent features is important since it suggests that the social sciences, which rely heavily on these features in characterizing all sorts of phenomena, can be objective.

The three features

Now we are ready to discuss the three features Searle says he needs to construct social reality. The first he calls the assignment of function. Roughly speaking, to assign a function to something is to put it to use on our own or someone else's behalf. The object assigned a function can be found in nature (as when a log is used as a bench, or a stone is used as a tool or weapon) or it can be something made by us (a chair, aeroplane, a medical drug). Some animals can assign certain objects a function (e.g. a monkey might use – that is, climb up – a tree in order to evade a ground predator) but humans are especially good functionizers. Think for a moment how numerous and varied functional objects are for humans. Typically, carpenters have hundreds of tools, each of which has at least one function. Chefs have scores of tools, instruments, spices, etc. In medicine, physicians also have tools by the thousands but in addition have supplies, medicines and procedures all with identifiable functions. Each human occupation has a long list of functional tools, instruments and procedures associated with it. Then there are the various means of transportation, each of which, again, has one or more function. In addition, there are hundreds of parts to each of these vehicles. With each part having one or more function – wheels and tyres to move us quickly and smoothly, brakes to stop us, pistons to help run the engine, lubricants to keep wear on engines at a minimum, seats to keep passengers in place and comfortable, etc. The home has its own myriad of functional objects from sofas, tables and chairs, through to somewhat smaller items such as radios, computers, telephones, TV sets and coffee makers to still smaller items such as spoons, napkins, towels, soaps and shampoos. We take these functional objects so much for granted that it is almost shocking to realize how many are around us even when we take the time to identify just a few.

However, the variety of the functional is not restricted to physical objects. Human institutions are functional "objects". Marriage as an institution has the purpose of providing a stable environment for the children that result from sexual activity; and the additional purpose of keeping sexual activity (somewhat) under control. Armies have the purpose, or function, of protecting society, courts to adjudicate disagreements among us, and business organizations the purpose of providing services and goods to the public and, on the side, profits for their owners. Language too is a functional object.

Searle distinguishes between what he calls agentive and non-agentive functions. The former concerns those objects, processes or institutions made functional by the intentional acts of humans (i.e. where humans are the agents), the latter not. So, to use Searle's example, to say that the heart functions to pump blood is to speak of the non-agentive function of this organ. Language falls under the agentive heading. Humans intentionally impose Intentionality on sounds that we utter, on marks that we make on paper or on motions of our body so that they have meaning (Searle 1995a: 21). We then use these meaningful sounds, marks and movements for the purpose of giving information to others, telling them what to do, etc. Once in position as a functional instrument, language serves, in a feed-back manner, as a functional multiplier. Because language makes it possible for us to write down our plans, it in turn helps create other functional objects. Thus, language helps us to design computers that in turn facilitate use of language that, in turn once again, helps create still more functional objects.

For the present purposes one more point needs to be made about the assignment of function. This assignment need not be done consciously. The assignment will always possess Intentionality, but it need not be done intentionally. In the distant past, a member of our tribe may have sat on a log because they were very tired. On another day another member sat down on the same log for the same reason. A storm may, next, have brought down second tree near by the first that tempted our original sitter to sit on it as well. Gradually, without any conscious decision, the tribe members may have found themselves sitting on these logs on a regular basis and, in so doing, turning them into (functional) benches.

Here it is not clear what assignment means. Are the logs benches because people sit on them regularly; or do they become benches when the tribe actually assigns the new concept of bench (i.e. their own version of our concept) to these logs? Searle allows for the former possibility and suggests this may be part of what some social scientists mean by latent function; and is what he means by a non-agentive function (1995a: 22). Very likely a concept will be assigned to the practice (that has a function), but concept assignment is not required for a functional object to exist.

The second of the three elements or features that Searle says he needs to account for social reality is collective intentionality. This feature appears to be the kind that all good hard-headed analytic philosophers like Searle should avoid like the plague. The temptation for these philosophers is to grab hold of these collective intentions, or so-called we-intentions, by the nape of the neck and reduce them to a series of I-intentions.

> The reason for this temptation is that if you think that collective intentionality is irreducible, you seem to be forced to postulate some sort of collective mental entity, some sort of overarching Hegelian World Spirit, some "we" that floats around mysteriously above us individuals and of which we as individuals are just expressions. But since all the intentionality I have is in my head and all you have is in your head, our puzzle is: How can it be the case that there is such a thing as irreducible, *collective* intentionality? (Searle 1998: 118)

Searle solves the puzzle by neither becoming a Hegelian, nor effecting some sort of reduction. As he says, the Hegelian option is too mysterious for him, so he rejects it out of hand. But he feels the need to explain his rejection of the reductionist option. A sample analysis of how that option might work involves Sam having an intention to pull a heavy wagon that he cannot pull by himself, Tom having the same intention, Tom recognizing that Sam has the intention to pull the wagon, Sam recognizing that Tom has the intention, Sam recognizing that Tom recognizes that Sam has the intention and so on. Searle grants that this regress to still another level of recognition need not be infinitely vicious since our minds will simply stop the process from fatigue or confusion. Still, since he thinks that this reductive analysis is too complex, he rejects it.

This is strange. As we saw in Chapter 1, some of the processes that Searle describes in his language theory where a speaker has an intention, which intention is recognized by another and which recognition is recognized by the speaker, etc., are also very complex. So, if we accept Searle's account of how language works, complexity by itself does not seem to be a very good reason for rejecting the reductionist theory of collective intentionality.

The better reason is that Searle thinks he has a simpler story to tell. He treats we-intentionality as a primitive concept. To appreciate his non-reductionist option it is helpful to turn once again to some of the speech acts he and Austin analyze in developing their language theories. Consider a declaration of war. The governmental leader of The Good Nation does not get up before his people and announce "I declare war on The Evil Empire". And it is not the case that following his declaration, each member of The Good Nation says "I am at war with the Evil Empire and I recognize that you are at war with The Evil Empire", etc. and, as a result, there is war. To be sure, the leader might say "I say we are at war" but the sense of what he is saying is that *we*, the people of The Good Nation, are at war.

Consider, once again, the example of Sam and Tom. Sam says to Tom "Let's pull together" and Tom agrees. There is a we-intention in each of their heads. Where else, Searle asks ironically, would their intentions be? Out in social space somewhere? But, he adds, it does not follow that just because intentions are in individual minds that the intentions themselves have to be individual. Or putting it linguistically, it does not follow that if Sam has an intention to work with Tom to pull the wagon that this intention needs to be expressed in the singular or I (or me) mode. Sam could very well have an intention that we (Tom and I) will work together. Tom can have a comparable we-intention. Sam can have his we-intention and, at the same time, have an I-intention that he will push as hard as he can from the left side of the cart. In turn, Tom can have a similar we-intention and also an I-intention to push from the right side.

Consider another example – by now a familiar one. The commander tells his troops "Let's take that hill (from the Evil Empire forces)". Here he doesn't have to wait for agreement from his troops. They are programmed to follow his orders. On Searle's account what the commander expresses is a we-intention. He says, we together will take the hill. It is easy to imagine still other examples of we-intentions and then come to realize how common they are. That is exactly what Searle wants us to do. I'll have more to say about these intentions in the next chapter, but for now let us grant Searle's point that primitive we-intentions exist. They exist, and because they do, they allow us to talk about what Searle calls social facts. Social facts are those facts that, by definition, involve collective intentionality (1995a: 26). Without we-intentions there can be no social facts.

The third element that Searle says he needs to explain social reality is the notion of constitutive rules. Searle introduced this notion, along with a small family of other notions, back in his *Speech Acts* (1969) days. Recall that constitutive rules are contrasted to regulative ones. Regulative rules help to control pre-existing kinds of behaviour. If there are rules about not walking in the street, passing other pedestrians coming from the opposite direction by keeping to the right, never walking in the street naked, these would be regulative rules.

In contrast, constitutive rules literally create forms of behaviour. By following a set of such rules people engage in activity that they never could have engaged in before. Basketball, historically, was not a game until over 100 years ago when Dr James Naismith said that tossing the ball in the basket under such and such conditions counts as two points, walking the ball down the court without bouncing it on the floor counts as a violation and will be punished by the loss of ball possession, and playing in accordance with these and other rules for a certain amount of time constitutes a game. Others of course had to accept most of Naismith's rules before the game was accepted as the game of basketball we know today.

Constitutive rules have much wider application than to help us invent games. They apply when we say certain things in certain settings such as "I will" and suddenly, and shockingly (for some), find ourselves married. They also apply when we find ourselves in a gathering of people as someone says "I call this meeting to order" and when standing before a green light which permits us to cross the street. As with we-intentions, much more needs to, and will, be about constitutive rules.

Simple forms of social reality

Consider the following setting. There are two tigers, a male and a female. Each hunts on its own. On a daily basis the male has essentially no social life, yet its experiences can be characterized in terms of Intentionality. It sees, hears, smells and touches all sorts of objects in its environment. It has desires for food and water. The former will drive it to attack and, if lucky, destroy other animals. Its relationship with these animals will in no sense be social in nature.

The female's life can also be characterized in terms of Intentionality but her life is different because of her cubs. Presumably she has to hunt more intensely since she has more mouths to feed. She has found a small and well hidden depression in the soil that serves to hide the cubs from predators and to some extent she has altered the depression by digging it out so now it resembles a cave. She feeds the cubs and watches them play with each other. She also watches over and plays with them. After the cubs are grown and leave the nest, she has another affair with her boyfriend and this eventually leads to a new generation of young ones.

In addition to Intentionality, which of the Searlian concepts apply to this setting? Certainly two forms of agentive functionality apply in so far as the female tiger finds a location and uses it for the purpose of nesting, and in so far as she modifies it to make it more suitable for that purpose. Of course the female, or even the male, tiger could have built the hiding place for its own security reasons. So the hiding place need not be part of their social life. It could serve just the opposite purpose of further isolating them from the rest of the world. But, let us assume that for the female at least the nest was built in anticipation of the cubs' arrival. Even so, there is no social reality as yet. Nor is it clear that social reality is present as the cubs are born and soon after.

When, then, does social reality make its first appearance? Most clearly when the cubs and the mother begin to respond to each other in the feeding process, in play and in whatever "strategies" they employ to secure the safety of all the animals. At this point Searle would say that we-intentions are present. About a different, still more complicated, setting involving animals Searle says:

> it takes no cultural apparatus, cultural convention, or language for animals to move together in a pack or to hunt together. When hyenas move in a pack to kill an isolated lion, no linguistic or cultural apparatus is necessary, even though the behavior of the hyenas is very skillfully coordinated and the hyenas are responsive not only to the lion but to each other. The selectional advantage of cooperative behavior is, I trust, obvious. Inclusive fitness is increased by cooperating with conspecifics. (1995a: 37–8)

So there is no doubt that on the non-linguistic level of animal life there are social facts. Presumably it is the same when two humans decide to pull the cart stuck in the mud together without saying anything. They too are exhibiting we-intentionality and are thus on the level of living that allow for social facts to be present. What is missing so far from all these settings is the notion of constitutive rules. Here language is required and so animals, with few exceptions, are left behind.

But before discussing those settings where constitutive rules are involved, it is useful to list and give an account of various kinds of judgments that involve social reality. As with the account of social reality given so far in this chapter, the listing proceeds from the most simple to the most complex and, in so far as it does, it fosters a greater appreciation of the more complex judgments.

Batch I
- A "That is a rock."
- B "The water is running rapidly down stream."
- C "The ice is melting."
- D " He is (I am) eating."
- E "He sees (I see) the mountain."
- F "He is in pain."

Batch I judgments have nothing to do with social reality. They correspond to what Searle calls brute facts in that they do not, by definition, involve observer relativity. His rough-and-ready test of his form of brutishness is that these events could take place even if no one observed them. Notice that E falls under this heading because someone could be seeing the mountain quite apart from whether anyone else "observed" him seeing it. The same can be said about F. The pain being suffered does not require anyone to observe or sense the suffering he is undergoing. Although the pain is transitory, as is the running water in B and the melting ice in C, it is nonetheless real. This way of putting it catches Searle's claim that Intentionality (e.g. seeing) is an intrinsic part of human nature just as hardness of a diamond and the length of a blade of grass are intrinsic parts of their nature. Examples of Batch I judgments serve as a contrast to the batches that exhibit more social reality.

Batch II
  A "They are walking together."
  B "They are playing together."
  C "The children are sleeping together."
  D "They are pulling (the cart) together."

With this batch we get judgments comparable to some of those we find with our tigers and hyenas. Walking is not inherently a social activity in that it can be done alone, but it can be done with others and thus be turned into a social activity. In Searle's terminology it would be a social fact if the two or more people walking together are doing so with collective (we-) intentions, rather than merely walking side-by-side by chance. Roughly the same can be said of B, C and D. Each activity can be done individually or by the two (or three or more) together. In addition, each judgment can reflect occurrent or dispositional reality. The present wording in Batch II suggests that an individual event is being talked about. However, with a slight change in wording (e.g. "They walk together") the speaker would naturally be taken as talking about a series of related events (i.e. a tendency or a disposition).

Batch III
  A "They are making love."
  B "They are giving each other a rub down."
  C "They are fighting (each other)."

Batch III differs from II in that the activity involved is necessarily social. The one possible exception is C. C would be social if the fight is being governed by a set of rules (e.g. issued by the boxing commission) or is in some sense ritualized. But if the fight is a no-holds-barred affair as it might in war, it probably does not represent any form of social activity. As with Batch II, the activity in Batch III could either be occurrent or dispositional although the present wording suggests the former interpretation. Also, as with II, this batch could represent judgments of either human or other-animal behaviour (again with animals C is probably an exception).

Batch IV
A "They are using that log over there as a bench."
B "They are both using sticks as tools to reach out for the food."
C "They have turned the pond into a swimming pool."

This batch returns to judgments of activities that could be done by individual but in fact are about activities being carried out under the heading of we-intentions. However what is added is functionality. All three judgments are about the use of found objects for human or other-animal purposes.

Batch V
A "The rule says that we are to drive on the right side of the road."
B "Following the rule we go to work at dawn and stop working at sunset."
C "We always hold the fork with our left hand when eating."

There is a significant difference in the level of social reality between Batch IV and V. With IV the activities might very well achieve a level of habit so as to be called regularities. But it would be inappropriate so say that Batch IV regularities involve rule-following. Batch V judgments are about rule-governed activities. These regulative rules govern already existing activities. We are already engaged in activities such as driving, going to work and eating. The rules tell us how to control such activities. Because rule-following involves the use of language, Batch V leaves animals behind. With Batch IV there was some overlapping between the social activities of humans and other animals. This is no longer so with the Batch V examples.

Batch VI
A "He gave him a $20 bill."
B "They got married."
C "He was excommunicated."
D "War was declared."

E "He promised to be at his office in the morning."
F " He hit a home run."

Batch VI's social facts are governed by constitutive rules. These are rules that follow the formula: "X counts as Y in C" where "X" is a place holder for all sorts of processes or activities that things undergo, "Y" stands for the status that X gains as the result of the razzle dazzle that X undergoes, and "C" stands for the context. In a context where there is a diamond shaped and fenced field with bases called first, second, third and another base called home plate; and in a context where there are batters with bats in their hands, pitchers who throw balls in the general direction of the batters, catchers, infielders and outfielders, etc.; in that context, when a batter hits the pitched ball over the far fence somewhere between first and third base (all this is X), hitting the ball will count as a home run (a Y). Similarly when a man and a woman stand in front of a religious or civil official, when there are witnesses, when neither the man nor the woman is already married, etc. (all this is C) and they and the official say and do certain things (all this is X), then it counts that they are married (a Y).

Rules about home runs, getting married and the like clearly differ from regulative rules since they help create new forms of human activity rather than regulate already established ones. Whereas regulative rules give us something new out of something that already exists, constitutive rules seem to give us something new out of nothing. There is an air of mystery about how this gets done; and this challenges Searle. He takes it as his task to explain how constitutive rules can help create what he calls institutional facts like those listed under the heading of Batch VI and, in the process, understand better what constitutive rules are, how they work and what their structure is. It is the task of the next chapter to answer these and other related questions.

However, before moving to that chapter it is worth reporting that Searle presents us with a taxonomy of facts that shows how he thinks the various batches of reports of facts relate to one another. The diagram is as he gives it to us in *Construction of Social Reality* (1995a: 121) except I have added where Batches I–III and Batches V and VI fit in. Notice that there is no place for Batch IV; I have indicated where it might be placed. Roughly speaking the level of social sophistication increases as we move from top to bottom. The most sophisticated levels dealing with institutional facts interests Searle the most since they beg for more explanation.

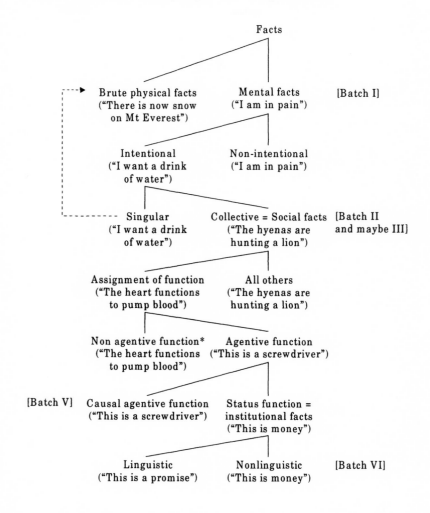

Facts

Brute physical facts   Mental facts   [Batch I]
("There is now snow   ("I am in pain")
on Mt Everest")

Intentional   Non-intentional
("I want a drink   ("I am in pain")
of water")

Singular   Collective = Social facts   [Batch II
("I want a drink   ("The hyenas are   and maybe III]
of water")   hunting a lion")

Assignment of function   All others
("The heart functions   ("The hyenas are
to pump blood")   hunting a lion")

Non agentive function*   Agentive function
("The heart functions   ("This is a screwdriver")
to pump blood")

[Batch V] Causal agentive function   Status function =
("This is a screwdriver")   institutional facts
                                        ("This is money")

Linguistic   Nonlinguistic   [Batch VI]
("This is a promise")   ("This is money")

* Functions are always ultimately assigned to brute phenomena, hence the line from the Assignment of Function to Brute Physical Facts.

Chapter 10

Institutions

The nature of institutions

What are institutions? Certainly if we follow ordinary usage, the American and the British governments count as institutions. Within each there are other institutions such as each country's military, medical and postal services as well as each country's legislative and judicial branches. Universities, whether public or private, also count as institutions as would other large schools, various kinds of museums, galleries and libraries. Our list of institutions also likely includes large corporations and businesses, large hospitals and hospital chains, large legal groups, symphony orchestras, opera companies, major theatre groups and major "think tanks". With each institution we are likely to associate some piece of real estate. Land, buildings or both, help us identify each one.

Searle's sense of institution is different. His sense is driven not so much by ordinary usage but by his formula for constitutive rules: "X counts as Y in C". Searle's preferred form of the formula is not important. Other versions that help explain its meaning are as follows: "X in (context) C becomes (or changes into) Y" or better yet "X in (context) C is given status (by the group) as Y". However it is stated, the formula allows the concept of "institution" to include much more than one might suppose. For example, Searle talks of money as an institution. But one might wonder whether money itself has that status; or whether the government is the institution and making money is just one of the functions it performs. The same can be said of games such as football and baseball. Are the games the institutions or are the organizations that authorize them to be played the institutions? Searle leans in the direction of the former interpretation. This is suggested by what he says about chess. If my king gets checked, its dire condition in the game represents what he calls an institutional fact. Being checked is an institutional fact presumably because the constitutive rule that helps make up the institution of chess says that if my king is in a certain position on the board, then it is in check (counts as being checked). So it appears that the game itself is an institution for Searle.

If we tie the meaning of institution to the X, Y and C formula as Searle does, rather than to usage, there will be other strange institutions. Almost all games will be, so will marriages, divorces, knighthood and (legal) punishment. Language itself is also an institution, as we will see shortly.

Beyond the formula, what makes these activities institutional is the *network* of (constitutive) rules that comprise them. Institutions evidently are systems of constitutive rules (Searle 1969: 51). A game is what it is not because of any one rule, but a family of rules. Chess is a game not just because of the rule concerned with checking, but also because of rules that dictate how rooks, pawns and the rest of the pieces are to be moved on, and removed from, the board. Similarly, if we think of the Senate as an institution in the United States government, we do so because of a variety of rules that govern how senators get elected, what powers they have on the floor of the Senate, how they gain committee assignments, etc. Evidently the buildings associated with the Senate represent just so much window dressing.

For Searle, then, "institution" means something like a cluster of related constitutive rules or practices. Indeed he might have done better to say that his theory of social reality is concerned with clusters of constitutive rules, or constitutive rules for short, and then go on to say that some of these rules are found in our social institutions while others are not. But terminological questions aside, once we realize what the special meaning he gives to "institution" is, no real harm gets done. We can go on to ask the next question.

Creating social reality

How do institutions bring about social reality? The quick answer is that they do so by helping us generate institutional facts. How this happens is most easily understood in the context of a just invented game. The game, played on a field something like that of American football, has three balls in play at the same time rather than the usual one. The balls are shaped like an American football only somewhat smaller. Their size facilitates hiding them from the opponent There are fifteen players on each side. Each side tries to score with one or more of the balls, while it tries to keep the other from scoring with one of the other balls. If each side scores on a play, the one who scores first gets four points; the one who scores second, three. If one side scores while the other side fails, five points are awarded to the scoring team, none to the other team. Scoring, like American football, comes about when, during play, a member of one side carries the ball over the end line of the field. The game is over when one side gets a lead of 24 points or more, or when one hour of actual play has elapsed. There are of course other rules in the game about uniforms, use of hands, kicking opponent players, tackling, substitutions, about other ways of scoring and about the role of the officials. The inventor of Chaos, as he calls his game, says it is more exciting than American football or football (soccer), and that it encourages athletes to develop a variety of skills for both offence and defence. He adds that the game more readily reflects how war is fought since both sides can strike an offensive blow at, or almost at, the same time.

As he sits down inventing his game and then writing down its rules he can, and let us suppose he does, express himself in accord with the Searlian formula: X in C counts as Y. If such and such happens in the game (X) while it is being played on the field where there are officials, etc.(C) that such and such will count as five points (Y).

Notice the objectivity that the rules of Chaos exhibit. In a practice game the Blue Team scores by moving one or more of the balls over the goal while the Red Team flounders with its offence. The scoring play itself is ontologically subjective since it involves an observer dependent fact. The score itself cannot be understood without taking into account the observer-known-rules. Any observer of the game cannot tell that the Blue Team scored its five points just by observing the bare fact of one Blues player crossing the goal with a ball in hand. Still, although observer dependent ontologically, the scoring play is epistemologically objective. Knowing that the Blue Team scored has nothing to do with the prejudices, preferences or desires of any observers. Anyone who knows the rules and who knows what happened during the play can objectively tell that the Blues scored in a certain way and therefore deserve to be awarded five points.

Actually there is another feature of social reality at play here. Even when the game is being played by the two practice teams on an experimental basis, the rules of the game will count as part of the game only if the players and those observing the game *accept* the rules. That is, what counts as a score, a "fiver" for example, involves not just carrying or catching a ball over or the goal line, but also an agreement by certain special people that carrying or catching a ball in the specified manner will receive a five point reward. We don't literally see the "fiver". All we see is a player from the Blue Team cross the goal. Of course an observer might say "I saw him score the fiver". But that is just a manner of speaking. "I saw him score a fiver" means something like "I saw him cross the goal in such a way as to satisfy the rules invented for Chaos and accepted by those playing and observing the game". In Searle's terminology "I saw him score a fiver" is an observer dependent judgment. Also, in Searle's terminology, the heavy involvement of we-intentions in these game activities is obvious. In accepting the rules of Chaos the players and coaches are in effect saying that we intend to play by the rules. On the level of rule acceptance both sides share in what they intend.

Searle calls this acceptance feature of social reality self-referentiality. It is a feature that for him helps to distinguish natural reality from the part of social reality that deals with institutions.

> Something can be a mountain even if no one believes it is a mountain; something can be a molecule even if no one thinks anything at all about it. But for social facts, the attitude that we take toward the phenomenon is partly constitutive of the phenomenon. If, for example, we give a big cocktail party, and invite everyone in Paris, and if things get out of hand, and it turns out that the casualty rate is greater than the Battle of Austerlitz – all the same, it is not a war; it is just one amazing cocktail party. Part of being a cocktail party is being thought to be a cocktail party; part of being a war is being thought to be a war. This is a remarkable feature of social facts; it has no analogue among physical facts. (1995a: 33–4)

The acceptance of Chaos's rules is not necessarily like the acceptance of constitutive rules in other social domains. With Chaos the rules are written down. Especially because the game is new, people will be staring at the rule book on a regular basis. So acceptance will be conscious and deliberate. Shortly we will see how this deliberate and conscious acceptance is different from that found in some of the other social domains and, thus, why it may be dangerous to focus too much on games in trying to understand social reality of institutional facts.

In addition to acceptance, another feature of social reality needs to be noted: viz., the normative component. This component can be expressed either in functional terms or by Searle's "counts" formula. In the former way anyone involved in the game of Chaos can say that the function (or purpose) of running or passing one or more of the balls over the other team's goal is to outscore it; and the function of outscoring it is to win. The goals of scoring and winning are artificial, of course, since they gain their meaning from within the rules of the game itself. But these goals are normative none the less. They represent what the team wants to achieve. What makes the goals in Chaos and many other games different from the goals in most other social domains of our lives is that they are quantifiable. A "fiver" is worth more than a "tray" or a "deuce" by a measurable amount. Expressed in terms of the "counts" formula the normative component shows itself in the transition from X to Y. In the formula, Y has status lacking in X. It has value by virtue of the fact that the rules (and the rule maker) give it value.

So there is no mystery about social reality when it comes to games like Chaos. Institutional judgments like "We scored a fiver" and "We won the game" achieve their objective institutional status because people decide what the standards of success in the game are, and then some players go out on the field in order to try to meet those standards. They score fivers and win games. Players on the other team accept the same set of rules, but they fail to meet as many standards and so they lose. But now, it might be asked, can we follow this same model for explaining social reality in realms other than games?

Let us look once again at the institution of marriage, more particularly the part having to do with getting married, to see if the game model works here as well. It certainly seems to. In both Chaos and getting married, rule citing is the order of the day. Like Chaos some people know the rules better than others. The officials at a wedding ceremony know the rules the best. The couple to be married and others participating in the wedding usually require instruction, while the witnesses don't even have to know or learn much about the wedding rules to play their secondary role in the proceedings. Presumably the reason rules need to be cited is that getting married is, unlike making promises for example, something one does (the hope is) once in a lifetime. Coupled with the fact that getting married represents a serious "status change" for individuals, it is important that one gets married properly. So the constitutive rules for getting married are cited to make sure things are done right and, in so far as they are, Searle's formula "X counts as Y in C" is present in the wedding scenario. Assignment of function is also present. The function (or purpose) of going through the ceremony is to achieve the status of being married; and achieving that status gives the couple certain rights and responsibilities. In turn, these rights and responsibilities allow normative concepts into the scenario. We can now say that if the husband finds time for an overnight visit with his old girlfriend, he is violating the institutional rules of marriage.

Collective intentionality is (we-intentions are) also here. The couple, the marriage officials, the other members of the marriage team and the witnesses collectively can all assent to the intention that can linguistically be expressed as "We intend to take part in this wedding". Their collective intentionality can be expressed in terms of a closely related concept. Their intention to participate expresses approval of the marriage. Those at the wedding approve of marriage as an institution but also approve of this particular marriage ceremony which is about to begin. Again notice that they express approval even though they do not necessarily know all the rules of the getting married game. Presumably they understand some of the rules. They at least know that neither participant in the wedding already has a spouse and that at a certain point in the ceremony the about-to-be-husband and the about-to-be-wife need to say something like "I do" or' "I will" before they actually become husband and wife.

One other feature found in the marriage ceremony matches closely a feature found in the Chaos game. Once the couple is married a new institutional fact emerges. Linguistically we express this by saying "Well, they are married now". This judgment about the new fact, much like the judgment about the Blue Team scoring a "fiver", is epistemologically objective. Since the couple went through the whole ceremony (X) and since all present at the wedding (and the society in general) approve of marriage, it is an objective fact that the couple has achieved Y status.

So Searle's model seems to work quite well not only with games but also with other institutional settings where the constitutive rules need to be known and recited. One should not underestimate the number of such settings. Constitutive rules are near the surface when we apply for our driver's licence, buy a home, car or refrigerator, go to school in order to receive a degree, vote in an election, run for public office, apply for a job, get hired, get promoted and get honoured for being a true and loyal employee. Presumably all these settings, and others like them, can be accounted for by Searle's model. His model tells us how the institutional facts that arise from these settings get generated.

However, there are other settings where the institutional facts emerge, but where the constitutive rules appear to be hiding. These sorts of institutional facts are generally more commonly met in everyday life than are those we find on special occasions such as weddings. When Captain Jones orders Private Smith to climb a hill, that institutional fact emerges with the help of somewhat hidden constitutive rules of the military. When John pays the bartender for his beer that institutional fact emerges with the help of the somewhat more hidden constitutive rules about money. And when Sally tells Sam to take the refuse out, that institutional fact emerges with the help of the even more hidden constitutive rules about language.

As these examples suggest there are degrees of hiddenness when it comes to constitutive rules. This fact poses a problem for Searle.

> How can it be that the rules of the institution play a role in our dealings with the institution, even though we are not following the rules either consciously or unconsciously? Of course, in some cases we actually are following the rules. I might teach you a new card game and you might memorize the rules and follow the rules of the game. But for many institutions, particularly after I have become expert at operating within the institution, I just know what to do. I know what the appropriate behavior is, without reference to the rules.   (1995a: 137)

Language is certainly the best example of an "institution" where we know what to do without making reference to the rules. Many of us do not even know the rules of our natural language, or perhaps know a few of them, and yet we have known how to use that language for a lifetime. It isn't that we don't know these rules now but knew them when we were in school. Rather, we never knew them. If this lack of knowledge describes the state of most language users, what sense can we make of Searle's claim that institutions are to be understood in terms of rule-following?

Back to the Background (and Network)

Searle begins to deal with this question by invoking the concept of Background once again. So far we have invoked that concept mainly in connection with the discussions of Intentionality, the mind and, more generally, the concept of context (in Ch. 6). The concept of Background is an old one for Searle. His earliest clear use of it is found in his article "Literal Meaning" that first saw the light of day in the late 1970s and is reprinted in *Expression and Meaning* (1979a: 117–36). It is in this article that he uses the "The cat-is-on-the-mat" example and where he asks whether we can understand whether the cat is on the mat without taking the context into account. Searle's answer, recall, is that we cannot, even though "The cat is on the mat" seems at first sight to be a contextless claim. But, he asks, what if the cat and the mat are out in space where there is no gravity and thus where it is difficult to know when the mat is on the cat or the cat on the mat? What if the cat is suspended by wires so it just barely touches the mat? What if the cat is heavily sedated and balanced on the edge of a mat has been stiffened and put on edge? Is the cat now on the mat? These unlikely scenarios remind us that when we say "The cat is on the mat" we take for granted that this claim is made on earth where gravity is at work, where cats are not normally suspended by wires and where mats are not stiff. We also take for granted that cats don't change into flowers and then change back again into cats after a few moments, mats don't change into cats, that floors on which we place mats don't collapse as the cat ambles over to the mat, and on and on. Searle's point is that even the simplest of statements lie in a bed of Background conditions that contribute to our understanding of them.

Consider again the Chaos setting. The rules of Chaos are not in the Background nor even the Network. Indeed those playing and observing the game must have the rules in the foreground simply because it is a new game. They wouldn't know how to begin playing or know who was winning the game unless its basic rules were explained. But that doesn't mean that the Background and Network are not at work even in this setting. Could the game have been played in outer space with players floating around in three rather than two dimensions? Would it be the same game if the players could be transformed into monsters at the will of their coaches? Could we determine who won if players had the ability to divide in two; and thus be in two places at the same time? Even when there are explicit rules that guide us in how to engage in some institutional activity, there are many things taken for granted that are not explicit such as that gravity is at work, the field is solid, players don't change radically from moment to moment etc.

Recall how it is that we are aware of or know about the Background. We don't know about "units" in the Background by forming a set of beliefs. But what then is the status of those "units" or "parts of" the Background?

> Intentional states only have the conditions of satisfaction [the conditions that allow us to assess them as true/false or correct/ incorrect] that they do, and thus are states that they are, against a Background of abilities that are not themselves Intentional states. In order that I can now have the Intentional states that I do I must have certain kinds of know-how: I must know how things are and I must know how to do things, but the kinds of "know-how" in question are not, in these cases, forms of "knowing that".   (Searle 1983: 143)

According to this account, a celebrated pianist does not say to himself "I am aware that these are the right rules and this is the right time to apply these rules". Instead he shows us that he knows how to play the piano by simply playing it. His skills are not cognitive in the sense of being representations of ideas in the mind but are, instead, abilities located in his fingers, muscles and neural system. If so, what role, if any, do rules have to play for our pianist? We saw in the Intentionality chapter (Ch. 5) and in the Chaos example that rules are useful when someone is learning to do something. When our pianist began to play the piano as a child, there was lots of rule recitation. At that time his teacher told him what to do and in the process recited a variety of rules. Then our young pianist practised, was told again what the rules were and then he practised some more. But, as we have seen, in time the rules disappear. They are replaced with abilities, tendencies, ways of reacting and other knowing-how capacities.

With language things are seemingly still worse for rules. Typically, children do not learn their native language with rule recitation and practice, and then more rule recitation and practice. They learn it instead on the go. They learn their native language by listening to others speak, speaking themselves, listening, speaking, listening and so on. Nonetheless, Searle insists that rules still have a role to play even in this seemingly rule-less environment. How can this be? Searle tells us that the know-how we have when we learn language and many other skills that find themselves in the Background is sensitive to, or as he sometimes puts it, is a reflection of, the constitutive rules.

> [one] doesn't need to know the rules of the institution and to follow them in order to conform to the rules; rather, he is just disposed to behave in a certain way, but he has acquired those unconscious dispositions and capacities in a way that is sensitive to the rule structure of the institution. To tie this down to a concrete case, we should not say that the experienced baseball player runs to first base because he wants to follow the rules of baseball, but we should say that because the rules require that he run to first base, he acquires a set of Background habits, skills, dispositions that are such that when he hits the ball, he runs to first base. (1995a: 144)

Such an account makes sense for baseball where someone, or some influential group, has articulated the rules of the game at one time or another, and then trained players to follow the rules. But when we are concerned with language, where very little rule teaching takes place, Searle's account sounds a bit mysterious. How does our know-how become sensitive to rules that have been articulated only by linguists and philosophers of language who, by and large, do not influence people in the process of learning (or speaking) their native language? That is, how can rules that have been articulated only (or mainly) by those outside of the learning loop play a causal role in teaching us to know how to use our language? Here is another attempt by Searle to explain the role of rules in these contexts where no one essentially cites rules in the learning process.

> I am saying that if you understand the complexity of the causation involved, you can see that often a person who behaves in a skillful way within an institution behaves as if he were follow-

ing the rules, but not because he is following the rules unconsciously nor because his behavior is caused by an undifferentiated mechanism that happens to look as if it were rule structured, but rather because *the mechanism has evolved precisely so that it will be sensitive to the rules.* The mechanism explains the behavior, and the mechanism is explained by the system of rules, but the mechanism need not itself be a system of rules. (1995a: 146)

The mechanism Searle is referring to in this passage is the neural system that carries (in some unknown way) the information that enables us to use our language and exhibit other skills whatever they might be. So the neural system (perhaps via parallel distributive processing) again is sensitive to the rules. With language, where the rule teachers are few and far between, these rules have to be implicit in the usage of parents and other adult users of the language who speak the language in front of children who are learning it. Of course, the rules of the language can be extracted by careful post-mortem analysis. But it is tempting to say that what is causing speakers to speak the way they do is not the implicit rules, but the speech patterns of the parents and other adults. Be that as it may, Searle evidently wants to think that the implicit rules have a causal role both in how adults speak and how they transmit their speech to the younger generation. I will have more to say about this issue shortly.

Additional features of social reality

Let us see where we stand. Social reality is found among animals as well as humans. Some animals are capable of having collective intentions and thus engage in activities that generate social facts. It is a social fact that those lions over there are hunting together for their next meal. It is a social fact that those birds on that tree are cooperating to build a nest for their offspring. With some of the social activity many animals engage in, they exhibit the ability to impose functions on objects. Such imposition can be social as it is with joint nest building, some not as when individual monkeys use branches as a tool to reach for food. As subtle and complicated as these forms of social reality can be, they pale to insignificance when compared to the social reality constructed by humans.

Humans can engage in those social activities common among animals beneath them on the evolutionary ladder, but they can do much more because they can make and (deliberately) follow rules.

Some of the rules they employ regulate behaviour humans engage in already. Although these regulative rules enable humans to engage in social activity unknown to animals, what really separates animals from humans is the latter's ability to make and use constitutive rules. Such rules take the form "X in C counts as Y". The move from X to Y confers new status on X. If X is a certain kind of paper produced by the government, etc., then it gains status as money. If X is an unmarried couple who say certain things like "I do" in a certain context then they gain new status as a married couple. The move from X to Y comes about because of collective agreement. The society as a whole has to approve of that kind of move for the change of status to take place. Institutions are formed when we have a system (or cluster) of accepted "X in C counts as Y" formulas. Clusters of rules are not always explicitly stated but when they are it is easy to understand what it means to follow rules and how such rule-following helps create institutional facts ("Yes that is a dollar bill and yes they are married"). However, much of our institutional life expresses itself in the Background, and this seems to pose a problem as to what it means to follow rules and also what it means to say that rules causally influence what we do.

Two closely related things need to be added to this account of social reality to more fully appreciate Searle's theory of the social world. The first has to do with how institutional facts relate to one another. Searle insists that institutional facts do not exist in isolation. Since institutional facts, by definition, are part of at least one institution and since institutions form up only when there exists a system of constitutive rules, individual institutional facts can only be understood and assessed within the system. Even in games such as basketball an institutional fact such as "He made a basket" can be understood only in relation to other rules of that game having to do with the height of the basket, dribbling the ball to the basket, pushing opponents out of position and so on. Institutional facts in life away from the playground are even more interrelated with other facts and rules. Searle talks about money to help make this point. If Susy spends $50.43 at the store in Atlanta, Georgia, that institutional fact presupposes that there is a system for exchanging goods in the United States (1995a: 35). There must also be a system having to do with property and property owner-ship. "Similarly, in order that societies should have marriages, they must have some form of contractual relationship. But in order that they can have contractual relationships, they have to under-stand such things as promises and obligations" (1995a: 35).

The interrelated nature of institutional facts goes hand in hand with the phenomenon of iteration. This phenomenon truly shows the complexity and subtlety of the human social world. We find iteration when, first, we use sounds in a certain way (X) to speak in English (Y). Then secondly, we speak certain words in English such as "I promise" (formerly Y, but now X) and saying that counts as making a promise (a new Y). Thirdly, if a young man and young woman both make a special promise (formerly Y but now X) they are married (new Y). But not quite. This piling on of one institu-tional fact upon the other (iteration) doesn't get the couple married because the context hasn't been fully specified. There is more itera-tion in this ceremony, but now it has to do with the official who marries them. That official had at one time to make sounds (X) in such a way as to speak in English (Y), so that he could say certain things in English (formerly Y, but now X) that would make him trained to be an official (a new Y), which training and the use of more English (formerly Y but now X) made him an official when he took an oath of office (a newer Y) which oath and the use of more English (formerly Y but now X) allowed him to say "I pronounce you man and wife" (Y). Now the couple is married if, addition, we keep in mind that others (e.g. witnesses) might be required to add other institutional facts to the ceremony in order to get the couple properly married.

With iteration and the close interrelationship of one institu-tional fact with another, we can appreciate even more than before the power and subtlety of the institutional structures humans are capable of creating. Yet, with all these interrelationships, there comes a nagging feeling that these structures are nothing more than houses of cards. Changing the status of some X to Y happens because humans jointly will it to happen. It is not as if God or nature creates some foundation upon which our institutions stand. And so if humans build these houses of cards, they can take them down. Or maybe circumstances can blow them down. Searle grants all this. Indeed, he insists that human institutions live only so long as humans support and use them. His motto here could be: Use (or accept) them or lose them.

The secret of understanding the continued existence of institutional facts is simply that the individuals directly involved and a sufficient number of the relevant community must continue to recognize and accept the existence of such facts. Because the status is constituted by its collective acceptance, and because the function, in order to be performed, requires the status, it is essential to the functioning that there be continued acceptance of that status. The moment, for example, that all or most of the members of a society refuse to acknowledge property rights, as in a revolution or other upheaval, property rights cease to exist in that society. (1995a: 117)

Although institutions and the facts they generate are not founded on solid rock, they nonetheless tend to be more stable than one might suppose. Keep in mind that many of these institutions manifest themselves in the Background. This means that we come to accept them to such a extent that what they ask us to do becomes second nature, habit or, we might say, addictive. Keep also in mind that when we articulate what the constitutive rules ask us to do, we do so in "deontic" terms. They tell us that we ought to behave this way or that it is right that we should behave in this way. The power of the language encourages us to treat our institutions as something more substantial and stable than houses of cards.

One other feature of institutional facts gives them a kind of substantive appearance. Recall that social facts can be talked about in epistemologically objective terms. Mary was married last Sunday, Charles paid for the groceries with a cheque, Sam was awarded his degree at graduation, and Bill and Anne sold their house to the Smiths last Sunday – all these are objective reports of what happened. Just because all these institutional facts are ontologically subjective (having person dependent content) does not mean that we cannot talk about them in terms equal to the way physicists talk about their brute facts in outer space.

Some problems

Searle recognizes that his theory faces some serious problems. To see why all one has to do is hark back to the notion of collective intentionality. Recall that such intentionality, talked of as we-intentions, seems strange. Searle asks how can there be we-intentions when in fact intentions can only be found in the head of individuals? His answer is that individually we can have intentions of the form "I intend . . ." but also "We intend . . ." We-intentions are in each of our heads. Then he adds that we-intentions are unanalyzable (1992b: 401–15; 1998: 118–21). They are fundamental. Having, then, satisfied that he has "explained" the nature of we-intentions he goes on to rely on these intentions and the related concept of collective agreement to show us how social reality is constructed.

But the problem is that he doesn't make a very convincing case for the unanalyzable status of we-intentions. Basically the case seems to be that: (a) it makes sense to talk about we-intentions; (b) these intentions can't be Hegelian-like; and (c) they can't be analyzed into I-intentions. So they must be unanalyzable. The argument for the unanalyzable status of we-intentions is arrived at by a process of elimination.

However, consider the following line of thinking. A distinction can be made between how we arrive at we-intentions and the we-intentions we arrive at. In thinking about the former it is clear that one very common way we arrive at such intentions is to work within the society's already existing institutions and organizations. A society, let us suppose, is considering outlawing the eating, possession and manufacture of candy. It proceeds by having the abolitionist law passed in its legislature, then signed by the society's chief executive officer and, finally, sanctioned by the highest religious body of the land. If all that is done, and if what was done mirrors the society's regular procedure for making new law, then that society has arrived at a new we-intention. Those in the legal system who have passed the new law can say things like "We (i.e. the society) mean business", "We will enforce this law (and save our children's teeth)" or even "We intend to enforce this law". The members of the society at large can say the same things even though they have not participated in the decision procedure in any way. Some can express these we-intention thoughts even though they personally oppose abolitionism. "We as a society have decided to accept the abolition of candy even though I personally like the stuff."

Notice, how under this line of thinking, we-intentions can be discussed even when the decision involves only two people. The couple say to their friends "We intend to go to the movies tonight". They can say this not just because each has an unanalyzed we-intention but because they, as a couple, have a procedure for deciding what "we" are going to do together. Each says to the other what he or she wants. If there is agreement then their method of deciding delivers for them a we-intention for the evening. If they disagree, they flip a coin to decide. That is their procedure for breaking ties. Having flipped the coin in favour of movie going, they now can speak of their "we-intention". Again, that is their we-intention even though one member of the couple is somewhat upset at the result of the coin flip.

But what difference does it make whether we-intentions are unanalyzable or analyzable? We can argue for a role for we-intentions under Searle's unanalyzable flag or under a flag of an analysis, as has been just outlined, that uses other social concepts to make sense of (many) we-intentions. What is important is the we-intentions concept itself. So long as the notion is accepted (perhaps for no other reason than that we regularly speak as if it makes sense, i.e. we say "We intend . . ." all the time), then that is all we need. We can then proceed, as Searle does, to argue that this notion is needed in order to construct all or some of social reality. In other words, it is no criticism of Searle's use of we-intentions in his attempt to construct social reality to point out that his unanalyzable notion of we-intentions is suspect because the use to which he puts we-intentions does not rest on his unanalyzability thesis.

That leads to the second problem. Even if the concept of we-intentions makes sense, are we-intentions actually needed to construct social reality? It certainly seems so. In those settings such as those discussed above where rules are explicitly approved of and where, once approved, they are explicitly appealed to in order to make decisions, we-intentions seem quite at home. When the rules committee of any sport deliberately makes a new rule it seems quite natural for anyone on the committee to express himself by saying "We have accepted this new rule" or "We intend to implement this new rule" or something of the sort. Prior to the decision one or more of the committee members could even have said "We intend to make a decision on this matter". So clearly the concept of we-intentions has a role to play in our thinking about social structure at least in some settings.

However, the problem is with those settings discussed above where rules are not explicitly accepted or explicitly cited such as when we use language. Recall that in these settings we operate on automatic. We learn our native language at our mother's knee without appealing to rules and, also, obviously, without explicitly approving these rules. The question is: Are there any rules or approvings to be found when we operate on automatic? It was noted earlier that, for one, rules can be extracted from these settings retrospectively. Presumably that is what Searle, other philosophers of language and linguists do for a living. We can always take a pattern of language use and express it as if it were rule-governed. That speakers of English (tend to) use a singular verb to go with a singular noun can be expressed as a rule as "When the noun is singular one ought to use a singular verb". But saying that rules can always be extracted from language use is not the same as saying they do any work for us in guiding our use of our language. The pattern of noun and verb correspondence may be just that, a pattern learned by children from their parents through very little coaching. Parents may simply talk in a certain way and the children may simply follow suit. They listen and learn.

But if that is the way things go, what role if any is there for we-intentions, agreements, we-acceptance or anything of the sort? There can be acceptance. Certainly not consciously in the sense that at puberty or some other key point in its life the child says "I accept my native language (even though I can't articulate any of its grammatical or semantical rules)". Rather the child accepts its natural language by adopting it and using it as its own. But need this acceptance involve we-acceptance? It does not seem so. The child's acceptance of the language in which it is born can be thought of simply as one person joining an already well established group. It is possible, later, as the child matures to see its acceptance of its language as we-intentioned. That is, it might gain an insight that language works only when it is accepted by the community. But before the child is likely to get that insight it might very well have long since accepted the language as an individual rather than as a member of a group. If other children accept the native language in the same way then we seem to be sustaining a social construction not so much by we-intentions and we-acceptance but more by one I-intentions and I-acceptance after another.

If these thoughts about constructing social reality make sense, they suggest that Searle's account of these phenomena is not wholly accurate. His account seemingly works well in those settings where deliberation is appropriate. It may also work well in those settings where, although deliberation isn't practised every moment, we can deliberate when called upon to do so. But as we gradually move to considering settings where people act out of habit (under the influence of the Background) Searle's account seems troubled. The problem may be in attempting to give any *one* overarching account of social reality. Searle's rule-driven account takes us only so far, but seems wanting in explaining what I have been calling automatic behaviour (Turner 1999). But a habit account that argues that rules are superfluous in explaining social reality, and thus intends to explain all our social behaviour without appealing to rules and their causal powers, may also be inadequate. The obvious place of rules in our social life in many settings seems to put the lie any such non-rule governed theory.

One last problem with Searle's theory of social construction needs to be considered. It is a problem he faces directly and deals with quickly and effectively. In fact it is not a serious problem, but discussing it helps in understanding Searle's overall position on social reality. It has to do with self-referentiality. As we have seen earlier in this chapter, a mountain is a mountain, for Searle, even if no one believes it is. Because the concept of mountain is mind independent we can define or characterize it without making reference to any mental concepts such as desires, preferences and intentions. Such is not the case with the main concepts discussed in this chapter. The concept of money is not mind independent in this way. In characterizing money we need to say that for something to be money, it needs to be believed to be money. If it is not believed to be money, then the paper money I am holding in my hands no longer is money. Language to be language also needs to be believed in or approved of to be language. If no one treats the noises that come out of my mouth or the marks I put on paper as language then those sounds and marks aren't language. Similarly presidents to be presidents need to be thought of as presidents. One isn't a president the way the mountain is a mountain. Being a president depends, in part at least, on someone or some group thinking of one as president. In other words, the social world with its self-referential feature presents us with circular definitions of social concepts. It is a bit like defining triangle as a triangular figure.

Searle's solution to this problem, or paradox as he calls it, is not to deny that institutional and other social concepts are self-referential or circular. You can't understand money without reference to that stuff being used as money. But he says that we don't have to use the word money in our account of what money is. Here is how he puts it.

> But the resolution of the paradox is quite simple. The word "money" marks one node in a whole network of practices, the practices of owning, buying, selling, earning, paying for services, paying off debts, etc.. As long as the object [e.g., a coin] is regarded as having that role in the practices, we do not actually need the word "money" in the definition of money, so there is no circularity or infinite regress . . . It is sufficient that one believes that the entities in question are media of exchange, repositories of value, payment for debts, salaries for services rendered, etc. (1995a: 52)

What goes for money goes for other social concepts. So long as we define or characterize them in a wide enough circle we have done all that can be expected of us in giving an account of a key social concept. If the circle is too tight so that X is explained in terms of Xing nothing is explained. But if we explain a concept of money in terms of some of the social concepts that surround it we gain the understanding that comes from knowing where the concept sits relative to other concepts.

Although not part of the problem of self-referentiality as such, it is worth mentioning in closing this discussion on social reality that the feature of self-referentiality has important implications to ethics. If money, the military, marriage and other institutions must be believed in and sustained in order to have the status as institutions, the ethical (and other) norms these institutions generate must also be believed in to be able to operate and continue to operate as norms. The rights of the wife in the married ceremony go hand in hand with the institution. If the marriage institution were abolished, her rights would be abolished too. The rights of the citizens would similarly evaporate if a revolution abolished the government and the other institutions in the society that had hitherto kept the citizens together. In such a chaotic setting citizens would become just a bunch of people, perhaps, even rabble.

At this point one might ask whether, on Searle's account, these people would have *any* rights left? Even if they have lost all their rights as citizens, would they have lost their rights as humans as well? Certainly not if one were to hold to a classic natural law view of rights. On such an account the rights one possesses have a status as rights quite independent of the society's legislative practices and quite independent from the follow-on support these rights receive from the society. There is no feature of self-referentiality at play in natural law theory since these laws are akin to Searle's brute facts. They are part of the real world.

But Searle is not a realist in ethics the way he is a realist about the physical world. He is a constructionist. We construct social reality and all the features that go with it. Thus, if Searle wants to talk about human rights, he would not do so because we have discovered them in nature. Rather, he would have to show us how we constructed them. That is, he would show us how we moved from X in context C to Y. As we have seen, a society can grant couples certain rights (and duties) within the bonds of marriage, and grant rights to its citizens to vote in elections. Within the framework of the government and/or the society it might even make sense to grant people human rights. But if, for whatever reason, the society were in the process of dissolving, it would seem to follow that one's human rights would dissolve with them.

Of course even if a society within certain borders were dissolving, there might still be an existent world society that could sustain the rights of the people. But on Searle's account, right or wrong, it would seem that if the world society were also dissolving (e.g. because of nuclear or biological war) it would be, strictly speaking, improper to say that people's human rights were being violated. When rights no longer exist (on any social level) they can no longer be violated, or defended.

Strictly speaking, then, if people said that our rights are being violated during this period of chaos, they would be uttering assertives with unhappy conditions of satisfaction. It just wouldn't be true that their rights are being violated. On Searle's account of social construction if they continued to say "Our rights are being violated" they could only be saying something, perhaps, on the order of "We want our rights back". Saying that would be an assertive whose conditions of satisfaction are more than likely satisfied. No doubt most of the people would want their rights back. Presumably what they would be doing linguistically in telling us about their wants is issuing some sort of indirect speech act. By way of asserting that they want their rights back, they would indirectly be issuing a directive like "Give them back to us". However one "translated" their claim that their rights are being violated, that claim would be seriously misleading since, presumably, the people believe they have rights (in this chaotic setting) when, in (institutional) fact, they cannot possibly have such rights.

Chapter 11

Ontology

External realism

Searle is not content to be a specialist. In Chapters 9 and 10 we saw him move away from his old haunts of philosophy of language and mind to deal with issues concerned with social reality. In this chapter we see how he moves still further away from his old studies to deal with issues concerned with what there is, that is, with ontology. In a way this moving away is not a moving away. In being concerned with ontology, he brings with him and uses most of the tools collected from his old studies. As was noted in the previous two chapters, it is almost as if he were not in position to deal systematically with ontological issues until he had completed his tool collection – one which includes important parts of his theory of language, Intentionality, Background, and the distinction between brute and institutional facts.

Searle calls his ontological position external realism. His initial characterization of it is as follows: "The world (or alternatively, reality or the universe) exists independently of our representations of it" (1995a: 150). Of representations he says:

> Human beings have a variety of interconnected ways of having access to and representing features of the world to themselves. These include perception, thought, language, beliefs and desires as well as pictures, maps, diagrams, etc. Just to have a general term I will call these collectively "representations." A feature of representations so defined is that they all have intentionality, both *intrinsic* intentionality, as in beliefs and

perceptions and *derived* intentionality, as in maps and
sentences.   (1995a: 150–51)

Searle's external realism has the consequence that if we humans,
and presumably other animals, had never existed so that there had
never been any representations, the world (universe, etc.) would
have been able to get along quite well without us. Similarly,
although we humans (and other animals) have in many ways
affected this particular world, if all of us were to disappear suddenly, the world and the universe would continue to exist pretty
much as before.

Opposition to external realism

In his writings on ontology, Searle typically begins his "defence" of
external realism (ER) by attacking the enemy. The "enemy" are
sometimes called antirealists and at other times sceptics. Actually
the two are allies, and direct their criticisms of Searle and his realist claims with several similar arguments.

One of the most serious Searle calls the argument from conceptual relativity. Here is a version of it as he presents it.

All of our concepts are made by us as human beings. There is
nothing inevitable about the concepts we have for describing
reality. But, so the antirealist argues, the relativity of our
concepts, if properly understood, shows that external realism
is false because we have no access to external reality except
through concepts. Different conceptual structures give
different descriptions of reality, and these descriptions are
inconsistent with each other.   (1998: 22–3)

Thus, I may describe my garden in terms of trees, bushes, flowers
and grass and then claim there are four things there. Or I may
identify each tree, bush and flower and then tediously count each
blade of grass. I may then claim that there are hundreds of thousands or, perhaps, millions of plants back there. Take another
example. One historian characterizes a people as mainly industri-
ous, another as mainly selfish, still another as mainly religious. It
appears as if there is no one way to describe them. It also appears
as if the feature each historian picks out is either arbitrary or a
function of the ideology brought to the description.

What is interesting about Searle's response to this criticism of realism is that he does not deny the doctrine of conceptual relativity. In truth, he cannot deny it. Recall what Searle was reported as saying in Chapter 7 about perspectivalism under the heading of aspectuality. He says that all Intentional judgments are made from some perspective. The perspective can be physical (e.g. "I see it from the left side, you from the right") or conceptual (e.g. "Adam is a Marxist so he sees class conflict, Bob is a libertarian and so he sees freedom and how governments take freedom away from people"). So part of what results when people come to a situation with a different perspective is that they apply one rather than another set of concepts to what they see is there. Recall, as well, that Searle used perspectivalism in his attack on those who claim to find deep unconscious rules in the mind. If these unconscious rules were truly there they would not be able (since they never can see the light of day) to work, as they must, from some perspective or other. So the doctrine of perspectivalism (aspectuality) and the closely related doctrine of conceptual relativism are both correct for Searle.

But then how does Searle avoid the conclusion that external realism is false? If we are always viewing the world through some perspective and/or from a set of ideological or arbitrary concepts, how can we get at reality? The way seems blocked by the concepts as they filter out and distort what might be out there, and present us instead with the unreal instead of the real. Searle begins his response by pointing out that external realism's claim that "Reality exists independently of our representations of it" is not directly contradicted by conceptual relativism's seemingly counter claim that "All our representations of reality are made relative to some more or less arbitrarily selected set of concepts" (1995a: 161). The former claim has to do with what things are out there, whatever they are; the latter with what concepts we select to talk about things out there, whatever they are. Here, clearly, he is making a sharp distinction between an ontological claim on behalf of external realism and claims about conceptual selection, matters having more to do with epistemology. He then says that whatever selection we make will not affect reality in any way. We can select our concepts or we can all die, and thus not select any concepts at all to talk about reality. Either way reality remains the same. Here is how he expresses these thoughts in *Construction of Social Reality*.

Think of the relation of realism and conceptual relativism like this. Take a corner of the world, say, the Himalayas, and think of it as it was prior to the existence of any human beings. Now imagine that humans come along and represent the facts in various different ways. They have different vocabularies, different systems for making maps, different ways of counting one mountain, two mountains, the same mountain, etc. Next, imagine that eventually the humans all cease to exist. Now what happens to the existence of the Himalayas and all the facts about the Himalayas in the course of all these vicissitudes? Absolutely nothing. Different descriptions of facts, objects, etc. came and went, but the facts, objects, etc. remained. (Does anyone really doubt this?) (1995a: 164)

A bit later in *Construction* Searle expresses this same general point somewhat differently. He says that how we interpret certain concepts such as "cat", "kilogram", or "canyon" may very well be arbitrary.

But once we have fixed the meaning of such terms in our vocabulary by arbitrary definitions, it is no longer a matter of any kind of relativism or arbitrariness whether representation-independent features of the world satisfy those definitions, because the features of the world that satisfy or fail to satisfy the definitions exist independently of those or any other definitions. (1995a: 166)

He adds that we don't make the universe, the world, reality, etc. with our use of concepts or language but use the concepts we choose to in order to describe what is out there. Again, what is out there is one thing; what we use to talk about what is out there is something else. The latter, whatever its character, cannot be used to impugn the former. Just because we can't get outside of our system of our concepts, whatever their nature, does not mean that our experiences are not *of* something outside the system.

Having attacked is his attackers' arguments, Searle can't resist attacking the attackers themselves – he can't resist appealing to a good old fashioned *ad hominem* argument. He thinks he knows the motives behind their argument that we can only think within the conceptual framework we have chosen and thereby show that realism is a flawed position (1995a: 19–20). Many of his attackers, he says, have a dislike for science. When scientists make discoveries they think that they have discovered something about the real world. Searle agrees with the scientists, as do most common people. But the science haters, many of whom are in the humanities or belong to groups preaching some political or religious ideology, realize that their own claims do not have this being-about-reality status. Understandably, then, as "postmodernist" opponents of science, these humanities people are motivated to look for arguments that bring science down to their level. "If I'm a sinner, I'll show that you're a sinner too." Everyone's a sinner! For critics of science, scientific claims can now be seen as no better than any other kind of claims. All are perspectival, all are relative. Having levelled the playing field by making all theories, scientific or whatever, relative to some conceptual scheme, it is presumably easier for the postmodernists to preach whatever ideology they might wish. Not being tied to some reality principle, they can now be as creative or coercive as they wish in order to get their way politically.

At this point Searle reminds them that it is not clear on what basis we should take any postmodernist pronouncements seriously. Having made all thinking relative to one or another conceptual scheme, one set of thoughts would seem to be as good as any other. Levelling the playing field has its costs for the postmodernists because now we have no reason to listen to their presentations, ways of looking at things or "arguments" any more than we have to listen to anybody else's.

Be that as it may, Searle thinks that the postmodernist dislike for science is wrong-headed. It fails to understand how science works especially with regard to its search for truths based on what is out there. Still, taking account of this dislike seems to help explain why there is opposition to realism, and explain as well why his opponents are willing to accept bad arguments such as conceptual relativity as a way of destroying realism.

Searle addresses a second line of criticism of external realism, one coming more from the two closely allied traditions of phenomenalism and scepticism. This criticism can be summarized as follows.

We can never be sure what it is we are experiencing. At this moment we might be experiencing some illusion (e.g. the road ahead looks wet but the light is such as to fool us), having an hallucinating (e.g. there is a pink elephant in the living room – big as life) or simply dreaming while we think we are not (e.g. we think it is wonderful that we won the £100,000,000 lottery prize – so now we can live happily ever after). The reason these and similar experiences raise doubt in our minds is that we don't really see things out in the world the way Searle claims we do. Rather we simply have experiences. It is experiences, in the form of sense data perhaps, that we are directly aware of. We can be sure we have a red sense impression of a car but we can't be sure we see the car. The criticism goes on to tell us that there is a kind of experience barrier between us and the supposed real world out there. So it is a fantasy to talk about the real world. If it were out there, we never could know it is.

This is the criticism or line of argument everyone meets when taking an introduction course in philosophy. Searle is not impressed with it. Of course, he admits we are deceived in our experiences from time to time. Yes, it felt wonderful to suppose that we won the £100,000,000, and it was very disappointing to discover that it was all a dream. Yes, the highway wasn't wet after all, and the elephant "went away" once we put enough coffee in our stomach to overcome the effects of alcohol. But these very examples dramatize the role of one of the sceptics' assumptions. Sceptics suppose that we need to assess the truth or falsity of some belief in isolation. The sceptic argues that, at the moment, in isolation, we can't tell whether we won all that money or are merely dreaming we did.

Quite so. But why suppose that judgments need to be made in isolation? Searle certainly does not make that supposition. His commitment to the Network and the Background tells us why. We make our judgments within a pattern that includes these two systems and in a pattern that also includes follow-on experiences. It is especially these follow-on experiences that tell us that, earlier, we were fooled in one way or another.

Searle also needs to reply to that part of the sceptics' argument that says all we see is our sense impressions, not those things out there. Nowadays this argument is often backed by a description of how we biologically come to see things via the retina, the visual cortex and ending in some sense experience deep in our brain (Searle 1998: 28). With the blessings of science the argument sounds more imposing than before. But Searle is, once again, not impressed. To give a scientific account of how things go with our vision and then conclude that external realism is false is to commit the genetic fallacy. He tells us that he learned 2 + 2 = 4 from his first grade teacher Miss Masters. She evidently strongly conditioned him to believe in this important mathematical truth.

But does knowing how he came to this belief show that this belief is nothing but a belief? The genesis of the belief is one thing, its truth is something else. To know the scientific genesis of our visual experiences does not say anything as such about whether these experiences report things that are true or not. Besides, the claim that all we have are our experiences, often translated into all we experience are our experiences or all we "see" are our own sense data, is wrong. We don't see sense data. We have experiences, and many of them (really most of them) are about something. These experiences exhibit Intentionality. If we follow Intentionality theory which happens to follow commonsense thinking, it makes more sense to say that we see the red car than to say we have a red sense impression of a car.

It is pretty clear from how Searle is dealing with the antirealists so far that many of his arguments will make little impact on them Using an *ad hominem* argument may be amusing but he knows full well that it is not a sound way to argue. The argument, he says, is more a diagnosis than a refutation (1995a: 33). From the worst of motives the opposition forces might still be right about their negative claims concerning reality. As to Searle's other arguments he also realizes that the most they show is that his own position is not implausible. The opposition's sceptical and conceptual relativist arguments don't disprove his position. But his counter arguments only show that his realism isn't obviously wrong. It seems that he needs to do something more by way of supporting his external realist stance than he has done so far.

Presentation of realism

Searle could avail himself of G. E. Moore's argument to justify his external realism. Famously, Moore held out one hand and said "[H]ere is one hand" and then held out his other hand and said "[A]nd here is another". He said he could have held out or pointed to other things. Presumably two elbows, socks, shoes, underpants, tables, trees all would do. But, having held out his two hands to show that he has them, Moore drew an inference that there are things outside of us (Moore 1959: 145–6). The inference is supposed to be like making an inference from "This is a triangle" to "This is a three sided figure" or "This is a hand" to "This is a biological entity".

But Searle is wary of Moore's proof (Searle 1995a: 180–81). He notes that Bishop Berkeley, a most famous antirealist, would also not deny that Moore has two hands, two elbows, socks, shoes and that that is a table and that over there is a tree. However, he would deny the inference Moore made. A phenomenalist like Berkeley would argue, instead, that the proper inference is not that there are things outside of us, but that we are having some experiences. So Moore is of no help to Searle even though he is a realist ally.

But why is this? What is wrong with Moore's proof? Two things. First, external realism is not proved or disproved in the same way that we prove that we have hands. To help us understand this point Searle makes an important distinction between truth conditions and conditions of intelligibility (1995a: 181). Truth conditions are like seeing something in clear light, seeing it when sober and the like. If we get these truth conditions right we can say "Yes, Moore has two hands". Conditions of intelligibility have to do with what we take for granted, with presuppositions. So these conditions take us back to the Network and the Background. Searle's claim about external realism is that it has more to do with conditions of intelligibility rather than truth conditions – with Background rather than foreground. Moore thought it had more to do with truth conditions, with foreground.

> The claim I make here is that ER [external realism] functions as a taken-for-granted part of the Background. Unless we take ER for granted, we cannot understand utterances the way we do normally. Furthermore we have to take ER for granted to engage in the sorts of discourse and thought that we have been engaging in. The presupposition of ER is thus a *necessary* presupposition for a large chunk of thought and language. We can't give it up as, for example, centuries ago we gave up our presupposition that the earth is flat.   (Searle 1995a: 181–2)

Secondly, Searle says, now that we see that external realism is not just another empirical claim but part of the Background, we can also see that it has no real ties to how we in fact conceive of objects and space out there in the real world. In the future we might alter the atomic theory radically or abandon Einstein's theory of relativity (of space) completely and, yet, that would not affect external realism. Searle reminds us at this point that: "Carefully stated, external realism is the thesis that there is a way things are that is independent of all representations of how things are" (1995a: 182). So, as such, external realism does not tell us how things are or that things are arranged in a certain way. Rather, it provides us with what Searle calls *a space of possibilities*. Moore is of no help, then, since in treating reality claims as if they were much like ordinary empirical claims, he fails to see that they fall into a totally different category.

If Moore's kind of argument is of no help in supporting realism, Searle might get help from some another source. He could avail himself of the so-called convergence argument to back up his external realism doctrine. But, again, he demurs. He does so for the same reasons as with Moore's argument. The convergence argument is supposed to provide us with an empirical proof for realism. If scientists working separately engage in research that leads to converging results this must, so the argument says, mean that realism is true. Realism is the best explanation for the convergence. Not so, says Searle. The argument does not prove that realism is true, rather it presupposes realism.

> In order for us even to raise the question whether scientific investigation does converge in the suggested fashion, we have to presuppose an independently existing reality of investigators engaging in investigations. These investigations either converge or fail to converge. (1995a: 179)

If they converge nothing is proved concerning realism. Convergence is merely a test for the truth of empirical claims. If they don't converge, as often happens in the social sciences, then all that it proves is that our tests for the truth of certain empirical claims have failed. Either way, realism is presupposed from the beginning. So Searle is not getting much help from his realist friends. But by showing how both Moore and the convergence theorists fail to "justify" external realism, he begins to show how the job can be done. Since external realism is a doctrine found in the Background, what is needed, he says, is a transcendental argument that first identifies some condition that obtains and then asks what that condition presupposes.

But with what condition should we start? As a philosopher raised in the ordinary language school of philosophy what could be more natural than to identify our *talk* about such life as the condition.

> The condition is that we do in fact attempt to communicate with each other by making certain sorts of utterances in a public language and the presupposition is external realism. To

> spell this out a little more precisely: the assumption we are making is that there is normal way of understanding utterances, and that when performing speech acts in a public language, speakers typically attempt to achieve normal understanding. The point we are attempting to show is that for a large class (to be specified further) a condition of intelligibility for the normal understanding of these utterances is that there is a way that things are that is independent of human representations. The consequence is that *when we attempt to communicate to achieve normal understanding with these sorts of utterances we must presuppose external realism.*
>
> (Searle 1995a: 183–4)

Searle's message here is, first, that the normal way of understanding utterances requires that we understand what we are saying in the same way (Baggini 1999). That seems fair enough. We would hardly have any language if there were not normal understanding of what was said. Presumably this normal understanding would include utterances having to do with mathematics and subjective feelings. Second, above and beyond these kinds of utterances, is our understanding of a (very) large group of utterances as making reference to phenomena outside of the speakers and hearers of the language. These are the ontologically objective claims concerned with brute facts (e.g. that mountain in Asia again). All this seems fair enough as well. It is hard to deny that a large part of our language is not being used to talk about what is out there. But, third, this means that the truth of the claims we make about the outside world is set not by our language, but by the world. We presuppose that the world makes our claims true; not the other way around. That too seems fair enough.

It is hard to argue against Searle's message given his starting point (i.e. what he calls a condition). Given a different starting point, perhaps we might very well arrive at different conclusions. However, Searle is clear that he knows his starting point isn't sacred or foundational. He says that normal understanding is our default position, that is where we start. Those who would start elsewhere need to give us an explanation as to why they start where they do.

In part because he realizes his starting point can be challenged Searle says that his argument, or better yet, his presentation, should not be thought of as a proof. It is also not a proof because external realism is not a theory. A theory needs to be defended by presenting evidence, showing how phenomena are explained by the theory, and showing that the theory explains things more simply than other theories do. If external realism were a theory it would be expressible on the speech act level as if it were true on the same level as other truths. We, then, could express our opinions about it if we wished (Searle 1998: 32). But if external realism is found in the Background, it is not a theory but a "framework within which it is possible to have theories (1998: 32). As a framework it is not committed to being true the way Darwinism, relativity, the atomic theory and other scientific theories or doctrines are. Any one or all of these theories could be true or false and external realism would still be there as a deep presupposition of the way we think when we use ordinary language.

What Searle has said thus far about his own position is presented with an eye toward the sceptics and/or those he calls phenomenalist idealists (Hume, Berkeley). These are the people who suppose that we are stuck with what is in our minds and have, as a result, a hard time saying anything about what is out there in the real world. In presenting his positive doctrine he next turns his eye, once again, toward the conceptual relativists, especially those in this group who are sometimes called social constructivists or postmodernists.

These theorists are not disturbed by Searle's account thus far. After all they are not opposed to talk about publicly accessible reality. We can say, for instance, "She is married" and "This is French money" in a public way. It can be verified publicly that she is married and that the money is, in fact, French. So the objection that the social constructionists mount against Searle's position is somewhat different from that mounted by the sceptics. The former will say that although our normal language is public, it is publicly or socially constructed through and through. All speech acts are socially constructed thus leaving no room for speech acts that have to do with naked reality. So Searle says he needs to complete his presentation in favour of realism by showing that some of what we talk about is naked or brute, that is, beyond the ways we have of representing. We need to find, he says, "a subclass of speech acts whose normal understanding requires a reality independent of *all* representation (1995a: 190). He needs an argument or presentation to take care of all the subversive postmodernist doctrines.

His argument is again transcendental. It is also suspect. The "condition" now is the application of his "X counts as Y in C" formula to something like money or marriage. The initial application of the rule may need to be "analyzed" in terms of another institutional concept. And that in turn into another. But, says Searle, eventually the X element of the lowest level institutional concept must "bottom out in an X element that is not itself an institutional construction" (1995a: 191). The institutional concept of money (the Y element in the formula) needs something like the brutish concept of paper [is paper brutish?] or metal (the X element). If there weren't this "bottoming out" we would get ourselves in an infinite regress or circular argument. So, the argument is, we can't understand institutional concepts and appreciate institutional facts unless, in the end, they rest on non-institutional bedrock. That means that the postmodernist argument that all thinking is institutional can't be right.

The reason this argument is suspect is that earlier (reported in Ch. 10 of this work) Searle found himself accepting a circular argument. He says in *Construction of Social Reality* (1995a: 52–3) when explaining institutional concepts that it would be wrong to accept the notion of money as an institutional concept if it were explained in terms of "believed to be money". That kind of circularity is too tight to have any explanatory power. But we are not to worry because we don't need the word "money" to explain money. As we have seen, so long as "money" is explained by other institutional concepts such as used as a medium of exchange and the like, then that account is acceptable. This wider account of "money" is also circular but the circle is wide enough to be acceptable. In other words, so long as one institutional concept is explained in terms of a wide set of institutional concepts no harm is done.

Certainly this same Searlian argument is available to the postmodernists. They could concede that their account is circular, but circular in the widest sense. So if they must explain one institutional use of language in terms of another institutional use, so be it. At best, then, Searle's argument concerned with circularity (or infinite regress) might make us suspicious of the postmodernist argument. It certainly does not refute it or embarrass it very much.

So Searle needs to say more to be convincing that not all speech acts (language uses) fall under the heading of culturally constructed social reality, that is, that not every use reports an institutional fact or creates an institutional rule. He seems to sense that there is a need here because he does present another argument. Actually it is a variation of one we would expect him to make. Throughout *Construction of Social Reality* he emphasizes how different brute facts are from institutional facts. Or putting it linguistically, he emphasizes how our reports about the former kind of facts are different from our reports about the latter. So now when he needs an argument against social constructivism (the postmodernists) he shows us an important difference between these two kinds of reports to help convince us that they all do not fall under the heading of institutional reports. Here is how he does it. He asks us to consider two ontologically objective claims of what he calls brute facts that contradict one another (1995a: 191–3).

1 " Mt. Everest has snow and ice near its summit."
2 "It is not the case that Mt. Everest has snow and ice near its summit."

We are next asked to consider two more contradictory claims, only now ones that report institutional facts.

3 "You owe me five dollars."
4 "It is not the case that you owe me five dollars."

Now Searle asks us to consider the following, rather strange but still meaningful, counterfactual claims.

A "In a world like ours, except that representations have never existed in it, Mt. Everest has snow and ice near the summit."
B "In a world like ours, except that representations have never existed in it, it is not the case that Mt. Everest has snow and ice near the summit."

Then, finally, we are to consider the following.

C "In a world like ours, except that representations have never existed in it, you owe me five dollars."
D "In a world like ours, except that representations have never existed in it, it is not the case that you owe me five dollars."

The cash value of a world without representations is something like a world without creatures in it who can have representations. His argument then is that there is a world of difference between A and B on one side and C and D on the other. With A and B our representations have nothing to do with the snow up there on that high mountain. The conditions up there are what they are no matter what we think of them or whether we think of them. Such is not the case with C and D. It is impossible for anyone to owe anyone else five dollars without representations. C and D require human rules and, in particular, rules in Searle's now familiar format of X counts as Y in C. To talk about owing money without human rules is like talking about baseball without (human) rules of the game (Searle 1995a: 193).

Searle's argument here is more convincing than his let's-avoid-circularity argument. It shows clearly that the "logic" of Mt. Everest type claims is quite different from claims about money. But his argument still depends on normal understanding or, as it might be put, it still depends on Searle doing some good old fashioned ordinary language philosophy. After all, it rests on how we as users understand one kind of claim as against another in our natural language. To the extent that many social constructionists work in literature and in social movements, and to the extent that they too rely on our natural language to express their views, they are vulnerable to Searle's argument. Their mistake, from Searle's perspective, is not to reject our normal understanding and usage but to misunderstand it. As a result they mistakenly lump together two kinds of assertive speech acts – one reporting brute facts and one reporting institutional facts into one.

Searle could have availed himself of another argument to help his cause on behalf of realism. In much of his writing (1995a: 37–8, 61–2, 70) he discusses animals and their Intentional powers. Animals can see, hear, have fear, experience anger, remember, believe and even organize themselves to act in social settings. They do all these things, and more, without language. To be sure, because they lack language they cannot engage in *institutional* social life. But in engaging in a wide variety of Intentional activities these animals help us to see that language isn't a necessary ingredient for coming into contact with the real world. And if animals can do it, so can humans. One can imagine a child raised by wild wolves, and thus devoid of any normal linguistic understanding, engaging in Intentional mental activity that very likely is even richer than the Intentional activity of its wolf family members. But what if, later in life, the wolf child comes into contact with humans who teach him some language skills? Are his experiences now so radically new or different that with the concept of size in his head he can for the first time see that one of his wolf family members is larger than the rest? With numbers like one, two and three now in his head is he able for the first time to recognize that his family is composed of four wolves and himself? And with the cluster of colour concepts now in his head are we going to say that he can recognize for the first time that one family member has dark brown eyes while the other members have light brown eyes?

What this argument involving animals and Searle's other arguments help to show is that if we employ normal public language (ordinary language, our natural language) we are committed to external realism. They also show that if we employ scientific language, which is also public and for Searle not really that different from our ordinary language, that we are also committed to external realism. However, since it is theoretically possible to avoid the commitments of realism by avoiding these languages, Searle has not proven that his realist ontological stance is correct. But adopting and living with this avoidance strategy is not easy. It involves adopting, as one option, the "for me" language of solipcism (and phenomenalism) and living with it. Or, as another option, it involves adopting the language of the conceptual relativists and then facing the "reality" of not readily being able to make objective moral and empirical judgments.

There is another difficulty inherent in this avoidance strategy. Opponents of external realism and the languages that presuppose it must not only avoid these languages but must proffer replacement languages that do not have realist commitments either hiding in the Background or facing us right there in the foreground. Keep in mind that these languages are, or have to be, invented by philosophers and their intellectual allies. They then have to be promulgated. Famously philosophers are not very good promulgators. Privately and with a small group of insiders they might communicate in their "superior" language. But probably they will not. They will write and read papers to one another at conferences about their new way of talking, but when the conferences are over they will lapse into using their "folk" language. They certainly will lapse into this talk when conversing with other philosophers and with their non-philosophical friends. Until they can promulgate the new way of talking, the old way will have to do. For practical reasons, even antirealists will find themselves talking in ways that have external realism built into the Background. So even if Searle has not straightforwardly refuted various forms of antirealism, he has shown that it is more difficult to act out the antirealist stance than we might suppose. Until antirealists make a convincing case for bringing about important changes in our way of speaking, it makes sense for someone like Searle to explore the

John Searle

foreground and Background of the way we speak and think, and, if it comes to that, point to the realist commitments that we actually live by.

Closing comments

In closing his discussion on ontology in *Construction of Social Reality* Searle makes two interesting comments. He notes, first of all, that his account helps explain why we are frustrated in trying to satisfy the demand for proving realism. Philosophers assume that realism, much like other ontological theories, is a theory. Supposedly, theories lend themselves to proofs or accounts in terms of "best explanation". But as we have seen, realism is not a theory like other theories. It is not a set of beliefs to be held and used to explain whatever theories explain. Instead, realism is found in the pre-intentional Background. We don't believe in a theory of realism; we have realistic presumptions. Given this status in the Background, we can show (via transcendental arguments) that it is difficult to avoid making realistic presumptions. But we cannot do more than that. Because thinkers suppose realism is a theory they don't understand this point. They therefore get frustrated when they try to prove or disprove realism.

Secondly, Searle comments on why exploring our ontological commitments is important. Some suppose it isn't important. Supposedly, holding one rather than another ontological theory makes no difference. William James probably believed in this no-difference doctrine. No matter what disagreements people have concerning their ontological theory they go about their business as if there were no disagreement. They all are concerned about eating during lunchtime, not getting killed while crossing a busy street and getting promoted at work. Life goes on in spite of philosophy. Reflecting this outlook, Searle quotes Wittgenstein as saying (somewhere) that these great debates between realism and anti-realism and between idealism and materialism as just so many battle cries (1995a: 196). However, Searle has a different take on ontology. In some ways he thinks it makes a tremendous difference whether one is a realist or not.

> In my observation, the rejection of realism, the denial of onto-
> logical objectivity, is an essential component of the attacks on

epistemic objectivity, rationality, truth, and intelligence in contemporary intellectual life. It is no accident that the various theories of language, literature, and even education that try to undermine the traditional conceptions of truth, epistemic objectivity, and rationality rely heavily on arguments against external realism. The first step in combating irrationalism . . . is a refutation of the arguments against external realism and a defense of external realism as a presupposition of large areas of discourse.   (1995a: 197)

Chapter 12

Truth, representation and epistemology

Truth and facts

In one sense, this chapter signals the end of the discussion of Searle's theory of social reality. Up to now, Searle's attention has been mainly on ontological issues. What is social reality? How does it differ from non-social reality? He is also concerned with the related question: How does social reality work? The answer to these questions goes like this. Social reality emerges from non-social reality and Intentionality. Humans create institutional facts from brute facts. For many institutional facts we need brute facts in the form of physical markers such as paper or pieces of metal to help create money. We also need we-intentions to get the job done. Whatever else is needed, it is clear that social reality emerges from simpler forms of reality in such a way that there is no sharp separation between the materials used to create social reality and that reality itself. For Searle there is one reality; not two, three or more.

But as presented so far, the discussion of social reality has not said much about how we represent that reality. That is, little has been said about how it is we talk about it; and how it is that we know that when we speak about social reality we speak truly of it. So now Searle turns to these topics to complete his picture of that reality. However, in another sense, this chapter turns to new subjects having more to do with philosophy of language, and even more to do with theory of knowledge, than anything else. It asks important questions such as "What is truth?" and "How do we know truth when we suppose we have found it?" In answering these questions, then, Searle not only completes his work on social reality but shows himself rounding out his overall philosophic stance to show, once again, that he is more than a one or two dimensioned philosopher.

Searle's analysis of "true" and "truth" takes him back, more or less, to his roots concerned with language analysis as it was done at Oxford after World War II. In particular, he says that his analysis is in terms of the Wittgensteinian concept of family resemblance and in terms of tracing how we actually use language

> There are not only true statements but true friends (real or genuine friends), true emotions (sincerely felt, not fake) true heirs (rightful and legitimate), as well as true north, true trout (the eastern brook trout is not a true trout; it is a char), knives cut true, and true believers. (Searle 1995a: 210)

The resemblances most of these uses share have to do with trust and reliability. Etymology supports this analysis. "True" is related to "trust" and "trustworthy" and all these expressions derive from the Indo-European word "deru" that stands for "tree" that, in turn, is supposed to be upright (and reliable).

Applied now to statements, a true statement is one that is upright and reliable. This uprightness can be expressed as follows:

s (e.g. "Snow is white") is true if and only if *p* (snow is white)

This formula establishes the criterion (criteria) for truth. The way Searle interprets this formula's application is as follows. Saying that the expression (in quotes) "Snow is white" is true is making a claim that it is upright. It can be trusted. Any person making such a claim is putting his credibility on the line by saying that what he has said is true. More than that, this speaker is telling us, in terms of the "p" portion of the formula, what it is that makes his claim true. It is true because, in the snow case, snow *is* white.

> This criterion of truth is sometimes called "disquotation," because the sentence quoted on the left-hand side occurs on the right with the quotation dropped. The substitution instances have come to be called "T-sentences".
> (Searle 1995a: 201)

Searle makes it clear that he disagrees with two popular analyses of the disquotation criterion. These analyses claim that the use of "true" in our language is either redundant (hence the redundant theory of truth) or deflationary (hence the deflationary theory). On the former theory the insertion of "true" and "truth" into "Snow is white" so that it reads "It's true that snow is white" or "Snow is white, that's the truth" adds nothing to the meaning of the original speech act. On the latter theory one is adding only a minimal amount to what is said. In contrast, for Searle, "true", "truth" and similar expressions add something significant. When properly inserted into speech acts, they tell us that there is evidence for whatever claim is being made; and that this evidence is of the most direct or "upright" kind. "Snow is white" is true because snow is, in fact, white.

But what is a fact? To answer this question, Searle does not so much engage in language analysis in the tradition of the Oxford school as he does in a bit more etymology. He tells us that fact is "derived from Latin 'factum,' which is the neuter past particle of the verb 'facere,' meaning 'to do' or 'to make'" (1995a: 210). In today's language "fact" has evolved into something like "*what* it is that makes a statement trustworthy or true". So in contrast to "true" which characterizes statements and beliefs, "fact" characterizes something out in the world. It is an ontological term.

A fact cannot be specified without language. Further a fact needs to be specified not by naming but by stating it. This is because a fact is a condition or a state of affairs – not a thing. A statement of fact contains the requirements that needs to be satisfied for the statement to be true. So there is a close connection between the statement of fact and the fact. That relationship, Searle says, is one of correspondence. Here he seems to be resuscitating the old correspondence theory of truth. That theory has come upon hard times lately largely because correspondence has often been interpreted as picturing. On this interpretation a statement of fact corresponds to some fact by picturing, mirroring or imaging it. Presumably, then, if a fact contains three parts, the statement corresponding to the fact would also contain three parts. This seemingly works with relational facts such as when Tom is to the left of Bill. It also seemingly works with two-part facts such as when a sheet of paper is red. But there are problems for the theory with so-called negative facts as when the paper is not red and the man not angry? How are these pictured? And what about contrary to fact conditional claims expressed linguistically as "I would have won the match had my leg not been injured"? How do they correspond with reality?

Picturing as a way of interpreting the correspondence theory has so many problems that it is no longer a viable theory for philosophers. But then how is one to interpret correspondence? Unfortunately there is no other intuitive interpretation. Yet, Searle insists that he needs an interpretation or conception of this theory "according to which there really are nonlinguistic facts in the world and statements are true because they really do stand in certain relations to these facts, relations that we variously describe as fitting, matching, stating, or corresponding to the facts" (1995a: 209). Putting it this way is not very helpful. "Fitting", and "matching" are just additional metaphors, as is "picturing", and need to be analyzed or explained. "Stating" isn't a metaphor, but it says nothing to help explain correspondence either. And "correspondence", of course, can't explain itself.

So again we have to ask: What is correspondence? Well, it has to be some relation between a statement and the world, more particularly, a *statement* about a condition in the world and the *condition* (state of affairs, fact) in the world. Although a statement needn't say anything about mirroring the world, it must contain its own conditions of success or satisfaction. This means that the statement itself tells us what it would take (what criteria need to be met) to make it true. "Roses are red" tells us that its primary condition of success is that roses are indeed red (out there in the world). When this condition as well as others are met we, then, say that it corresponds to the facts.

The details of this theory of correspondence are as follows. First, the standard way to express what criteria need to be met to achieve correspondence is with disquotation claims. "The roses are red" is true if and only if roses (really) are red. The use of "true", as already reported, tells us that the statement has met the standard that is expressed on the right side of the formula. When the standard is met the disquotation formula can be restated in explicit correspondence terms as "Roses are red" is true if and only if it corresponds to the fact that roses are red.

Second, statements not only correspond with the facts but they are made true by the facts (Searle 1995a: 219). The making here is not causal in nature in the sense that one billiard-ball causes another to move. Rather, facts make statements true because we have arranged language to work that way.

Third, there is no one to one correspondence between the statement that is true and the facts. This is because different statements can describe the same fact. Searle's example of this is when we have more than one name for the same red-headed person as in "Jim lost his job" and "Red lost his job".

Fourth, we can find correspondence not only between statements and the facts but between beliefs and the facts. Searle does not discuss this point but we can infer that correspondence is present when he says "'True' is the adjective for assessing statements (as well as, e.g., beliefs, that like statements have the mind-to-world or word-to-world direction of fit)" (1995a: 219). As this quote suggests, there is not going to be a problem in extending correspondence to human psychic states since human beliefs can be expressed linguistically. So, the belief that I have that Amelia is in her dog pen with her brother Lindy is true because it corresponds to the fact that she and he are in the pen – even if I do not bother to put this thought into words. But if Amelia herself has a belief that Lindy is in the pen with her (let us say while her eyes are closed but while she is awake) presumably that belief, if true, corresponds with the facts even though she cannot ever put her thoughts in words. Of course I can put her thoughts in words, as I have just done. But, the point is, correspondence seems to be fully in place even when on a first-person (first-dog) basis something is believed to be true.

Fifth, correspondence will also be in place when we deal with social as well as "brute" reality. The difference between them will be mainly one of complexity. Statements will (truly) correspond with brute facts when, roughly speaking, the physical world is in this or that condition. "That is a rock" is true when (it is a fact) that is a rock. In contrast, statements will (truly) correspond with social facts when, roughly speaking, the physical as well as the linguistic world is in this or that condition. It is true that we can express the correspondence when reporting social facts as if they are exactly like reports of brute facts. Thus we can say "He won the fifth set in the championship match at the French Open" is true when he won the fifth set at the French Open. This is why social facts fool us into not seeing how they are different from brute facts. But, as we have seen in the chapters on social reality, in reporting the truth of what happened in the fifth set one must know something about the rules of tennis as well as see what happened on the brutish level.

Sixth, because facts are about conditions in the world not things out there, Searle's version of the correspondence theory can deal with problems that overwhelm the picturing version of that theory. If facts were things then we would have a problem talking about the fact that there are no ghosts in my bedroom. What things are we talking about when there is nothing there to talk about? But if facts are conditions, it makes sense to say that there is a condition in my bedroom such that there is nothing there resembling ghosts.

In sum, a necessary condition for the correspondence theory being correct is a separation between statements about the facts (the conditions out there in the world) and the facts. Given that separation, we can talk about the correspondence of the statement with the facts when the statement's conditions of satisfaction are satisfied. In effect, statements make demands. They tell us that what we say is true when the facts we demand are actually out there in the world. We achieve correspondence by linguistically representing the facts out there.

It is only a question of a name, but summarizing Searle's position this way suggests that he is ill advised to insist on characterizing his position as the correspondence theory of truth. An ordinary language analyst should understand that correspondence in its most primary sense implies similarity. Two things correspond when they are similar to one another in at least one important respect. So it is understandable that the classical version of the correspondence theory is tied to such notions as picturing and mirroring. But Searle wants his theory to have no truck with these notions. For him the relation between statements (assertive speech acts) and the facts is one where the former represents the latter and where there is not necessarily any similarity between the representation and what is represented. It might have been better then had he called his theory the representation theory of truth (even though that theory has also had a history of being associated with mirroring and other like notions), or if he had picked a totally different name.

Epistemology

Compared to the attention he gives to the philosophies of language, the mind, culture, to ontology and to such concepts as truth, Searle must be suffering from attention deficit syndrome when it comes to epistemology. There is barely a reference for "epistemology" in the indexes of his various books. When discussing epistemology in these books and his articles it always seems as if he were doing so on the way to discussing some other subject. It is as if he is reacting against the primacy of epistemology in contemporary analytic philosophy by saying to his readers: See we can do a lot of good philosophy without first getting immersed in epistemology. Indeed, immersion here quickly leads to over-immersion – where we find ourselves drowning in scepticism, deconstruction and other similar disgusting lines of thinking.

Nonetheless, in spite of his neglect of epistemology it is possible to characterize some aspects of Searle's views on the subject. The best place to begin is with perception since, for him, it is (along with action) one of the two primary forms of Intentionality (Searle 1983: 36). In being primary, the various ways we perceive things provide us with a "reality check". Perceptual experiences possess conditions of satisfaction (in propositional form) that show us (they don't literally tell us) what it takes for the experience to represent knowledge. These conditions include the now familiar ones that the direction of fit must be mind (or word) to world and that the experience must be caused by the object experienced. The causal direction of fit is world to mind (word). I see (and hear) the car in part because the car itself makes me see it.

All perception is aspectual and this means that we see, hear, etc. what is out there from a certain point of view. The car perceived is seen from a certain angle, as a beautiful machine, as something to enjoy while travelling between here and there or simply as a means of transportation. Still, aspectuality does not undermine perception. The car seen first from one angle and then another is still the same car. Of course mistakes can be made. Our perceptions can be fooled by various environmental conditions or the conditions of our mind (e.g. one has been drinking too much). But mistakes can be corrected. In part this is done by taking the Network and Background into account. By nesting any one knowledge claim into the Network and Background we are better able to assess it. "Yes I really didn't win the lottery, it was all a dream as I can now tell by how my dream fits in with my other experiences." But also, in part, mistakes can be corrected by taking an objective attitude toward any claim I might make. Being objective means not letting personal wants, desires, prejudices influence our judgments. It is not easy to be objective but, then, it is not impossible either.

That perceptions put us in touch with reality and that these perceptions can be corrected makes the various sciences possible.

The sciences cannot be "devalued" as some sceptics and deconstructionists argue. They yield truths and thus are not just systems of thought on a par with, for example, political agendas. It is true that the modern sciences are more complicated than we supposed they were at the end of the nineteenth century, thanks to theories such as relativity and quantum mechanics. But they are "truthful" enough so that Searle feels that he can appeal to them in forming many of his views, especially when it comes to understanding the mind. Science has given us evolution, and evolution has made it possible for Searle to say things such as that consciousness is a real but subjective property that emerged from brain processes.

In contrast to direct knowledge that comes to us from perception one might suppose that the indirect knowledge or understanding found in scientific theories would be suspect. After all, Searle attacks many important cognitivists because of their theorizing practices One might suppose then that Searle is shy about theorizing. But that is not the case. His attacks on the cognitivists is aimed only at a particular kind of theory, one that explains our everyday mental processes by postulating unconscious mental processes that mirror the everyday processes. That is, he opposes those explanations of the mind that postulate a second inner mind – an anthropos inside the anthropos – that is in principle inaccessible.

Far from being shy about theories in science and other fields, Searle treats theorizing as a most important part of thinking and research. Indeed, as noted above, he not only fully accepts modern theories in physics, chemistry, biology and the social sciences but insists that his own thinking, especially in the philosophy of mind, take theories such as evolution into account. He places at least two constraints on theories. First, they must be tied to sets of observations (perceptions). More than one theory may explain the observations (data) but at the very least the theory must be compatible with the observations. Secondly, theories must possess the feature of simplicity. They must live in accordance with Occam's Razor. Searle may very well place other constraints on theory construction. It is difficult to tell since he typically writes about these matters only in passing. Still, what he says directly and between the lines about theory and theory formation sounds pretty much like "standard stuff".

There is one other kind of knowledge that needs mention since it clearly does not represent "standard stuff". For Searle there is first-person as well as third-person knowledge. The latter is what we gain mostly through perception. It is uncontroversial. If Winston sees the bank robber up close and in good light, what he sees counts as evidence. Winston would make a good witness if and when the robber is caught and tried. What is controversial is first-person knowledge where no evidence need be provided (Searle 1983: 119). I know that I caused my arm to go up without having to observe myself raising my arm. I know that I am looking at a mountain without having to observe myself looking. I know what I intend to do without waiting to see what exactly I am going to do. It is such first-person knowledge that behaviourists, functionalists and their allies cannot, or simply do not, countenance in their study of the mind. They don't see how such knowledge can count as knowledge simply because it *is* subjective. But, as we have seen more than once, Searle insists that it should count. If I am the one whose behaviour we are trying to understand it is very important that I know what I am doing. The first-person information that I have is certainly different from that had by others, but it is information nonetheless.

By allowing first-person knowledge Searle means to extend the "data" provided to science for doing its work. Such knowledge, strange though it is, is still part of the natural world for Searle. But for his opponents the extension affords them reason to think that he does not truly work within the scientific tradition. Subjective data is just what science doesn't need. Instead, what it needs is objectivity not subjectivity.

Searle's reply should be familiar by now. The subjectivity of the mind has ontological status. It is the nature of the beast that conscious mental processes are subjective. But that does not prevent scientists from looking at our subjectivity in an epistemologically objective way. Searle, then, thinks of himself as a strong supporter of science. What he doesn't support is a certain vision of science that excludes *ex cathedra* the subjective part of nature from scientific study. For him, this purely third-person vision undermines the efforts of the social sciences. Supporters of this misguided view of science are, of course, not themselves anti-science, but, nonetheless, they are doing science much harm.

Here is how Searle expresses himself on this misguided view and especially how this view expresses itself in the area of philosophy of mind. He first makes the familiar distinctions between ontology, causation and epistemology.

1. What is its mode of existence? (ontology)
2. What does it do? (causation)
3. How do we find out about it? (epistemology)

(1989a: 194)

Then he says:

> The history of the philosophy of mind in recent decades is in large part a series of confusions between these three questions. Thus, behaviorism confuses the epistemology of the mental with the ontology (we find out about mental states by observing behavior, so mental sates just consists in behavior and dispositions to behavior). And functionalism consists in confusing the causation with the ontology (mental states have causal relations to input stimuli, other mental states, and output behavior, so mental states just consist in having these causal relations. (1989a: 195)

This passage is paradigmatically Searlian. It may not be very important that Searle spend as much time as many of his contemporaries do studying and writing about epistemology. But it is important that he makes distinctions. For Searle the distinction, sharply made, between epistemology (and causation), on the one side, and ontology, on the other, is crucial not only for being clear about issues flowing around philosophy of mind, but also for many other areas of philosophy.

Chapter 13

Summing up

Ontology

The main thrust of Searle's philosophical writings is in ontology. This already sets him apart from many of his Anglo-American peers who favour epistemology and who, as a result, argue that issues concerning how we know must be settled before settling issues concerned with what we know. Searle is not particularly impressed with this line of thinking possibly because what we know is, for him, obvious in many cases. There is no need for endless rallies around the epistemological flag in order to say certain things about what is out there in the world. Indeed, Searle says "that I think our obsession with epistemology was a three hundred year mistake" (Baggini 1999). Our ordinary powers are good enough to tell us about most of what we know. To be sure, these powers can be fooled in certain situations. But when they lead us to believe that stars, mountains, rain, trees, grass, deer, cats, dogs, ants and, even, consciousness are real we should be reluctant to doubt these beliefs.

Instead of doubting the existence of all these things we should be engaging in processes of thinking that gain us understanding of their nature and structure. We do this in two ways. One we call philosophy, the other science. The two ways are not really separate. Philosophy represents ways of thinking and gaining understanding that are more informal than science. Philosophy often gets us underway in coming to understand a certain subject matter. Then it steps aside in favour of one of the sciences. This happened to speech act theory that was (at least in the tradition of analytic philosophy) started by John Austin, continued by Searle himself and then handed over to linguists. Going from philosophy to science is not the only direction our thinking can take.[1] Philosophy can start us thinking down a path, science can give us new insights that then send us back in the general direction whence we came. This back and forth strolling characterizes what Searle himself engages in when he is concerned with understanding the nature of the mind. Searle thus thinks of himself as heavily engaged in ontological thinking that begins with ordinary, everyday, common things that we know about but, then, is also willing to appeal to science (properly understood) to gain insights and rigour.

The particular views Searle holds in ontology can be understood best in terms of his philosophy of mind writings. This is because the mind is such a central concept in his ontology and also because the mind is seamlessly tied to the rest of nature. Those we call dualists do not hold to the seamless theory. They treat the mind as something so special that they find it difficult to say anything intelligent about the relations between the mind, on the one hand, and the body and the rest of nature on the other. Searle himself concedes that the mind is special in many ways. It possesses features such as consciousness, subjectivity and (intrinsic) Intentionality that are found nowhere else in nature. It possesses important causal powers to boot. Still, since the mind is an outgrowth of the body, more specifically the brain and its associated parts, it has to be understood in terms of the body. Searle's standard way of expressing this is to say that mental processes are caused by the behaviour of the brain and are realized in its structure. This being so, there is no reason to be shy about studying the mind scientifically. We need to recognize that the mind is ontologically subjective, but can still be studied objectively.

The ontology of the mind

In summary form here is how Searle goes about this study. He begins by distinguishing between our mental powers' basic features and how these features are related empirically to one another and to other features in the world. The empirical relations are for scientists to uncover. They can engage in research that tells us the extent to which our perceptions are affected by our wishes or our expectations. They can also tell us how our perceptions are affected by camouflage of various sorts, or even why changes in our nervous system cause pain and then later, after we have taken some medication, why the pain goes away.

However, it is not the business of science to explain away our basic mental features. Even if science provides a causal reduction of the mind by explaining in detail how the mind "emerges" from neuronal, etc. activity, the mental features are still there. These features have their separate existence and therefore cannot be reduced to something else. Causal reduction does not automatically give us ontological reduction (Searle 1991b: 182). The mind still has its own features which, in fact, it is the duty of the scientist to describe and explain. It is much the same as it is in physics when some causal reduction is given of a material such as glass. The structure of glass can be accounted for in terms of crystal formation and crystal formation accounted for in terms of molecules and so on. But glass itself can be still studied. Glass shaped in certain ways refracts various wave lengths of light one way rather than another, certain coloured glass reflects some light and allows other light to pass through, and some kinds of glass shatter more readily than others. Reduced causally or not, glass is still glass. In the same vein, the mind is still the mind reduced physically or not. Its basic features of intrinsic Intentionality, consciousness, subjectivity and causality are not to be denied. Denial is a tempting move if one's ideology of science demands that only third-person phenomena be treated as the proper subject matter of science and, therefore, demands that first-person consciousness be excluded. Denial might also be present if one indeed has made the mistake of assuming that causal reduction is the same as (reducible to) ontological reduction. But such denial is self-refuting. Denial of the mind is possible only within the framework of mental activity. Denying anything is, after all, an example of a conscious, subjective and Intentional mental state. But such clever philosophical arguments aside, it just seems incomprehensible (crazy?) that anyone would deny the existence, richness and variety of our experiences.

If not denial, Searlian opponents might simply choose to play down the importance of mental experience. They might do this, as Dennett does, by, on the one hand, claiming that consciousness is important but, on the other, arguing that it is best not to begin the study of the mind by focusing on consciousness (Dennett 1993:

194). Consciousness, with its subjectivity, is just too hard to deal with scientifically. But the effect is the same as it would have been had Dennett simply denied the existence of consciousness. As Ned Block suggests in his review of Dennett's *Consciousness Explained*, Dennett might have better titled his book *Consciousness Ignored* (Block 1993: 181).

However they go about discounting the consciousness of the mind, one way Searle's opponents might effect their discounting strategy is by challenging the mind's causal efficacy and claiming, beyond that, that causes are better found in the deep recesses of the permanent unconscious rather than in the conscious mind. Dennett's strategy of avoiding consciousness for now may be an example here. But as we have seen, Searle has arguments against these "cognitivist" arguments, one among them involving the use of Occam's Razor (Searle 1984: 51). He thinks that neurophysiological plus the mental states themselves give us all the causes we need in order to explain mental phenomena. There is, thus, no need to appeal to mysterious (and permanent) unconscious forces or entities.. Science tells us that mental experiences are caused by the neuronal system in our bodies, and everyday experiences tell us that the mind causes physical changes in our bodies and cause as well, via the neuronal system, changes in other (later) mental states. That is all we need to understand the workings of the mind.

Searle's criticisms of his opponents with respect to issues surrounding the mind can be put under three headings. The first has to do with his opponents' strong commitment to the study of behaviour. His criticism is not that psychology and related sciences should not study behaviour but that they should not do so to the exclusion of the study of consciousness. Studying pain is not just the study of pain behaviour. It is true that when Sally perceives Sam in pain all she sees are his writhings and all she hears are his screams. This is an epistemological point. But Searle is making an ontological point. He wants to say that the pain behaviour is caused by the pain. Pain is a genuine phenomenon with causal and, therefore, explanatory powers. If the concept of pain were reduced (totally) to pain behaviour we would be hard put to come up with any explanation of that behaviour. How, for example, would neuronal activity (minus the pain) explain writhings and screams?

In a similar vein, studying fear is not just the study of fear behaviour, and studying learning is not just the study of learning behaviour. There are genuine mental phenomena behind these two kinds of behaviour and these phenomena possess their own causal powers. One consequence of this criticism of those who downgrade the role of consciousness is that just because a machine exhibits behaviour like that of a human being, a chimp or a dog, we should not automatically suppose that the machine is experiencing pain, fear or has a learning experience. In order to experience pain, as against merely exhibiting pain behaviour, the machine would have to possess a structure with causal powers equal to those creatures who do experience pain. That structure could be biologically similar to these creatures or it could be different. However, given what we know about the kind of machines in our employ at present, there is no reason to believe that they have the requisite powers to exhibit consciousness.

The second criticism has to do with his opponent's penchant for finding explanations of behaviour in the deep and unfathomable unconscious. By postulating unconscious thoughts that cannot in principle ever reach the surface, Searle's opponents cannot explain the mind's intrinsic feature of aspectuality. In addition, by inventing these unconscious processes, these critics tend to anthropomorphize the mind and, in the process, give us explanations we don't need (i.e. they fail to use Occam's Razor).

Whereas the first criticism is concerned with end results, that is, with behaviour, and the second with what is in the middle, the third is concerned with what is at the front end. For Searle the study of psychology and related fields is not just a matter of monitoring up-front external stimuli. There is something more to attend to. The following diagram helps to show how these criticisms relate to one another, and to point to what this something more is.

Level 2

sensory experience		response experience		

Level 1

outside stimuli	internal sensors	mental processor	internal reactors	gross responses
	(neuron firings)	(the deep Unconscious)	(neuron firings)	

Searle's opponents want to work as philosophers of mind, psychologists, cognitive scientists, etc. on Level 1 exclusively or almost exclusively. Of course they disagree among themselves on how to interpret Level 1. Some will not appeal to the deep unconscious, others will. Some will attend to outside stimuli more than internal sensors and so on. Still, they will agree that Level 1 alone shows promise for success in their various fields of study.

Searle insists that these fields should be studied in a way that takes account of both Levels 1 and 2. Far from not being important to psychology, etc., Level 2 phenomena represent what is the most important. These *are* the phenomena that we need to understand and explain. They are the "something more". Even at our present low level of Level 2 understanding, Searle thinks it is clear that the phenomena on this level have causal powers that belie what the Level 1 enthusiasts want to say. Thus, to leave out Level 2 phenomena from whatever account of the mind we give is to tell only part of the story and, therefore, to invite more failure in a field like psychology than we need countenance (Searle 1991e: 336).

Not all thinkers who owe their primary allegiance to Level 1 thinking are willing to be completely loyal to that level. Recently, evidently, the mind *has* been rediscovered (McGinn 1999). The impact of Searle's writing, along with those of McGinn, Nagel and others has made thinkers in the area of philosophy of mind at least somewhat more sensitive to the (possible) limitations of Level 1 thinking. Here is what McGinn, excitedly, has to say about the this rediscovery in his review of Searle's *Mind, Language and Society*.

> Recently, consciousness has leaped naked from the closet, streaking across the intellectual landscape. People are conscious – all of them! The deep, dark secret is out. Even animals carry their own distinctive quantum of consciousness, their own inner life. You can almost hear the sigh of relief across the learned world as theorists let loose and openly acknowledge what they have repressed for so long. The Nineties are to consciousness what the Sixties were to sex.   (McGinn 1999: 44)

Given this changes of scenery in favour of consciousness, it should not be surprising that at least one Level 1 thinker should emerge who feels the need to say something more about Level 2 than he might have in the past. One such thinker is David Chalmers (1996). It is interesting to see how he incorporates Level 2 thinking into his theory of the mind and how that incorporation contrasts with Searle's views.

On Level 1 Chalmers is a functionalist. One "feels pain" (i.e. physically "senses") the heat from the stove and as a result removes one hand to avoid being harmed. On this functional account a robot could react in the same way. To this Level 1 account, Chalmers adds a Level 2 account that is quite separate from Level 1. It is so separate that he talks as if there are two pains involved when touching the stove There is the functional pain known to all in terms of how the organism and robot behave (i.e. via third-person knowledge) and the subjective pain. For Chalmers the separation is so great that there is no causal connection between the two levels (Chalmers 1996: 158–9). Indeed, the only causal talk necessary for understanding our mental life takes place solely on Level 1. Causally, consciousness is superfluous for Chalmers.

Not surprisingly Searle finds Chalmers's attempt to employ Level 2 as well as Level 1 concepts into a theory of the mind totally unsatisfactory (Searle 1997: 135–76). For Searle, since the mind is an outgrowth of the body it represents a perfectly natural phenomenon. However, as an emergent outgrowth, it possesses features of its own; and because these features are emergent they have their own causal powers. To say, then, as Chalmers does, that Level 2 mental concepts have a non-causal place (i.e. an epiphenomenal role) is not good enough. What Searle wants is a fully participating mind in the casual world. He wants a mind that neither leads to a conceptual dualism that bifurcates the world in such a way as to leave the relationship between the mind and the body a total mystery, nor to materialism that ignores the mind and thus gives us no account of the nature of the mind and how it works.

The ontology of the social world

If the mind (consciousness, subjectivity and all the rest) emerges from the brain, social reality emerges from the mind. But the two emergings are not alike. The former is not under our control. We have powerful minds because biological processes have evolved to present us with them. In contrast, the latter is our doing. Humans create or construct social reality by employing their mental powers. They construct various kinds of social reality. All involve we-intentions. Even the most simple and temporary forms of social reality, such as two people joining together for a minute or two in order to push a car, involve we-intentions. Hyenas and other pack hunting animals are also able to construct this form of social reality. However, as we move to more sophisticated social constructions, animals get left behind. Because they have few language skills, they cannot enter into social behaviour governed even by regulative rules. Beyond that, however, they lack the abilities to govern their social behaviour by constitutive rules.

These latter rules take the form of X counts as Y in C or, as it might be expressed, in context C, X becomes Y. Thus in a military context (C) where a colonel is on record as having successfully led various military units in battle and where at this moment various units are assembled on the parade grounds, saying certain words and doing certain things, transforms the colonel (who is X) into a general (he becomes a Y). This transformation or "becoming" happens, according to Searle only if the society affected by the transformation has the proper we-intentions. It is these collective intentions that show us how social reality is created. Without the approval of the society, generals cease to be generals. Indeed without the approval of the society the whole cluster of institutions that form the larger institution of the military ceases to exist. However if the society supports the transformation of colonels to generals, the transformation of certain pieces of paper into money, the transformation of simply hitting balls over a fence into hitting home runs, and the transformation of couples into a married couple, massive status changes take place.

With these changes comes what Searle calls the assignment of function. We go to the trouble of creating institutions, which often become layered, because we wish to accomplish certain things. The function of the general is to assemble, organize and command large military units so that they can act against the enemy in a concerted fashion. The function of money (the reason for giving it the status it has) is to enable people to buy and sell commodities in an efficient manner. So it goes with the other institutions created via the magical Searlian formula X counts as Y in C.

Once the constitutive rules, and the institutions that go with them, are in place people obviously put these rules to use in specific settings. Generals give orders, money is exchanged for goods and so on. But beyond that, constitutive rules make it possible for people to talk about the institutions they have been created and are sustaining. It thus becomes possible to discuss institutional facts. These facts contrast with brute facts. Brute facts report X kind of events and are about X kind of objects. This is an apple, this a rock, this a human organism, this is rain all report brute facts. These facts report about or talk about the ontologically objective world. Institutional facts report about or talk about the ontologically subjective world – the world of Y. She is married, he is a general, he ordered his troops to attack, the bottle of Scotch I bought was expensive, she was promoted, he was baptized and the nation is at war all report institutional facts.

Although these facts do not have a brutish ontological character, they can have epistemological objective character. This seems peculiar at first since institutional facts get generated from constitutive rules that in turn get generated from our subjective (we) intentions. But the epistemological objective status of institutional facts is less suspect than the comparable status of ontologically subjective events such as having a pain, or feeling a tickle. These latter events are so suspect that, as we have seen, whole traditions in psychology and related sciences such as behaviourism and functionalism no longer even attempt to talk about these inner experiences. Searle, as we have also seen, thinks that these traditions are mistaken. Nonetheless this form of subjectivity has proven to be difficult for everyone who is concerned with understanding the mind to deal with. The reason the subjectivity found in institutional facts is less daunting is that it is more remote. On the societal level, subjectivity plays a role in the creation of an institution and in the efforts it takes to sustain that institution. But most of the institutional facts we are concerned with do not deal with either one of these phenomena. In reporting that Sally was married yesterday we take the institution of marriage for granted. We assume it has been and still is being supported by the proper kind of we-intentions. What matters instead is: Was the public marriage ceremony done properly? "Yes it was done in the church, the good Father O'Leary was in charge, there were witnesses there, the documents needed to get married were properly signed . . ." In short, the events that led to saying that Sally was married yesterday can all be expressed in third-person terminology. Other institutional facts can be talked about in a similar fashion.

Philosophy of language

In spite of the subjectivity found in social reality, then, there is no reason why the social sciences cannot be studied objectively just as the physical sciences are. The same point applies to the study of language. Language is governed by hordes of constitutive rules and thus, when used, generates an open-ended number of institutional facts that can also be studied objectively. That is what makes the study of philosophy of language and linguistics possible.

Once these disciplines get underway we come to realize that language holds a special place in the social world.

> This fact, that language is also a matter of institutional facts, will make it sound as if language is just one more human institution among others. But language is special in ways that we need to explain . . . I believe that language is the fundamental human institution in the sense that other institutions, such as money, government, private property, marriage, and games, require language, at least language-like forms of symbolism, in a way that language does not require the other institutions for its existence. (Searle 1998: 153)

Although Searle doesn't say so explicitly, language is special in being the most sophisticated of social institutions. Compared to other institutions, its (constitutive) rules are the most numerous, most complex and most layered. It is not surprising, therefore, that even Searle finds himself mis-characterizing language in one way or another. For example, one would suppose, and evidently at one time he himself supposed, that language meaning is explained in terms of communication. His analysis of certain speech acts, of directives, commissives, expressives and declarations especially, would lead one to make this supposition. After all, the point of these speech acts is to reach out to the hearer in one way or another. However, listen to what he has to say in *Intentionality*.

> We need to have a clear distinction between representation and communication. Characteristically a man who makes a statement both intends to represent some fact or state of affairs and intends to communicate this representation to his hearers. But his representing intention is not the same as his communication intention. Communicating is a matter of producing certain effects on one's hearers, but one can intend to represent something without caring at all about the effects on one's hearers. One can make a statement without intending to produce conviction or belief in one's hearers or without intending to get them to believe that the speaker believes what

he says or indeed without even intending to get them to understand at all. There are, therefore, two aspects to meaning intentions, the intention to represent and intention to communicate. The traditional discussion of these problems, my own work included, suffers from a failure to distinguish between them and from the assumption that the whole account of meaning can be given in terms of communication intentions. On the present account, representation is prior to communication and representation intentions are prior to communication intentions.   (1983: 165–6)

Searle makes the same point in his reply to Jonathan Bennett's criticism of his theory of language (Bennett 1991). He says, now expressing himself in terms of meaning instead of representation "we must separate the intention which is the essence of meaning from the intention to communicate" (Searle 1991a: 86). With this distinction between meaning and communication in hand, Searle can now explain how it is possible for one can keep a diary that is not intended for anyone's eyes (and will not even be read by oneself) and how one can talk meaningfully to someone who is comatose.

The power of Searle's theory of language can account for a variety of other linguistic phenomena and uses. Lying is possible because of the role of what Searle calls a double level of intentions found in speech. A speaker has an intention to impose the conditions of satisfaction (e.g. of some belief such as that it is raining) on his utterance. But there is also a second intention present to actually issue the utterance. The main condition of satisfaction of this intention is simply that the utterance be issued. One can, then, issue the utterance (successfully), but not believe what the utterance says one should believe (Searle 1991a: 86–7).

As we have seen, other linguistic phenomena that Searle's theory of language can account for include metaphor, irony, and indirect speech. All these phenomena rely heavily on the distinction between word (sentence) meaning and speaker meaning which Searle champions. They also rely on the rules and strategies that Searle articulates on how we can hear the words such as "You're stepping on my foot" and yet "hear" what the speaker means as "Please move your foot off of mine".

Beyond explaining these phenomena, Searle's theory explains how "language" is a general name for an indefinite number of "games" or institutions and yet is a name for only a handful such games. On the one side, speech acts can differ from one another in any one or more of 12 ways. They may have different "points" or "purposes," direction of fit, expressed psychological state, strength, and they may differ in the status or position of the hearer or speaker. In addition they may differ in how the utterance relates to the speaker, in the relation the utterance has to the rest of the discourse, as to propositional content, in whether the acts must be speech acts, in whether they require extra-linguistic institutional support, in whether the verb in the speech act has a performative verb, and in the style in which the speech act is issued. With all these dimensions in place it is no wonder that language gives the appearance of a confusing array of one and then another type of speech act.

Yet, Searle tells us, if we focus on only a few key dimensions such as the point of a speech act, the direction of fit, the expressed psychological mode and the content we begin to see order in our language. We see dimensions such as strength as not contributing to generating new basic speech acts but merely encouraging variation in the basic types. Indeed, for Searle, there are only five basic games or types of speech acts: assertives, directives, commissives, expressives and declarations. Everything else represents linguistic moves that we make within these games. So if we keep our eye on the basic dimensions of difference, language will not befuddle us. Rather we should see it as the name for five games or institutions that, in fact, actually share much in common. They can for example share in their content as in "The door is shut" (an assertive), "I promise to shut the door" (a commissive) and "Please shut the door" (a directive). In so far as they share content, speech acts can also share in the referring work they do.

Having his taxonomy in place, Searle's theory of language can be used to explain how we can move from issuing individual speech acts to engaging in speech activity (operating on the discourse level). Supplemented by concepts such as master speech acts his theory can easily give an account of the flow of language use for everyday speech activity. Searle himself does not spend much time doing this speech activity work except to tell us about fiction. Even so, he shows us the power of his analysis of language by explaining how fiction is "logically" dependent upon normal language use. Overall, then, Searle presents his readers with a comprehensive theory of how ordinary language works and how variations on that language such as fiction and scientific discourse operates.

Searle's interest in language goes beyond the area he circumscribes as the philosophy of language. He is also a philosopher who engages in linguistic philosophy. No doubt this is a carry over from his earlier training at Oxford. At times the Oxford touch is firm and out in the open as when he discusses perception, intentions and Intentionality (see Ch. 5 of this work). At other times the touch is more subtle. There is no direct appeal to language but what he says about the mind, especially, tends to run in parallel with what he says about the language we use to talk about the mind. It is as if he keeps one eye on language to help him understand better how various distinctions concerning the mind should be articulated.

There is more to Searle's method of doing philosophy than following the Oxford tradition of ordinary language analysis. It also involves playing the "let's pretend" games in Chinese rooms, games with cats-on-the-mat-on-the-moon and the like to help him deal with opponent's arguments. In addition part of his method, especially in his work in philosophy of mind, takes scientific results into account. Whatever he says about the mind, and culture as well, is to be put in the Network of things that science tells us. All in all, Searle employs a variety of methodological tools to arrive at his philosophical position. Late in his career, here is what he says about his methodology.

> The methods I employ are more adequately described, at least in the first stages, as logical or conceptual analysis. I try to find the constitutive elements of consciousness, intentionality, speech acts, and social institutions by taking them apart and seeing how they work. But, truth to tell, even that is a distortion of the actual methodology in practice. In practice, I use any weapon that I can lay my hands on, and I stick with any weapon that works. (1998: 160)

Last words

John Searle's work in philosophy of mind, culture, language and ontology show him to be both an analytic philosopher and system builder. His methods are analytic in the best sense of that tradition. He is rightfully renowned for the clarity of his thought in dealing with specific problems such as those found in the study of language, mind and society.

Yet, not content to deal "analytically" with this and then that problem, Searle holds to what he calls the Enlightenment vision. That vision transforms him into a system builder. The physical world, the mind and culture all form a seamless web of reality. There are no sharp fissures separating these areas of concern. If there were, our understanding of the relationship such as that between the physical world and the mind would be mysterious. We could then wallow in mystery as do McGinn and Nagel, or simply do away with the mystery by denying or devaluing the existence of the mind as do Dennett and the Churchlands. By denying that reality is fissured Searle is in position to avoid the dilemma of living with mysteries or eliminating important segments of reality as if they did not exist.

As a system builder Searle also sees himself in opposition to an assortment of thinkers who have doubts about what it is we can know. Thomas Kuhn is one such thinker (Kuhn 1970). Searle says that Kuhn "was taken to have shown that a major scientific revolution is not just a new description of the same reality, but that it creates a different 'reality'" (Searle 1998: 4). Possibly Ludwig Wittgenstein is another. He has been "taken by many to have shown that our discourse is a series of mutually untranslatable and incommensurable language games" so as to raise questions about existence of "universal standards of rationality ... and intelligibility" (Searle 1998: 4) Many anthropologists and, of course, the deconstructionists are immersed in this sort of scepticism as well. All these people preach some version of relativism that undermines not only science but also our everyday objective judgments.

For Searle in contrast, a necessary condition for a system builder to do his work is that reality should be knowable. Searle thinks it is.

> I accept the Enlightenment vision. I think that the universe exists quite independently of our minds and that, within the limits set by our evolutionary endowments, we can come to comprehend nature. I believe that the real change since the nineteenth century is not that the world has become unintelligible in some exciting and apocalyptic way, but that it is a lot harder to understand for the rather boring and unexciting reason that you have to be smarter and you have to know a lot more. (1998: 4)

As a defender of the Enlightenment vision Searle has found himself in a minority position among many (most?) of his intellectual peers. It is a position he seems to relish and, more than that, thrive on. As a result, his defence of the vision is dogged and, given his many skills as a philosopher, it is articulate and imaginative. One cannot help but feel grateful that a philosopher of John Searle's calibre appeared on the scene late in the twentieth century to make a case for a vision of life and the world that its critics have been trying to bury – prematurely.

Notes

1. See Nira Reiss' *Speech Act Taxonomy as a Tool for Ethnographic Description* (1985). Reiss uses, and somewhat modifies, Searle's taxonomy. Refer to Chapter 1, *n.* 4, of the present work to see that not all work done in the area of speech acts has *not* been handed over to linguists.

Bibliography

Works by Searle

1969. *Speech Acts: An Essay in the Philosophy of Language*. Cambridge: Cambridge University Press.

1971. (ed.) *The Philosophy of Language*. Oxford: Oxford University Press.

1972. Chomsky's Revolution in Linguistics. *New York Review of Books* (29 June), 16–24.

1977. Reiterating the Differences: A Reply to Derrida. *Glyph*, 198–208.

1979a. *Expression and Meaning: Studies in the Theory of Speech Acts*. Cambridge: Cambridge University Press.

1979b. What Is an Intentional State? *Mind* **LXXXVIII**(349), 74–92.

1980a. Minds, Brains and Programs. *Behavior and Brain Science* **3**, 417–24.

1980b. Intrinsic Intentionality. *Behavior and Brain Science* **3**, 450–56.

1980c. Analytic Philosophy and Mental Phenomena. *Midwest Studies in Philosophy* **5**, 405–23.

1982. The Myth of the Computer. *New York Review of Books* **XXIX**(7), 3–6.

1983. *Intentionality: An Essay in the Philosophy of Mind*. Cambridge: Cambridge University Press.

1984. *Minds, Brains and Science*. Cambridge, MA: Harvard University Press.

1985. (co-authored with D. Vanderveken) *Foundations of Illocutionary Logic*. Cambridge: Cambridge University Press.

1989a. Consciousness, Unconsciousness and Intentionality. *Philosophical Topics* **XVII**(1), 193–209.

1989b. How Performatives Work. *Linguistics and Philosophy* **12**(5), 535–58.

1989c. Reply to Jacquette. *Philosophy and Phenomenological Research* **XLIX**(4), 701–8.

1991a. Response: Meaning, Intentionality, and Speech Acts. In *John Searle and His Critics*, E. Lepore & R. Van Gulick (eds), 81–102. Cambridge, MA and Oxford: Basil Blackwell.

1991b. Response: Perception and the Satisfactions of Intentionality. See Lepore & Van Gulick (1991), 181–92.

1991c. Response: Reference and Intentionality. See Lepore & Van Gulick (1991), 227–41.

1991d. Response: The Background of Intentionality and Action. See Lepore & Van Gulick (1991), 289–99.

1991e. Intentionalistic Explanations in the Social Sciences. *Philosophy of the Social Sciences* **21**(3), 332–44.

1992a. *The Rediscovery of the Mind*. Cambridge, MA and London: MIT Press.

1992b. Collective Intentions and Actions. In *Intentions in Communication*, P. R. Cohen, J. Morgan, M. E. Pollack (eds), 401–15. Cambridge, MA and London: MIT Press.

1995a. *Construction of Social Reality*. New York and London: The Free Press.

1995b. Consciousness, the Brain and the Connection Principle. *Philosophy and Phenomenological Research* **LV**(1), 217–32.

1997. *The Mystery of Consciousness*, including exchanges with Daniel C. Dennett and David J. Chalmers. New York: *New York Review*.

1998. *Mind, Language and Society: Philosophy in the Real World*. New York: Basic Books.

References

Alfino, M. 1991. Another Look at the Derrida-Searle Debate. *Philosophy and Rhetoric* **24**(2), 43–52.

Alston, W. P. 1970. Review of: *Speech Acts: An Essay in the Philosophy of Language. Philosophical Quarterly* (April), 172–79.

Alston, W. P. 1991. Searle on Illocutionary Acts. See Lepore & Van Gulick (1991), 57–80.

Anderson, J. R. 1976. *Language, Memory and Thought*. Hillsdale, NJ: Erlbaum.

Apel, K. O. 1991. Is Intentionality more Basic than Linguistic Meaning? See Lepore & Van Gulick (1991), 31–55.

Aristotle. *Rhetoric and Poetics*.

Armstrong, D. H. 1991. Intentionality, Perception and Causality: Reflections on John Searle's *Intentionality*. See Lepore & Van Gulick (1991), 149–58.

Austin, J. L. 1975. *How To Do Things With Words*, 2nd edn, J. O. Urmson & M. Sbisa (eds). Cambridge, MA: Harvard University Press. [This volume was first presented at Harvard University as The William James Lectures in 1955.]

Ayer, A. J. 1952. *Language, Truth and Logic*, 2nd edn. New York: Dover Publications.

Baggini, J. 1999. Painting the Bigger Picture: an Interview with John Searle. *Philosophers' Magazine* (Autumn), 37–9.

Beardsley, M. C. 1962. The Metaphorical Twist. *Philosophy and Phenomenological Research* **22**(3), 293–307.

Bechtel, W. & R. McCauley 1999. Heuristic Identity Theory (or Back to the Future): The Mind Body Problem Against the Background of Research Strategies in Cognitive Neuroscience. *Proceedings of the Twenty-First Meeting of the Cognitive Science Society*, M. Hahn & S. C. Stones (eds), 67–72. Mahway, NJ: Erlbaum.

Bennett, J. 1991. How Do Gestures Succeed? See Lepore & Van Gulick (1991), 3–15.

Bertolet, R. 1994. Are There Indirect Speech Acts? In *Foundations of Speech Act Theory: Philosophical and Linguistics Perspectives*, S. L. Tsohatzidis (ed.), 335–49. London and New York: Routledge.

Black, M. 1962. Metaphor. In *Models and Metaphors*, 25–47. Ithaca, NY: Cornell University Press.

Black, M. 1993. More About Metaphor. See Ortony (1993), 19–41.

Block, N. 1993. A review of Dennett's *Consciousness Explained. Journal of Philosophy* **XC**(4), 181–93.

Bransford, J. D. & M. K. Johnson 1972. Contextual Prerequisites for Understanding. *Journal of Verbal Learning and Verbal Behavior* **11**, 717–26.

Brown, R. & J. Kulik 1977. Flashbulb Memories. *Cognition* **5**, 73–99.

Burkhardt, A. 1990. Searle on Metaphor. In *Speech Acts, Meaning and Intentions: Critical Approaches to the Philosophy of John R. Searle*, A. Burkhardt (ed.), 303–35. Berlin and New York: Walter de Gruyter.

Chalmers, D. J. 1996. *The Conscious Mind: In Search of a Fundamental Theory*. Oxford: Oxford University Press.

Chomsky, N. 1965. *Aspects of the Theory of Syntax* Cambridge, MA: MIT Press.

Chomsky, N. 1986. *Knowledge of Language: Its Nature, Origin and Use*. New York and Philadelphia: Praeger Special Studies.

Churchland, P. S. 1981. Eliminative Materialism and the Propositional Attitudes. *Journal of Philosophy* **78**, 67–90.

Croft, W. 1994. Speech Act Classification, Language Typology and Cognition. See Tsohatzidis (1994), 460–77.

Culler, J. 1989. Convention and Meaning: Derrida and Austin. In *Contemporary Literary Criticism*, 2nd edn, R. C. Davis & R. Schleifer (eds), 216–28. New York: Longman.

Dennett, D. C. 1991. *Consciousness Explained*. Boston, MA: Little, Brown.

Dennett, D. C. 1993. A review of Searle's *Rediscovery of the Mind. Journal of Philosophy* **VC**(4), 193–205.

Donnellan, K. 1974. Speaking of Nothing *Philosophical Review* **83** (January), 3–32.

Flanagan, O. 1992. *Consciousness Reconsidered*. Cambridge, MA and London: MIT Press.

Fodor, J. 1975. *The Language of Thought*. New York: Thomas Y. Crowell.

Fotion, N. 1971. Master Speech Acts. *Philosophical Quarterly* (July), 232–43.

Fotion, N. 1979. Speech Activity and Language Use. *Philosophia* **8**(4), 615–37.

Freud, S. 1949. *The Origins and Development of Psychoanalysis*. Chicago, Ill.: Regnery.

Freud, S. 1959. The Unconscious in Psychoanalysis. *Collected Papers*, vol. 4, J. Riviere (trans.), 98–136. New York: Basic Books.

Freud, S. 1966. *Introductory Lectures to Psychoanalysis*, J. Strachey (ed. and trans.). New York: Norton.

Grice, H. P. 1989. *Studies in the Way of Words*. Cambridge, MA and London: Harvard University Press.

Habermas, J. 1991. Comments on John Searle: "Meaning, Communication, and Representation". See Lepore & Van Gulick (1991), 17–29.

Hancher, M. 1979. The Classification of Cooperative Illocutionary Acts. *Language in Society* **8**, 1–14.

Hare, R. M. 1952. *The Language of Morals*. Oxford: Oxford University Press.

Hempel. C. 1949. The Logical Analysis of Psychology. In *Readings in Philososophical Analysis*, H. Feigl & W. Sellars (eds), 373–84. New York: Appleton Century Crofts.

Henle, P. (ed.) 1965. *Language, Thought and Culture*. Ann Arbor, Mich.: University of Michigan Press.

Hobbs, J. R. 1990. Matter, Levels, and Consciousness. *Behavioral and Brain Sciences* **13**(4), 197–220.

Holdcroft, D. 1978. *Words and Deeds: Problems in the Theory of Speech Acts*. Oxford: Clarendon Press.

Holdcroft, D. 1994. Indirect Speech Acts and Propositional Content. See Tsohatzidis (1994), 350–64.

Hull, C. L. 1943. *Principles of Behavior*. New York: Appleton-Century.

Jackson, F. 1997. "Epiphenomenal Qualia," *A Historical Introduction to the Philosophy of Mind*, P. A. Morton (ed.), 401–8. Peterborough, Ontario: Broadview Press.

Jacquette, D. 1989. Adventures in the Chinese Room. *Philosophy and Phenomenological Research* **XLIX**(4), 605–23.

Kripke, S. 1972. Naming and Necessity. In *Semantics of Natural Language*, G. Harmon & D. Davidson (eds), 253–355. Dordrecht: Reidel Publishing.

Kuhn, T. 1970. *The Structure of Scientific Revolutions*, 2nd edn, Chicago, Ill.: University of Chicago Press.

Lakoff, G. & M. Johnson 1980. *Metaphors We Live By*. Chicago, Ill.: University of Chicago Press.

Lepore, E. & R. Van Gulick (eds) 1991. *John Searle and His Critics*. Cambridge, MA and Oxford: Basil Blackwell.

Levinson, S. C. (1983) *Pragmatics*. Cambridge: Cambridge University Press.

Loftus, E. F. & J. C. Palmer 1974. Reconstruction of Automobile Destruction: An Example of the Interaction Between Language and Memory. *Journal of Verbal Learning and Verbal Behavior* **13**, 585–9.

Lycan, W. G. 1987.*Consciousness*. Cambridge, MA: MIT Press.

Marcel, A. J. 1983. Conscious and Unconscious Perception: Experiments on Visual Masking and Word Recognition. *Cognitive Psychology* **15**, 197–237.

Marr, D. 1982. *Vision*. San Francisco, Calif.: W. H. Freeman.

McCloskey, M., C. G. Wible, N. J. Cohen 1988. Is There a Special Flashbulb Memory Mechanism? *Journal of Experimental Psychology: General* **117**, 171–81.

McGinn, C. 1991. *The Problem of Consciousness*. Oxford: Basil Blackwell.

McGinn, C. 1999. Can We Ever Understand Consciousness? (a review of Searle's *Mind, Language and Society* and Paul and Patricia Churchland's *On the Contrary: Critical Essays, 1987–1997*), *New York Review of Books* **XLVI**(10), 44–8.

Miller, G. 1993. Images and Models, Similes and Metaphors. See Ortony (1993), 357–400.

Moore, G. E. 1959. Proof of an External World. *Philosophical Papers*. London: George Allen and Unwin.

Nagel, T. 1974. What is it Like to be a Bat? *Philosophical Review* **LXXXIII**(4), 435–50.

Nagel, T. 1986. *The View from Nowhere*. Oxford: Oxford University Press.

Newell, A. 1982. The Knowledge Level. *Artificial Intelligence* **18**, 87–127.

Norman, D. A. 1981. Categorization of Action Slips. *Psychological Review* **88**, 1–15.

Ortony, A. (ed.) 1993. *Metaphor and Thought*, 2nd edn. Cambridge: Cambridge University Press.

Place, U. T. 1956. Is Consciousness a Brain Process? *British Journal of Psychology* **47**, 44–50.

Reason, J. 1984. Lapses of Attention in Everyday Life. In *Varieties of Attention*, R. Parasuraman & D. R. Davies (eds), 515–49. Orlando, FL: Academic Press.

Reiss, N. 1985. *Speech Act Taxonomy as a Tool for Ethnographic Description: An Analysis Based on Videotapes of Continuous Behavior in Two New York Households*. Amsterdam and Philadelphia: John Benjamins Publishing.

Rock, I. 1984. *Perception*. New York: W. H. Freeman, Scientific American Library.

Rorty, R. (ed.) 1970. *The Linguistic Turn*. Chicago, Ill.: University of Chicago Press.

Rorty, R. 1984. What is it About? review of John Searle's *Intentionality*. *London Review of Books* (May 17–June 6), 3–4.

Ryle, G. 1949. *The Concept of Mind*. New York: Barnes and Noble.

Ryle, G. 1952. Systematically Misleading Expressions. In *Logic and Language*, First Series, A. Flew (ed.), 11–36. Oxford: Basil Blackwell. [This article also appears in *The Linguistic Turn*, R. Rorty (ed.), 85–100. Chicago, Ill.: University of Chicago Press.]

Skinner, B. F. 1953. *Science and Human Behavior*. New York: Macmillan.

Smart, J. J. C. 1959. Sensations and Brain Processes. *Philosophical Review* **68**, 141–56.

Squire, L. R. 1987. *Memory and Brain*. Oxford and New York: Oxford University Press.

Squire, L. R. & E. R. Kandel 1999. *Memory: From Mind to Molecules*. New York: Scientific American Library.

Stevenson, C. 1945. *Ethics and Language*. New Haven, CN: Yale University Press.

Stich, S. P. 1983. *From Folk Psychology to Cognitive Science: The Case Against Belief*. Cambridge, MA: MIT Press.

Stroud, B. 1991. The Background of Thought. See Lepore & Van Gulick (1991), 245–58.

Titchener, E. B. 1896. *An Outline of Psychology*. New York: Macmillan.

Treisman, A. & S. Gormican 1988. Feature Analysis in Early Vision: Evidence from Search Asymmetries. *Psychological Review* **95**, 15–48.

Tsohatzidis, S. L. (ed.) 1994. *Foundations of Speech Act Theory: Philosophical and Linguistic Perspectives*. London and New York: Routledge.

Tulving, E. 1972. Episodic and Semantic Memory. In *Organization of Memory*, E. Tulving & W. Donaldson (eds), 382–403. New York: Academic Press.

Tulving, E. 1985. Memory and Consciousness. *Canadian Psychology* **26**, 1–12.

Tulving, E. 1986. What Kind of a Hypothesis is the Distinction Between Episodic and Semantic Memory? *Journal of Experimental Psychology: Learning, Memory and Cognition* **12**, 307–11.

Tulving, E. & D. M. Thomson 1973. Encoding Specificity and Retrieval Processes in Episodic Memory. *Psychological Review* **80**, 352–73.

Turner, S. P. 1999. Searle's Social Reality. *History and Theory* **38**(2), 211–31.

Vanderveken, D. 1990–1. *Meaning and Speech Acts*, vols 1 & 2. Cambridge: Cambridge University Press.

Van Gulick, R. 1995. Why the Connection Argument Doesn't Work. *Philosophy and Phenomenological Research* **LV**(1), 201–7.

Vanderveken, D. 1991. Non-literal Speech Acts and Conversational Maxims. See Lepore & Van Gulick (1991), 371–84.

Watson, J. B. 1913. Psychology as the Behaviorist Views It. *Psychological Review* **20**, 158–77.

Watson, J. B. 1919. *Psychology From the Standpoint of a Behaviorist*. Philadelphia: Lippincott.

Weber, M. 1998. *The Protestant Ethic and the Spirit of Protestantism*, 2nd edn, T. Parsons (trans.). Los Angeles: Roxbury.

Wittgenstein, L. 1953. *Philosophical Investigations*, G. E. M. Anscombe, R. Rhees, G. H. von Wright (eds), G. E. M. Anscombe (trans.). Oxford: Oxford University Press.

Wouk, H. 1971. *The Winds of War*. Boston and Toronto: Little, Brown.

Wouk, H. 1978. *War and Remembrance*, vols 1 & 2. Boston and Toronto: Little, Brown.

Wundt, W. 1912. *An Introduction to Psychology*. New York: Arno Press [republished in 1973].

Index

Printed in the United States
87951LV00002B/94/A

9 780691 057125